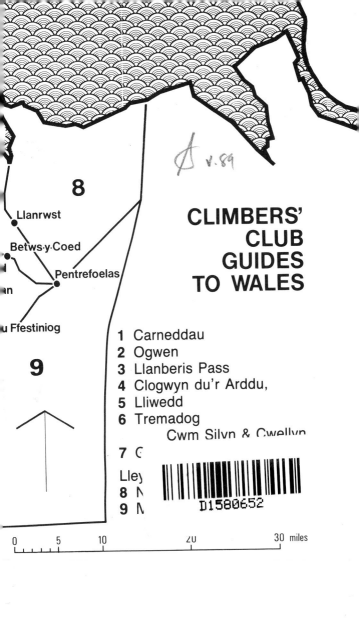

8

Llanrwst

Betws·y·Coed

Pentrefoelas

u Ffestiniog

9

CLIMBERS'
CLUB
GUIDES
TO WALES

1 Carneddau
2 Ogwen
3 Llanberis Pass
4 Clogwyn du'r Arddu,
5 Lliwedd
6 Tremadog
   Cwm Silyn & Cwellyn

7 ᴄ

Lley

8 ᴎ

9 ᴎ

D1580652

| 0 | 5 | 10 | 20 | 30 miles |

Jill Sumner on Shade of Pale, Craig Cywarch.　　　Photo: John Sumner

CLIMBERS' CLUB GUIDES TO WALES
Edited by Geoff Milburn

9

Mid-Wales

by **John Sumner**

Diagrams by **Phil Gibson**
      and Robin Thorndyke

Historical by **Geoff Milburn**

Front cover photograph by **Geoff Cope**
Back cover photograph by **John Sumner**

Published by the **CLIMBERS' CLUB**

1958 *Craig Cowarch by R E Lambe*
Published by The Mountain Club of Stafford

1964 *Craig Cowarch by R E Lambe and A B Knox*
Published by The Mountain Club of Stafford

1966 *Craig Cowarch by R E Lambe and A B Knox*
Published by The Mountain Club of Stafford

1973 *Central Wales by John A Sumner*
Published by West Col

1975 *Dolgellau Area by John A Sumner*
Published by West Col

1988 *Mid-Wales by John A Sumner*
Published by the Climbers' Club

© The Climbers' Club 1988

Sumner, John
  Mid-Wales. — (Climbers' Club guides)
  1. Rock climbing — Mid-Wales
  I. Title   II. Climbers' Club
  III. Sumner, John   IV. Series

  ISBN 0-901-601-42-X

front cover:

Photo: Darker Angel, Craig Cau, Cader. John Sumner leaving the stance between the two 5c pitches.

back cover:
Photo: Chris Nunn on Wingeing Pom, Craig Rhiwarth.

Prepared for printing by: Synergy, Royal Oak Barn, Cartmel, Cumbria, LA11 6BQ.
Produced by The Ernest Press, Glasgow.
Distributed by Cordee, 3a De Montfort Street, Leicester, LE1 7HD.

CONTENTS

6

PHOTOGRAPHS

Colour

Black and White

Jill Sumner of King of Maybe, VS, 4c, Craig Rhiwarth.

DIAGRAMS

ACKNOWLEDGEMENTS

I would like to thank everyone who has helped in the production of this guidebook and especially: Jackie Short for the original typing of this manuscript and Les and Jean Ainsworth for the huge task of attacking a mangled typescript – twice (!) – and of course to my mentor, Geoff Milburn, for his unflagging enthusiasm, who has produced the historical section and put the text into a modern format. Our meetings at The Rock near the Roches formed a foundation to produce this C.C. guidebook.

Also I should like to thank Nick Smyth for dealing with access problems, Alun Hughes, a part-time National Park Warden, for extensive work to obtain Welsh crag names, and to Mark Hutchinson and Bill Wright of the BMC for their work on Access.

Robin Thorndyke helped by drawing earlier diagrams when the guidebook was originally going to be published by West Col (which published the two predecessors to this guide-book). More recently Phil Gibson produced the remaining superb diagrams which were done in a remarkably short time over the Christmas period in 1987.

Several others deserve a mention: Geoff Cope for the great front cover photograph, Robin Collomb for taking on the original guidebooks, and the Stafford M.C. for Bryn Hafod the base from which I worked, and not least my wife Jill who has encouraged me throughout the work for this guidebook.

J.A. Sumner 1988

Introduction

Although Cader Idris was first explored by the rock-climber during the last century the area has largely remained a backwater as far as the climber is concerned. Northerners going down to Wales largely restrict themselves to Snowdonia, or since the 1980s have opted for the long drive down to the limestone crags of Pembrokeshire. The same may be said of the southerner and there is no doubt that mid-Wales has mainly been the preserve of climbers from the Midlands. In the cwms it is rare for climbers to find others on the crag and only in Winter do the numbers of climbers increase. Consequently many of the crags tend to carry a great deal of vegetation which is rather off-putting for some, but to others this is in itself a challenge allowing routes of a more mountaineering nature to be sought out.

Certain routes of a scrappy or vegetated nature have been reduced to briefer notes and full detail may be found in the previous Central Wales and Dolgellau Area guides. Another change since the last guides is that many of the crag names in Cwm Cywarch have been corrected. This information has been collected from the farmers in the valley by Alun Huges who is a part-time warden with the Snowdonia National Park. The current guidebook contains the Craig Cywarch complex, the Arans, the Cader Idris area crags, Bird Rock and the Berwyns.

Route Grades
The standard adjectival grading system has been used and the grades are as follows:

Easy	Severe
Moderate	Hard Severe
Difficult	Very Severe
Very Difficult	Hard Very Severe
	Extremely Severe

The Extremely Severe grade is now an open-ended system represented by the symbols E1, E2, E3, E4, E5, E6, E7 etc and the E grades give an overall impression of the difficulty of a climb, be it a desperate well-protected physical effort or a thin and poorly protected affair which requires nerves of steel.

E1 corresponds to Mild Extremely Severe.
E2, E3 and E4 correspond to Extremely Severe.
E5 and E6 correspond to Hard Extremely Severe.

Numerical Pitch Grades have been included in the text; they are 4a, 4b, 4c, 5a, 5b, 5c, 6a, 6b, and 6c. So far none of the hardest routes ranks with the hardest in other areas of the country.

Wherever aid of any form has been used, the minimum number of points of aid for each climb is given in brackets after the grade of the route, e.g. Hard Very Severe (1 pt. aid). The nature of the aid will be made clear in the route description. Much of the aid in the area has now been eliminated but a few points of aid still remain. The word peg is used in three contexts; 'peg' means that the peg is used for a runner only; 'aid peg' and 'peg belay'. Nearly all the pegs should be found in place.

The familiar 'star' system is used to indicate the quality of routes irrespective of grades. A route must be excellent in all respects to qualify for ★★★ and even a ★ route must be out of the ordinary.
The absence of stars does not mean that a climb is unsatis-factory, as poor climbs are specifically described as such. A dagger in front of the route name indicates it probably hasn't had a second ascent therefore the grade could be incorrect. These routes have obviously not been included in the graded list.

Access — (A Statement by the British Mountaineering Council)

Most, but not all, of the crags in this guidebook are situated within the Snowdonia National Park. However, the designation of a National Park does not confer access rights and most of the crags are on private land, where the goodwill of landowners in permitting access is extremely important. Since the publication of the previous mid-Wales guide in 1973, there have been very considerable access difficulties encountered, in particular to both the hills and crags of the Aran range.

In 1982 the National Park concluded access agreements with the landowners concerned for a footpath over the main Aran ridge, with access from Llanuwchllyn and Dinas Mawddwy. This path now provides the agreed access route to Gist Ddu and Craig-y-Geifr.

Most of the difficulties over access to crags have hopefully now been solved, largely as the result of much patient negotiation. The access details for each crag have been included in the crag introductory sections with careful explanations of the ap-proaches, parking and other arrangements where these have been agreed. It is extremely important in the interests of maintaining access that where such agreements have been made they are closely followed.

It is also essential that climbers observe the very highest standards of behaviour, both in the interests of conserving the hill and crag environment, and of maintaining a spirit of good will between climber and landowner.

Please observe the following code:

1. Leave no litter or rubbish
2. Take care not to damage walls or fences
3. Close all gates
4. Don't light fires
5. Don't take dogs
6. Park cars considerately – don't block access
7. Avoid disturbance to wildlife or vegetation
8. Try to avoid disturbing sheep, particulary in the lambing season – during February, March and April

For up to date information on access contact the National Park Office, Penrhyndeudraeth, Gwynedd – tel: (0766) 770274; or the BMC, Crawford House, Precinct Centre, Booth Street East, Manchester – tel: 061-273 5835.

THE INCLUSION OF A CRAG OR ROUTES UPON IT IN THIS GUIDEBOOK DOES NOT MEAN THAT ANY MEMBER OF THE PUBLIC HAS A RIGHT OF ACCESS TO THE CRAG OR THE RIGHT TO CLIMB UPON IT.

Campsites, Huts etc.

For the south side of Cader there is an excellent campsite with good facilities at the farm Cwmrhwyddfor, owned by a Mr. Nutting, OS reference SH 738120.

For the north side of Cader there is a campsite at the farm along the side of the National Park car park O.S. ref. SH 698152. Also at the start of the pony track up Cader, there is a National Park bunkhouse.

The climbing hut Bryn Hafod is also bookable at weekends by climbing clubs.

New Routes

Descriptions of all new routes should be sent to: J A Sumner, Pear Tree Cottages, 188 Main Road, Milford, Stafford, ST17 0UN.

Historical by Geoff Milburn

HISTORICAL

The hills of mid-Wales have for hundreds of years been known to travellers but it was not until 1767 that there was a record of an ascent of Cader Idris. Although we do not know the full name of the initials L.N. we do know that the number of subsequent ascents increased rapidly in the early 1800s and the mountain was even climbed in 1863 by Prince Arthur. Legend has it that Cader Idris is the chair of Idris, the giant. It is said that anyone passing the night in his chair (a hollow in a rock near the summit) will either become frenzied with madness, die in the night, or be thenceforward gifted with supernatural genius.

At the beginning of the 19th century moonlight mountaineering became a fashion and inebriated parties used to wander up the mountain with food hampers and bottles in hand. They used to spend hilarious nights among the summit boulders relating weird tales until dawn. It was also at this time that the first tourists were exploring Welsh mountains and guides from Dolgellau used to take them to the summit of Cader. The most celebrated of the guides was Robin Edwards who guided his clients to the top for over forty years. Richard Pugh seems to have been the most enterprising for he built a summit hut in the 1830s which proved to be a great asset. It even had a hut keeper living there. Late in the century it was reported that on one day there were 100 people on the summit after 40 people had gone up for dawn. There was even much talk about the possibility of a mule track and a hotel on the summit. In the Climbers' Club Journal there was a cutting comment:

'Is not the sacrifice of Snowdon sufficient. Must it be that Cader Idris too will be given over to the hotel builder, and made sacred to bottle hurlers and sardine tin sprinklers.'

The first rock-climb in the area was almost certainly the alluring cleft of the *Central Gully* of Pen-y-Gadair which was done pre-1880. It is not known who made the ascent but perhaps it might have been F H Bowring as he was known to have regularly explored the north face over a period of many years. At one time the gully was even thought of as a popular route. Early dates of first ascents are few but certainly several members of the Alpine Club worked their way up the direct route from Llyn y Gadair in 1881 and during the 1880 the artist H.G. Willink explored the mountain.

Well before he became famous, Owen Glynne Jones soloed the *Eastern Arête of Cyfrwy* in May, 1888. Nothing much else was done over the next few years but several routes were added to

Mynydd Moel. W.P. Haskett Smith was active in the area however and had looked at the upper section of the *Great Gully* of Craig y Cae as early as 1890. He returned with O.G. Jones in May 1895 to complete the route which was described as being scenically the most dramatic gully known in Britain. The route soon attained a great reputation and Jones's enthusiasm about it was both infectious and overpowering. Some time later George Abraham commented about Jones:

'It is many years now, but I remember how, one Christmas at Wastdale, our appreciation of the best of the Cumberland climbs was always interrupted by some remark about the Great Gully of Craig y Cae.

"Ah," he would say disparagingly, "this is not bad, but wait until you see Craig y Cae"; or "Oh yes, this pitch is all right as pitches go" (he was now sitting on the top of the Great Chimney in Deep Ghyll), "but it is nothing to one I know in Wales."'

The day after Great Gully they also did *East Gully*.

Five years passed then in 1900 T.K. and F.W. Rose ascended the *North Arête* of Cyfrwy. Routes were slowly being discovered and *The East* and *West Gully* on Twr Du were then climbed in 1902 by S. Ridsdale and party. The classic Pencoed Pillar was accomplished in 1903 by the Dalton brothers two splendidly eccentric characters who were better known in the Lake District.

The Arans were first mentioned in the guidebook 'Climbing in the British Isles' by W.P. Haskett Smith in 1895. O.G. Jones had reviewed the area and described it in the following words:

'Climbers are often asked, "Where can a man start practising rock work?" The Arans are first rate for this. Whatever the difficulty on the mountain, a few minutes traversing will generally take one out of it, if direct ascent or descent be considered undesirable. The mountain face is so broken up that we have no gullies or arêtes separated by impossible walls from the easy parts of the mountain. In short, from the enthusiastic shin-scraper's point of view the architecture of the Aran face is defective.'

Climbing in the Arans really first began in 1907 when the Rucksack Club led by C.H. Pickstone paid a visit to Craig Cywarch. Pickstone knew of the crag as he had lived at Aber Cywarch as a boy. The three main gullies were climbed and teams did a great amount of indiscriminate scrambling on the faces. South Buttress was tried by two parties but without success and George Ewen later had a distinct recollection of anxious moments on a tiny ledge while the leader endeavoured to retrace his steps from 'an absolute impasse'. After a further Easter visit to the crag when nothing new was achieved Pickstone wrote in the Rucksack Club Journal:

'In view of the meticulous accuracy with which every potty little crack in Cumberland has been exploited – with variations – it is inexplicable why this fine crag remains neglected.'

The Rucksack Club had made a good start but their advice about the potential of the crag was to remain ignored for a very long time. This was partly due to the development taking place in North Wales and the Lake District but a key factor was that the area was poorly served by public transport until long after the Second World War. One climber who did venture into the area was Charles Evans who explored Aran Benllyn in 1941 and did three routes on Gist Ddu, the best of which was *Devious*. These routes went unrecorded and were unknown for over twenty years. Another isolated route was *Steric Slab* on Cyfrwy by E.L. Furness and J.H. Gilham in 1942. In 1951 R.E. Davies and H.E. Chatham added a further route to the same buttress. About that time Edward Pyatt reported that a Ken Mascary had climbed many new routes all over Cader in 1948 – unfortunately details have not yet been traced.

In the 1940s, after the war, no exploration took place in mid-Wales and it was not until 1950 that a close look at Craig Cywarch was taken. Peter Harding and N.L. Horsfield investigated the possibilities and picked out the obvious Shark's Fin, Main Hier, where they climbed *Kurzweg*. Harding also attacked the North Buttress and eventually completed a line with D. Kay in 1952. Sadly the line was not recorded and has not been established since then. 1952 was a significant year as R.E. 'Larry' Lambe and other members of The Mountain Club were attracted by a photograph of Craig Cywarch taken by W.A. Poucher. They began exploring at Cywarch and in addition to Lambe who was starting a phase of development both Eric Byne and Ernie Marshall led new routes. A meet held in November 1954 led to the acquisition of Tyn-y-Twll – a farmhouse at the head of the valley. The hut was essential for a long-term exploration of the local crags as when camping in the valley tents and rucksacks were apt to be ripped apart by packs of farm dogs in search of food.

When the hut opened early in 1955 it meant that serious exploration could begin and during the mid-1950s some well-known names were to appear on the Cywarch new route scene: John Sumner, Tony Moulam, Barry Knox, Don Roscoe, John Vereker, Peter Biven, Trevor Peck, Dave Adcock and John Downes to name but a few. In a two-year period about thirty routes were climbed, often as a result of repeated visits and extensive gardening. The big breakthrough however was the creation of routes on the highly impressive North Buttress. Sumner and Adcock made the first strike with *Stygian Wall* which has an extremely intimidating and airy second pitch. Later Adcock was to claim *Styx* and a third route was *Midlander* by Biven and Peck. The hardest route however was undoubtedly *Archeron* which was subjugated by Tony Moulam and Larry Lambe.

About that time aid routes were appearing in Derbyshire, Yorkshire and on outlying Welsh crags and the 'locals' were quick to notice a big overhanging crack on Tap-y-Gigfran. This provided *Purge* a full-blooded A2 complete with pegs and etriers. The two pitches were done by Sumner/Chisholm and Chisholm/Knox although Sumner made the first complete ascent with Dave Adcock in July 1956. Amazingly Sumner was to free the route some 23 years later in 1979.

After 1956 the spate of frenzied activity subsided and at the end of 1957 the lease on Tyn-y-Twll was terminated as the cottage was needed by the owner for a farm worker. With a total of about 50 routes in the valley it was decided to produce a guidebook to the Craig Cywarch area and this was duly completed by R.E. Lambe in 1958.

The year after the guidebook appeared Knox and Adcock were working on a big new line on the North East Buttress and they eventually cleaned the hard pitch from above, leaving the route for their next visit. An unsuspecting villain then showed up — one Chris Bonington. Not knowing that the line had not then been completed he promptly made an ascent of *Hades* which was the first Extreme done in mid-Wales.

The Mountain Club had tried unsuccessfully to find another cottage in the valley and eventually in desperation took the decision to reconstruct a ruined mine building at the head of the valley. With a five-year plan in mind the club began the work in the summer of 1960.

While a minor route explosion was taking place at Cywarch in the 1950s there was no similar activity on Cader Idris. Ray Handley and Bowden Black were the main leaders looking for new lines in the area from about 1954 onwards. There were two outstanding routes from this period: Bowden Black's classic slab climb *Obsession* and Handley's fine *Triad* on Twr Ddu. In the late 1950s Nat Allen with Derek Burgess also produced several new lines such as *Route 2*, and inevitably Joe Brown turned up on Mynydd Moel in 1959 to climb *Route Central*. He didn't stop however as there were bigger plans afoot in Snowdonia. Brown did however return with various partners in 1963 to grab five routes on Gist Ddu. The best of these is *Sloose*, a 300-foot corner which is rarely in good condition. On another route, *The Trench*, so much vegetation was removed from the crux section of the groove that eventually a 15-foot pile of debris built up at the foot of the crag.

Although people had scrambled on Craig Aderyn (Bird Rock) in the 1800s little of note was done and the crag remained until it was discovered by instructors from the outdoor pursuit schools in the area. While at the army school at Tywyn Chris Bonington did a few new routes on the Eastern face including the striking line of *Guano Pinnacle*. He also tried the diamond-shaped wall of The Bastion but failed to complete the route which had to wait until the 1970s for an ascent. During 1964 climbers from University College of North Wales, Aberystwyth and the Rimmon Mountaineering Club began to explore Bird Rock. Tony Howard, mainly with Alan Waterhouse, accounted for *The Beak, The Gizzard* and *The Talon*. L.K. Forsey and D. Davies added the hardest route up to that time with the bold line of *Daisy Belle*. Later, in 1967, R.A. Wilson and P. Surfleet were to climb several routes including *The Girdle of The Bastion*.

Martin Boysen and members of the Black and Tan Club went down to mid-Wales in 1966 and their exploration resulted in two classic HVS routes: *Plank Walk* on Cywarch's North Face and *Aardvark*, a superb arête on Gist Ddu.

Over the years from the mid-1960s to the mid-1970s the new route scene in the Arans was dominated by the Stafford-based Mountain Club. Some of the many outstanding achievements during that time were: *The Gem* (Sumner) and *The Grafter* (Sumner and J. Kirkam) on Tap-y-Gigfran; *Doom* (Sumner) and *Man of Kent* (R. Thorndike) on North Buttress; *Keel Haul* (Sumner) on the North Face; *The Scythe* (Knox and I.R. Tapley) on North-East Buttress); *Scimitar* (Sumner), *Obvious* (Thorndike) and *Moai Man* (Sumner) on Gist Ddu. Also during that time the fine V.Diff. *Will-o'-the-Wisp* (Sumner) was climbed on Cywarch's South Buttress.

During the 1960s much of the development at Cywarch had been done under the watchful eyes of R.E. Larry Lambe and Barry Knox and throughout their reign they produced two further guidebooks, in 1964 and 1966. Their names will always be firmly associated with Cywarch, but it is John Sumner who has virtually made the mid-Wales scene his own. After six new routes in the mid-1950s there was a gap of ten years, then from 1966 onwards Sumner began a long relationship with the surrounding crags; his name consequently figures prominently in the list of first ascents. It was also logical that he should take on the responsibility of keeping a record of all that had been

Kurt Sumner on Lanchester, Craig Cywarch. Photo: John Sumner

Jill Sumner on Will-o'-the Wisp, Craig Cywarch. Photo: John Sumner

done on the crags. This led to plans for a new guidebook which was eventually published in 1973 by Robin Collomb (West Col Productions).

After the Central Wales guidebook, there was a more pressing project. As yet no guidebook had been written for Cader Idris and while Sumner was working on this there was considerable activity on the Cader crags. In addition to Sumner, two other names kept cropping up on the new route scene – Keith Bentham and Dave Shaw. Undoubtedly their finest route was the magnificent *Darker Angel*, on the Great Gully Wall of the Pencoed Pillar, one of the best routes in Wales; but there were plenty of other classics such as *Crack of Cau*. Eventually in 1975 the guide to the 'Dolgellau Area' made its appearance.

In the late 1970s and early 1980s a whole new set of dedicated young climbers arrived – still mainly from The Mountain Club – and they were to push the standards in the area to a far higher level than ever before. New routes began to appear on the blank walls between the old natural lines but it was not only the youngsters who were having a field day, the old hands were there as well – ready to grab the gems if the opportunity arose. Craig Cywarch's North-facing cliffs in particular continued to yield superb routes such as *Strobe, Hard Rain* (both G.R. Herus and Sumner) and *Heretic* (John Codling). On the Southern Crag there was *Bear Cage* (Gary Gibson) and *Sweet Baby James* (Sumner). Some of the best discoveries were on Cywarch's sunshine crag – Tap-y-Gigfran; star routes such as: *Beggar's Banquet* (Sumner and Knox), *Dream Racer* (Sumner) *Crozzley Wall* (Sumner and Phil Gibson), *Rolair* and *Heist* (Sumner) and *Tumblin' Dice* (Herus and Bob Bradley).

In hard route terms Cader Idris did not keep pace with the action in the Arans but things were to change in the early 1980s. Firstly there were one or two classic routes done such as *Idris Corner* (Sumner) the open book corner low down on Craig Cau and *Gwydrin* (Sumner) probably the best slab climb in mid-Wales. Two climbs by John Codling were to raise the standards to new heights and both came firmly in the E5 bracket. *Rabble Rouser* was found on Mynydd Moel while *Messiah* was created on Craig Cau.

Later in the 1980s there was a definite reduction in the new routes produced at Cywarch but there was an increase in other areas. Gist Ddu for example at the opposite end of the Aran range yielded many superb new climbs: amongst these *Voie Suisse* and *Hungry Hearts* are destined for classic status.

The Cader Idris area came in for a thorough inspection and many of the low-lying crags around its base were opened up. Some, such as Craig-y-Llam and Craig Rhwyddfor, had probably not been climbed on before. John Sumner in particular stepped in for such gems as *Ice Man* and *Tyburn Gate*.

Farther afield the crags of Rhiwarth and Craig-y-Mwn on the southern end of the Berwyn were also to come out of obscurity. Rhiwarth had obviously been climbed on for many years and it is likely that the pioneers did not record their routes. Later teams from Oswestry and Reading claimed some of the lines and it was left for the Stafford based Mountaineering Club to methodically climb and grade all the lines. They also produced some very fine lines of their own. At Rhiwarth C. Nunn found his *Eden* and Sumner had plenty to smile about with *The Cheshire Cat*. On Craig-y-Mwn the team of Andy Grondowski, Little and Sumner had a particular good day with *Pardon me for Breathing* and *Brothers in Arms*.

Looking ahead to the future it is absolutely clear to those in the know that the new route possibilities in Mid-Wales are still enormous when compared to other areas. Crags such as Craig-y-Mwn in the Berwyns could easily have the number of routes doubled – and all would be of good quality. There is no doubt that the future of Mid-Wales climbing is going to be exciting as more and more climbers discover its true potential.

THE CRAIG CYWARCH AREA

Craig Cywarch

O.S. ref. SH 845190

Lying at the head of Cwm Cywarch this fascinating cliff complex has the largest concentration of rock-climbs in Mid-Wales. In fact the Cywarch crags cover well over 1½ miles with a variety of buttresses, walls and ridges – some of which are well hidden up in cwms and deep gullies.

This network of crags can be put to an advantage if climbs of a similar standard are linked together. For example a good day at VS could be had by starting up Lanchester, then continuing up The Gem on Tap-y-Gigfran. By finishing with the Girdle of Tap Rhygan Ddu it would give a total of some 600 feet of climbing.

The longest routes, some well over 400 feet, are found at the northern end of the cliffs where Acheron and Doom are located.

The crags mainly face south-east and north-east and are described starting from the south and then working north (left to right when facing the cliffs).

Good nut protection exists throughout the whole of the Cywarch crags and in particular the rock lends itself to good small nut protection.

Approach
From Dinas Mawddwy on the A470 Dolgellau – Machynlleth road take the minor road to Aber-Cywarch then follow the signposted road up the Cywarch valley. The Common at the end of the valley is customarily used for parking cars although this is not an official car-park (see sketch map). The crags are best approached by taking the track marked to Rhydymain which by-passes the last farm in the valley at Blaencywarch. Follow this track for approximately ⅓ of a mile to where a sheep track leads up to a small crag of Esgair Felen Isaf. Tracks then lead to the various parts of the crag (see sketch).

PANT LYGOG
The hanging valley of Pant Lygog has many broken buttresses the best of which are KEEP BUTTRESS and THE FORTRESS. To the left of these at the south-west end of the crags where the rock deteriorates there are some overlapping slabs. **S & D**, 250 feet, (1958), Very Difficult, takes the largest of the slabs.

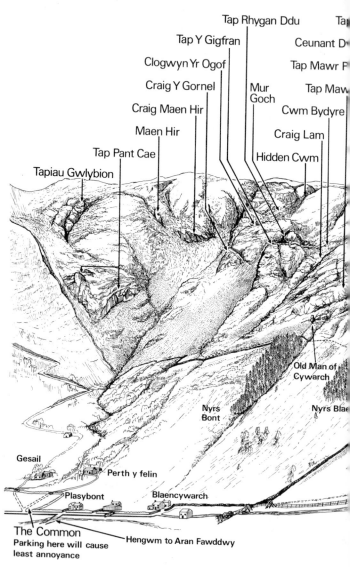

Tap Rhygan Ddu

Tap Y Gigfran

Ceunant D

Clogwyn Yr Ogof

Tap Mawr P

Craig Y Gornel

Mur
Goch

Tap Maw

Craig Maen Hir

Cwm Bydyre

Maen Hir

Craig Lam

Tap Pant Cae

Hidden Cwm

Tapiau Gwlybion

Old Man of
Cywarch

Nyrs Blae

Nyrs
Bont

Gesail

Perth y felin

Plasybont

Blaencywarch

The Common
Parking here will cause
least annoyance

Hengwm to Aran Fawddwy

Craig Cowarch

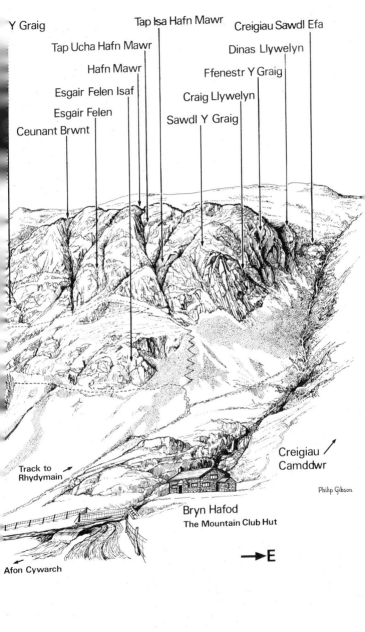

Y Graig

Tap Isa Hafn Mawr

Creigiau Sawdl Efa

Tap Ucha Hafn Mawr

Dinas Llywelyn

Hafn Mawr

Ffenestr Y Graig

Esgair Felen Isaf

Craig Llywelyn

Esgair Felen

Sawdl Y Graig

Ceunant Brwnt

Track to
Rhydymain

Creigiau
Camddwr

Philip Gibson

Bryn Hafod
The Mountain Club Hut

Afon Cywarch

➡ E

KEEP BUTTRESS is the small steep and vegetated buttress which starts from the scree to the left of the gully which contains the overlapping slabs of THE FORTRESS. **Portcullis**, 140 feet, Severe, is a vegetated line up cracks in KEEP BUTTRESS.

TAPIAU GWLYBION (THE FORTRESS)

The striking V-shaped buttress in the first gully that is encountered when entering the Hanging Valley.

* Stronghold   330 feet   Severe   (1970)
A delicate slab with a well-maintained standard throughout. Start at the lowest point of the buttress.
1   90 feet. Ascend an easy slab until it steepens then slant right to a bracket on the arête. Climb the arête for a few feet to a ledge on the left. Go back right to the arête and follow a crack just left of the arête to a long narrow ledge under a short steep wall. Go left along the ledge to a heather ledge. Stance and belay.
2   40 feet. Return back right a few feet to a weakness in the short steep wall. Ascend this and climb a slab above to a large heather ledge.
3   90 feet. From the left-hand end of the heather ledge a subsidiary slab gives access to the main slab above. Climb this with a delicate exit onto the main slab, then ascend the main slab direct to a heather ledge on the left.
4   40 feet. Return right and continue up the slab to a ledge then traverse right and go up easily to a large grassy ledge.
5   70 feet. An obvious chimney and a crack in the slab above provide the finish.

Battlements   350 feet   Hard Severe   (1970)
Quite a good slab route but with greater exposure than Stronghold.
1   130 feet. As for Stronghold to the long narrow ledge under a short steep wall. Return right along the ledge to the arête, then climb a groove to steep heather and a tree; continue to a large heather ledge. Good spike belay on a steep wall.
2   100 feet. Crux. Climb a steep broken groove just right of the spike belay to the slab above. Make an airy traverse right for 20 feet to a groove. Climb this to a heather ledge and continue to another heather ledge and a tree. Belay.
3   50 feet. Take a little wall directly behind the tree to climb another slab and exit right to a large grassy ledge.
4   70 feet. Finish up the right edge of the slab above.

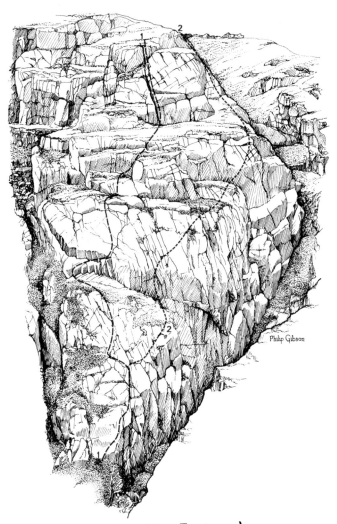

Philip Gibson

Tapiau Gwlybion (The Fortress)

1 Stronghold   S
2 Battlements   HS

1	White Ribbon	HS
2	The Wizard	S
3	Green Wall	E2
4	Dunsinane	HS

TAP PANT CAE (CRAIG TYN-Y-FEDW)

A rather wet and vegetated crag except for an area near a greenish wall on the East Face and an obvious smooth wall on its North Face.

EAST FACE

* **White Ribbon**   140 feet   Hard Severe   (1963)
A good route which is varied and exposed. Just left of the green wall a grass terrace runs out into the face. Below the right-hand end of this terrace is a small block above a hawthorn tree. Start at the block at a cairn.

5   Paper Back   HVS
6   Room at the Top   HS

1 70 feet. 4a. From the block make a rising traverse right for a few feet to move up left into a groove. Ascend the groove for a few feet then traverse left into the base of a narrow chimney and climb this on reasonable holds. The top of the chimney is choked with vegetation, so a bulge on the left is climbed to reach a ledge.
2 70 feet. A reasonably clean slab is climbed fairly directly on small incut holds to the top.

The Wizard 120 feet Severe   (1968)
A good line which is often wet. Start as for White Ribbon.
1 40 feet. From the block traverse right to a slab, cross the slab to the right and move right across the slab to a tree.
2 30 feet. Move up just to the right of the tree and climb a ramp, trending back left to another tree and grassy ledges.
3 50 feet. Ascend a short chimney, then go slightly left up to a large spike. Go over the spike and finish up the wall above.

* Green Wall   120 feet   E2   (1981)
A direct way up the obvious green wall which is the outstanding feature of the crag.
1   120 feet. 5c. Climb with increasing difficulty via cracks directly up the steep wall. Gain a ledge on the left beneath a steep little corner then move left to enter a scoop, then go straight up from the scoop using a good pocket hold to reach easier ground.

Dunsinane, (1968) a vegetated first pitch starts 30 feet right of **White Ribbon** (150 feet, Hard Severe, 4a). The second pitch takes a hidden chimney on the right of the green wall.

The Sting   180 feet   Hard Very Severe   (1 pt. aid)   (1974)
The climb follows the steep section of rock about 90 feet down and to the right of the conspicuous green wall. Rather vegetated in the upper section. Start directly beneath the steep wall at a crack.
1   80 feet. 5a. Climb the crack in the centre of the steep wall to a little groove below a steepening. Use the aid peg above to reach good holds up on the left to gain a slab. Go up the corner to the slab above and move right, then climb to a grassy ledge with a block belay.
2   35 feet. 4a. Climb the wall on the left of the block belay to a bulge which is overcome by spike holds on the right and so to a heathery ledge.
3   65 feet. 4c. Ascend the wall between two towers to the overhang. Climb the wide crack in the centre. Above the overhang move right to an arête, then go up to easier ground.

Gryptych, 170 feet, Hard Severe, 4b, 4a, (1973) is a vegetated route right of The Sting. **Clubs**, 105 feet, Severe, (1955) is farther right at the lowest point of the buttress, starting to the left of a wall. Ascend a broken slab and overhanging block on the right to a ledge. The climb then deteriorates.

Above and right of the lowest point of the buttress is a smooth, steep wall with an obvious corner crack on its right, with a large overhanging capstone. Room at the Top takes the corner and Paper Back the smooth wall on its left.

Paper Back   90 feet   Hard Very Severe   (1969)
The clean fine-looking diagonal crack left of the centre of the smooth wall. Start 10 feet left at a second vegetated crack.
1   90 feet. 5b. Climb the crack with increasing difficulty to a pinnacle on the right. Step off the pinnacle top and climb a short wall to a ledge; continue up the short steep wall above.

Room at the Top   90 feet   Hard Severe   (1969)
The corner crack with an interesting top pitch; climbers of small frame will find it easier than its grade. Start at the corner crack.

1 60 feet. Climb the wide crack on the right of the corner, on good holds, to a ledge beneath the capstone.
2 30 feet. Ascend the wide crack above by the through route.

Higher up the Cwm to the right are several small buttresses. All have routes on them. A pinnacle known as Maen Hir has four climbs. The short side of the pinnacle gives **Kurzweg**, a 20-foot Difficult, (1950).

CWM-YR-YCHEN (CWM RHYCHAIN)

MAEN HIR (THE SHARK'S FIN)

Steilweg 60 feet Severe   (1953)
Start on the east side of the pinnacle, a short distance down the gully from the neck.
1 60 feet. Ascend diagonally right to a quartz bulge, then gain a small ledge above it. Move delicately right and pull onto a bilberry ledge on the front of the pinnacle. Move round onto the other face and gain the sharp edge above which is followed to the top.

Schnellweg 50 feet Severe   (1970)
Start by a traverse out below the neck on the western side of the pinnacle.
1 50 feet. Traverse horizontally left on good handholds to reach a small ledge, move up and left to reach the arête and ascend this to finish.

CRAIG-Y-GORNEL

A rather disappointing crag at the head of Cwm yr Ychen, which has an obvious gully near its centre. The right-hand wall of the gully, which is not obvious from a distance, has one worthwhile route.

Taranu Crack 90 feet Hard Very Severe   (1969)
A little way in the gully on the right wall is a rather steep overhanging crack. Start below this.
1 90 feet. 5a. Climb the crack with the crux in the centre where the crack constricts.

Other routes have been done on the lower section of the crag.

Flashback, 150 feet, Hard Severe, 4b, 4a (1976) takes a line up the middle of the slabs finishing by a long traverse right to a projecting pedestal.

Cwm yr Ychen (Cwm Rhychain)

Maen Hir (The Shark's Fin)
1 Steilweg   S
2 The Wall   HVS

Philip Gibson

HIDDEN CWM

A cwm between Craig-y-Gornel and Tap Rhygan Ddu has produced several short routes of a rather scrappy nature except for Knockdown which takes an arête line on the left (an obvious feature) just past the narrow entrance to the cwm at a fork in the gully.

Knockdown 200 feet Hard Difficult   (1975)
Start 15 feet to the right of the lowest point of the crag of Mur Goch.
1 90 feet. Move up on flakes then climb the slab above until it is possible to move out to the right onto the nose of the arête. Climb this on good holds to a small ledge and spike belay.
2 30 feet. Move right into a corner, then traverse diagonally up left across a slab to join the arête again at a small ledge.

3 40 feet. Go up the arête to a small corner, move round to the left, then climb the slab above to a heather terrace. Large belay block on the left.
4 40 feet. Go over the belay block then move up left to the top of the crag.

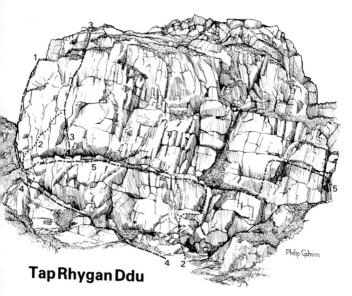

Philip Gibson

Tap Rhygan Ddu

1	Darkness on the Edge of Town	E3
2	Baptême de L'air	E1
3	Chariots of Fire	E2
4	Shady Saunter	S
5	The Girdle Traverse	VS

TAP RHYGAN DDU

An obvious feature of this crag is the horizontal gash which has a large overhang above and an overhanging wall beneath it.

** **Darkness on the Edge of Town** 80 feet E3 (1982)
Start at the finishing ledge of Shady Saunter and The Girdle at the left-hand side of the crag, below a rust coloured wall.
1 80 feet. 6a. Climb the wall for 10 feet then traverse left on side pulls to a peg. Step left to a bottomless V-groove and ascend this (crux) with difficulty to good holds. Step left to a ledge. Climb the wall above, passing hollow flakes, to the top. Big hexes for belay.

** **Baptême de L'air** 350 feet E1 (1984)
A rather wandering route but with some good climbing. Start at the lowest point of the crag as for Shady Saunter.

1 75 feet. 5b. From a cave step left onto a nose of rock, move left again to a crack and ascend this to gain a ramp on the right. Traverse along the ramp to a crack in a corner and climb this to join the girdle line.
2 145 feet. 4b. Traverse left along the sensational last pitch of the girdle to its end at the sloping finishing ledge of Shady Saunter.
3 130 feet. 5a. Move right then go up to a traverse line above that of the girdle. Traverse right along this to a big spike on the edge. Make an awkward move right then follow a rising traverse right on good holds to a ledge. Take the wall above and finish up the easiest line.

* Chariots of Fire   120 feet   E2   (1984)
A worthwhile pitch taking the main break through the overhangs above the traverse line of the girdle.
1 120 feet. 5c. From the huge nest on the last pitch of the girdle where a small pillar bridges the overhangs climb the steep overhanging corner above the pillar (peg), exiting left to a ledge. Continue up a flaky crack then the wall above to the top.

Shady Saunter   170 feet   Severe   (1957)
Takes the ramp under the lower overhanging wall. Some bad rock. Start at the lowest point of the buttress, below and just left of a cave.
1 50 feet. Traverse easily left round an edge to gain the ramp below the overhanging wall. Nut belays.
2 120 feet. Continue along the ramp to a bulge, surmount this and the slab above to a steep corner. Climb this on doubtful rock to the ledge above. Nut belay well back.

* Girdle Traverse   250 feet   Very Severe   (1968)
Follows the obvious horizontal gash from right to left. Start at an easy-angled vegetated groove 40 feet right of a wet chimney. The gash starts above the wet chimney. Originally the gash was gained via the chimney. Not recommended.
1 90 feet. 4a. Climb the vegetated groove to gain the traversing line to the left. Follow this to where a wedge and sling in a horizontal crack (in place) enable an abseil to be made to the holly bush.
2 80 feet. 4a. Traverse left to a corner, descend 10 feet and traverse the pleasant slabs to their end. Nut belays under the overhang.
3 80 feet. 4b. A sensational pitch. Follow the gash starting with an awkward move round a wedged block. Continue in the same line round an exposed pillar to a gigantic nest. Continue leftwards making some final thin moves to the sloping finishing ledge of Shady Saunter. Nut belay well back.

General Galtieri   60 feet   Hard Severe   (1982)
A diagonal line rightwards on the clean right edge of the
buttress. Start 7 feet left of the undercut base of the right-hand
edge of the buttress.
1 60 feet. 4a. Make a rising traverse right to a ledge on the
edge. Climb a slab for three feet then step right to a groove.
Ascend the groove then move right climbing a slab to a niche;
move left to a small tree. Stance. Exit right to vegetation.

TAP-Y-GIGFRAN

The crag has faces to the south and east and forms the division
between Cwm-yr-Ychen and Cwm Bydyre. Its impressive south
face overlooking Cwm-yr-Ychen is one of Cywarch's better cliffs,
giving routes among the best in the valley. Some of the harder
climbs have the unique merit of staying dry in wet weather. The
most obvious feature of this face is the great overhanging corner
of Purge.

TAP-Y-GIGFRAN (SOUTH FACE)

The maximum height of the south face is 300 feet; unfortunately
the lower 150 feet are very broken and vegetated. From a small
sheep track passing below the face just above the scree, the
broken lower section rises to a wide grassy ramp crossing the
whole face diagonally from the bottom right-hand corner to
roughly mid-height. This is known as The Ramp and has sections
of Very Difficult climbing. Above The Ramp a very steep wall
rises to the top of the crag. This wall is split mid-way by a large
ledge; and from its left-hand end rises the overhanging corner
of the second pitch of Purge.

The Ramp affords the best approach to Dream Racer, Purge, The
Grafter, Heist, etc., and is easily gained at about one-third height
by a grassy terrace.

The best way off the top of the south face is to scramble up
heather and rock leftwards to a hidden short gully. Descending
to the left continue traversing leftwards across scree and grass
slopes until beneath the crag of Tap Rhygan Ddu. Descend steep
grass to the small track beneath the face.

Descent from routes ending on the large mid-way ledge, i.e.
Tumblin' Dice, The Crab, Heist, etc., is by making a 75-foot abseil
from a steel spike on the large sloping ledge under pitch 2 of
Purge.

High on the extreme left side of the south face is a steep grassy
gully with a steep headwall; this is **Concorde**, 120 feet, Severe,

Dream Racer, E1 5b with John Sumner climbing. *Photo: Dave Clilverd*

Geoff Cope on Sweet Baby James, Craig Cywarch.   Photo: John Sumner

2 pitches. **South West Arête**, 135 feet, Hard Very Difficult is a vegetated climb on broken rib forming the left ledge of the south face, and starts from the bottom of the gully leading to Concorde.

** **Beggars Banquet**   164 feet   Hard Very Severe   (1981)
Start beneath the square-cut corner topped by a triangular roof, best approached from the left via a grassy rake. A very good second pitch.
1 65 feet. 5a. Ascend the corner, but before reaching the roof step right to a foothold on the right edge; move round this and go up to a ledge. Continue moving up right to the big grassy ledge under a steep wall.
2 99 feet. 5b. Starting 17 feet left of the spike block in the centre of the ledge, climb the ragged vertical crack above to an overhung slab. Ascend this keeping to its right edge at the top.

** **Buzzard's Balcony**   150 feet   Severe   (1955)
A good climb, taking a line through the overhang. Start beneath the corner with the triangular roof, as reached by Beggars Banquet.
Alternatively climb The Ramp (V Diff) to its highest point at some blocks.
1 45 feet. Traverse right from the corner to a line of weakness trending up right. (This same point can be gained from the blocks at the top of The Ramp by making a short traverse left.) Climb the weakness with a short traverse right at the top to reach a big ledge on the right. Large nut belays behind a big block below a corner.
2 25 feet. Ascend the corner above to a large ledge on the left.
3 60 feet. Climb on to the end of the projecting rock on the right then make a long stride on to a rightward slanting slab and climb this to its top via some cracks. Small stance at the top of the slab with good nut belays and spike above.
4 20 feet. Go up a short easy wall above to the large terrace. Block belays well back.

** **Little Red Rooster**   194 feet   E2   (1981)
An excellent climb which is the quickest drying route on the crag. Start as for Dream Racer.
1 94 feet. 5a. Climb the wall of Dream Racer to the ledge. Continue up the corner above to the big ledge on the left with a huge spike block in its centre.
2 100 feet. 5c. Climb the overhanging wall just right of the spike block to a short ramp on the left then climb rightwards to a slab (rest place). Traverse upwards and leftwards to a large foothold on the prow. Continue up the prow to the top.

Tap-y-Gigfran (South Face)

1	Beggars Banquet	HVS
2	Little Red Rooster	E2
3	Lucy in the Sky	HVS
4	Buzzard's Balcony	S
5	Dream Racer	E2
6	Alecto	E3
7	Purge	E3

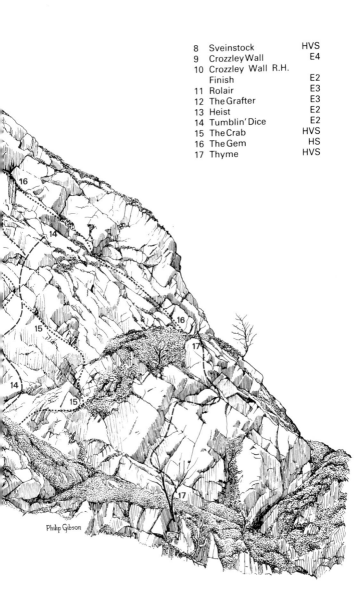

Philip Gibson

*** **Dream Racer**   180 feet   E2   (1981)

A superb route. Start at the top of The Ramp just left of a tree beneath a cleaned wall.

1   80 feet. 5a. Make a short rising traverse right then climb the wall direct to its highest point.

2   100 feet. 5b. Above on the right is a huge prow. The pitch follows the edge of this. From a flake just right of the corner step on to the wall, moving right to a peg. Move up to a crack then gain a ledge above on the edge of the prow, peg runner. Move up diagonally right to gain a niche above the overhang. Move up left to an arête leading to an easy slab. Belay at the top of the slab.

Lucy in the Sky   220 feet   Hard Very Severe   (1975)

Start 10 feet left of the belay block of Purge, beneath a steep wall bounded by a slight corner to its left and an arête to the right. Good small thread at the base of the corner.

1   70 feet. 5a. Good handholds to start lead up the steep strenuous wall to a resting place at 20 feet. Step right and follow a narrow exposed slab to a large ledge. Nut belays in a corner up to the left.

2   25 feet. Pitch 2, Buzzard's Balcony. Ascend the corner to a large ledge on the left.

3   70 feet. 5a. Climb on to the projecting rock on the right then gain a ramp on the left. Follow it until it is possible to make a move to a steep crack trending rightwards beneath the overhangs. Follow the crack with a final difficult move to reach the stance.

4   55 feet. Ascend the steep groove above then exit left to a grass area and tree belay.

* **Alecto**   185 feet   E3   (1 pt. aid)   (1975/1980)

Start as for Purge.

1   75 feet. 5b. From the belay block climb directly to a crack. Step left to a sloping ledge in the corner, and climb this for a few feet to an undercut flake. Traverse to the right-hand end of the flake (protection peg) and climb a very steep broken crack above to a large ledge.

2   110 feet. 6a. Just left of pitch 2 of Purge is a system of cracks in the overhanging prow; start below these. From the doubtful flake spike gain the large spike, then move slightly left to a crack with 2 pegs. Use the upper peg for aid, passing a peg runner on the right to reach a poor flake on the left. Make a difficult move to reach a large jug, then move up and left to gain the niche above. Climb easier ground to a slab and follow this to the top.

*** **Purge**   200 feet   E3   (1969/1979)

The classic of the crag. Start at a large block near the top of The Ramp, about 80 feet above the ash tree (start of The Grafter). If this route is done using the protection pegs for aid the standard becomes Hard Very Severe, 5a, 5a.

1   80 feet. 5c. Make a long step right off the large detached block then move up and right to a good ledge on the right, below a steep triangular wall formed by two cracks which merge in an overhanging groove. Climb the triangular wall and the overhanging groove (2 pegs) to the niche above. Move out left above the niche to a large ledge under an imposing corner.
2   70 feet. Climb the steep crack in the corner to a bulge. Move right to a peg then go up to a good hold; move delicately right again to reach the large sloping ledge. Move back left and climb the crack in the corner to a grassy ledge and block belay.
3   50 feet. Easy rock leads to the top.

* Sveinstock   210 feet   Hard Very Severe   (1968)
Start at a crack 30 feet right of the large detached block at the foot of Purge.
1   80 feet. 5a. Step up right on to a block. Make an awkward move up left to gain a sloping ledge below a groove. Climb the groove to a platform on the left. (Junction with Purge.) Traverse right for 20 feet to a slab slanting right. Climb this to a large spike in a corner.
2   130 feet. 4b. As for pitch 3, The Grafter. Take a crack line trending right above the belay spike until the wall steepens. Pull into a shallow niche, move out of this right (crux of The Gem) and continue up the wall above to easier ground. Continue trending left to the top of the crag.

*** Crozzley Wall   150 feet   E4   (1980)
A direct, sustained and brilliant route. Pitch 1 takes the abseil line from the steel spike under pitch 2 of Purge. Start 10 feet right of Sveinstock below a thin overhanging crack. Very small wires are needed for protection on pitch 1.
1   75 fee. 5c. Climb the overhanging crack with difficulty to a flake and reach the ledge above. Climb the next short steep wall to another ledge, then climb the wall direct to the big ledge under pitch 2 of Purge.
2   75 feet. 5c. Climb the wall above, starting 6 feet right of the abseil spike, to a protection peg under a little overlap. Step left and climb the wall above to the peg on Purge. Continue, taking the crux of Purge, to the sloping ledge on the right. Move back left and climb the crack in the corner to a grassy ledge and a block belay.

Crozzley Right-Hand Finish   75 feet   E2   †   (1982)
Variation finish to pitch 2, Crozzley Wall.
1   75 feet. 5c. Climb Crozzley Wall pitch 2 to the peg in the horizontal break then go up the wall directly above to a final bulge.

*** Rolair   100 feet   E3

(1982)

A stunning pitch which follows the steep ramp above the diagonal line of The Grafter. Start by a small stunted tree a short distance up left from the start of The Grafter.

1   100 feet. 6a. Climb the steep wall just right of the tree, past a peg, to a shallow niche. Traverse right from the niche to a sloping ledge. Step round a rib on the right and climb diagonally up right passing pegs, to good underpulls below and to the right of the last peg. Follow these right round a shield of rock to reach the ramp on pitch 2 of The Grafter. Follow the ramp up left for a few yards then go straight up via a crack to reach a big sloping ledge.

** The Grafter   285 feet   E3

(1968/1980)

A good route which takes the diagonal traversing line under the overhangs. Start at an ash tree growing against the overhanging wall roughly three-quarters of the way up The Ramp. If this route is done using the peg on pitch 1 for aid the standard becomes E1, 5b.

1   70 feet. 6a. Shin up the tree growing against the wall to a ledge. Move left into a niche at the start of the diagonal traversing line. Traverse right on this line to a short groove with a peg; continue moving right to a niche and a large spike belay.

2   75 feet. 5a. Climb the ramp trending left to its top, then move up to a large spike belay in a corner.

3   140 feet. 4b. Ascend the wall taking the crack line, trending right, then continue as for pitch 3 of The Gem. A better finish is pitch 2 of Crozzley Wall.

** Heist   115 feet   E2

(1981)

Finds an easier start and finish to the excellent middle section of Tumblin' Dice. Start at the ash tree, as for The Grafter.

1   115 feet. 5c. Climb the ash tree then traverse right via a large green flake to a sloping ledge with a peg. Move up and right to a broken flake (good tape). 5 feet above the flake reach a hidden jug. Step right using good little pockets to a short groove. Reach a good hold up right and gain a small ledge beneath a large spike. From the top of the spike climb directly up on good side pulls until stopped by a short steep wall. Traverse left past a peg to a short crack; go up this to a big sloping ledge. This pitch could be split at the large spike. Pitches would then be 5c, 5a. Finish up The Grafter or abseil from the steel spike under pitch 2 of Purge.

** Tumblin' Dice   135 feet   E2

(1978)

Start 30 feet right and down from The Grafter, at an undercut crack.

1   80 feet. 5c. Layback rightwards up the undercut crack to a small bramble ledge beneath an overhang. Pull over this on doubtful holds and gain a sloping ledge above by some technical

moves; peg. Move up and right across the wall to the bottom of a short groove, and follow this to the spike belay on The Grafter.
2   55 feet. 5c. From the top of the belay spike go straight up to attain a position at the bottom of a very small groove/pod on the right. Exit awkwardly right (peg on the left) onto a slab. Nut belays. Way off: Go easily up the short slab on the left, and traverse leftwards over large sloping ledges to the steel abseil spike under pitch 2 of Purge.

* **The Crab**   185 feet   Hard Very Severe   (1980)
The big ramp slanting right to left above the very steep wall of The Grafter and Tumblin' Dice. Poor protection on pitch 1. Start just below the start of Tumblin' Dice, beside a vegetated ramp that goes off right.
1   110 feet. 5a. Climb the ramp until a cleaned line can be taken up to the start of the ramp line. Follow this to the large spike belay on The Grafter.
2   75 feet. 5a. From the top of the spike make an awkward traverse left to gain the ramp line continuation. Follow this to its top, exiting left using a good side pull. A short easy arête leads to a large spike belay (pitch 2 of The Grafter). Continue as for The Grafter or abseil from the steel spike under Purge.

* **Thyme**   115 feet   Hard Very Severe   (1984)
Lower down the ramp line well below and right of The Crab are two very steep grooves. Start to the right of the left-hand one.
1   115 feet. 5b. Go easily up a slab to the left-hand groove which is overhung (peg at its foot). Climb the right wall of the groove to good jugs below a holly bush. Traverse right to a short arête under a V-notch, climb through the notch then take a slab and arête on the right to the top.

** **Lanchester**   125 feet   Very Severe   (1982)
A quality route which starts from the lowest point of The Ramp under the south face. Scramble up 23 feet of vegetated corner to a huge block on the right wall. Gain the top of the block.
1   125 feet. 4b. Step left across a slab to reach a spike. Ascend left again to reach jugs on the right; move right and go up to a niche. Traverse the slab up left below an overhang to a wide crack. Go left again to the end of the slab and step left on to the front of the wall; climb this trending slightly right to a scoop and the base of a groove trending leftwards. Take this to the top. Descent: 6 feet above the top of the route descend a ramp to the left into an overhung corner then go down a groove.

TAP-Y-GIGFRAN

This face consists of vegetated slabs and walls cut by gullies. The largest area of slabs are those sweeping down to the lowest point of the crag, and are known as the Eastern Slabs. Their left edge drops away to form the south face. Right of the Eastern Slabs a vegetated gully rises the full height of the face. Right of this two slabby buttresses, one above the other, form the North Wing. The steeper Tower Buttress is split on its right-hand side by a square-cut gully.

Ways off the Eastern Slabs and the upper North Wing are as for the south face. Descent from the North Wing Lower Buttress is by grassy slopes to the right of the crag, i.e. towards Cwm Bydyre or by descending the square-cut gully.

Tap-y-Gigfran (East Face)

1	Incapability	M
2	The Gem	HS
3	Jack O' Diamonds	HVD
4	Hot Pants	HD

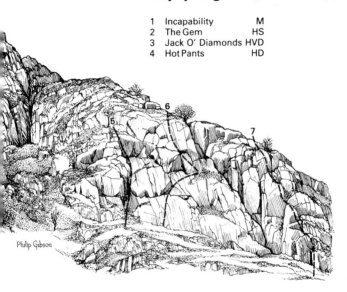

Philip Gibson

EASTERN SLABS

The vegetated arête found by the south face and Eastern Slabs is **Incapability**, 300 feet, Moderate, (1953), finishing on a grassy terrace where Jack o' Diamonds starts. This terrace, above the lower scrappy section, can be reached from the shallow gully on the right.

** **The Gem**   250 feet   Hard Severe   (1968)
The big right-angled corner topped by a square overhang high up on the left-hand edge of the Eastern Slabs. A leftward traverse from the overhang gives an exposed finish above the steep south face. Start from the left-hand end of a ledge, directly below the corner, to the left of the top of pitch 1 of Jack o' Diamonds.

1 60 feet. Climb the corner to a holly tree at 20 feet. Continue up the slabby corner to a large rock ledge beneath an overhang. Nut belay in overhang, small spike above.
2 60 feet. 4a. Make an awkward move over the overhang to reach the upper slab. Go delicately up the slab to the large square overhang, then traverse left to the arête. Stance and belay.
3 130 feet. 4b. Traverse leftwards on big holds for 20 feet to a rightward slanting crack. Go up this to a niche, pull out of this to the right, then go more easily up to the arête. Climb easily up this to the top of the crag.

* **Jack o' Diamonds** 350 feet Hard Very Difficult (1956)
Start in the middle of the grass terrace reached by climbing Incapability, or from the shallow gully on the right.
1 60 feet. Climb a short slab to a ledge below a steeper slab. Climb this to a grassy ledge.
2 60 feet. Climb the undercut slab taking a line of weakness diagonally up right to a ledge in a corner beneath a steep wall; traverse right for a few feet to another ledge with spike belays above.
3 80 feet. Traverse back diagonally up left across the steep wall on good holds to continue by the slab above to a ledge on the left. Spike belay.
4 100 feet. Easy slab work to a large heather ledge.
5 50 feet. Scrambling to the top remains.

NORTH WING UPPER BUTTRESS

This is the wedge-shaped buttress high to the right of the Eastern Slabs, framed by two gullies.

Hot Pants 300 feet Hard Difficult (1971)
A line up the centre of the buttress. Start at the toe of the buttress, above a mountain ash tree in the gully.
1 100 feet. Go directly up the wall via cracks for 80 feet. A heather terrace then leads to the start of the slabs, nut belay.
2 90 feet. A rising traverse to the left leads to a spike. Move up the open slab to an overhanging nose. Climb this on the right then go back left into a corner. Stance, and nut belays.
3 110 feet. Ascend the broken slab on the right of the corner, and continue direct to the top of the buttress.

NORTH WING LOWER BUTTRESS

Best examined and approached from the ruined hut in Cwm Bydyre. It is cleaner and steeper than the upper buttress with a square-cut gully on its right-hand side. A corner near the left-hand side of the buttress, formed by a large leaning tower, marks the start of **Wright's Route** (130 feet, Severe, 1965) which takes the corner for 20 feet then traverse left under an overhang to the arête. Finish up this.

Sifta 130 feet Severe   (1956)
Start 3 feet right of the corner noted above.
1 100 feet. Climb the wall and small groove above until a step left can be made into the crack in the corner. Ascend the crack to the overhang, traverse left to the arête and follow this to a stance and a small tree belay.
2 30 feet. Easy slabs lead to the top.

                                                           (1955)
* **Cerebos** 130 feet Severe
Start approximately at about the centre of the slabs.
1 70 feet. Ascend the steep slab to a small ledge, thread runner in the crack above. A small overhang above is climbed using the crack on the left and an obvious line is followed to a pinnacle up on the right. Stance and belay farther right.
2 60 feet. Move back left above the pinnacle on to an exposed slab. Climb this to a steep heather finish.

Square-cut Gully, 300 feet, Moderate, is normally used as a descent.

Square Chimney, 160 feet, Very Difficult, starts on the right side of the gully where a large block forms the side of a square chimney; 2 pitches, following the chimney line.

TAP MAWR (FAR SOUTH BUTTRESS)
This is the large triangular-shaped buttress lying between Cwm Bydyre and Little Gully, and above the second fir tree plantation. The buttress has an upper and lower tier. The split is formed by a large grassy terrace going right across the buttress. From this terrace two grassy rakes cut diagonally down leftwards ending above overhanging rock. The lower tier is very steep with roofs and overhangs; unfortunately the grassy rakes almost ruin any chance of continuous rock, the only exception being a central clean area with an obvious overlap line on its right. Left of the central clean area is a heavily vegetated section with a line trending left following trees; this is Sheep's Climb. Left of this the crag steepens with an area of wet black overhangs before the buttress degenerates into vegetation.

Descent is made by following the large horizontal terrace above the lower tier in either direction to Little Gully or Cwm Bydyre.

Migraine 178 feet Hard Very Severe   (1976)
Start 60 feet left of Black Wall below an obvious steep chimney just left of the black overhangs.

Tap Mawr (Far South Buttress)

1	Jungle	MVS
2	Short Circuit	VS
3	The Graveyard	HVS
4	Frigid Pink	E1
5	Scourge	E1
6	The Mind's Eye	E4

Philip Gibson

1 58 feet. 4c. Climb the crack to the steep chimney; ascend this moving out left then go up a steep wall to a ledge and belay.
2 100 feet. 5a. Climb the crack behind the belay to a ledge and tree. Move up to a huge flake and gain the scoop above (crux). Steep climbing from the scoop, going slightly right, leads to a ledge and belay.
3 20 feet. The steep wall above leads to the top.

Black Wall 220 feet Very Severe   (1956)
Start at the right-hand side of the large dark overhangs. A band of black rock runs up vertically. The climb follows this black band, starting where an easy-angled slab and a steep wall meet.
1 40 feet. 4b. Ascend the small black slab to a corner, climb this for 3 feet then traverse 10 feet right on good holds, and move up to a stance and doubtful tree belay.
2 60 feet. 4c. Surmount the chockstone in the back wall of the stance and climb awkwardly up and trend left to a small ledge below a quartz corner. Avoid the corner by a delicate traverse left for 15 feet, then ascend to a large grassy rake with a stance and belay.
3 60 feet. 4b. Walk up the rake for 40 feet and climb an arête, still on the black rock, to another good stance and belay.
4 60 feet. A short black wall ahead and a slab above lead to grass and a stance by a large tree.

Delli, 220 feet, Hard Severe, (1970), a vegetated route, starts approximately 8 feet right of the corner taken by Black Wall. Climb a steepening slab to a ledge line full of trees. Walk along this to its right-hand end and climb the left side of a corner to finish on vegetation. **Sheep's Climb**, 200 feet, Moderate, (1966).

Jungle 190 feet Mild Very Severe   (1956)
Sparse protection. Start from the huge block with a tree growing out of it just right of Sheep's Climb, on the left extremity of the clean central wall.
1 90 feet. 4b. Step off right from the top of the block and move right to a rib; climb this moving right to a short corner. Move out right above the corner and climb a short wall to trees.
2 100 feet. Climb the vegetated corner behind the trees until it is possible to move onto the right-hand wall at some cracked blocks. Traverse right for 3 feet then go up to the large grassy terrace.

* Short Circuit 165 feet Very Severe   (1982)
Start at the lowest point of the wall 15 feet right of the huge block with a tree growing out of it.
1 85 feet. 4b. Climb the wall on good incuts, trending left to a light-coloured ramp, and follow this left and go up to a short corner. Move right above the corner and climb a short wall to a ledge with large dead trees.

2 80 feet. 4a. Go to the right-hand end of the ledge, past a hawthorn tree in a corner, and step down and round the arête, then climb straight up the buttress front to the top.

The Graveyard 165 feet Hard Very Severe (1975)
A crack-line midway between Scourge and Jungle. Start directly beneath the crack.
1 85 feet. 5a. Ascend easily to the first bulge, then go awkwardly over this to a resting position beneath the second steeper bulge. Climb this (crux) to a small ledge and an easier-angled section; continue following the vague crack-line to vegetation and trees.
2 80 feet. 4a. Move horizontally right past a hawthorn tree in a corner, to climb the front of the buttress to the top. Pitch 2 of Short Circuit.

Frigid Pink 90 feet E1 (1980)
A devious line between Scourge and The Graveyard. Start 3 feet right of The Graveyard.
1 90 feet. 5b. Climb the slab to a good nut crack in the wall above; traverse right and gain a sloping ledge beneath a quartz wall. Make a move up the quartz wall (good nut crack high on the right), then traverse back left to a niche with a downward pointing fang of rock. Climb the groove just left of the fang to an easier-angled wall above. Climb this direct to a niche; pull out of the niche to a stance with a tree on the left. Either continue as for pitch 2, of The Graveyard, or abseil from the tree.

* **Scourge** 110 feet E1 (1969)
Start at the crack to the left of the overlap line.
1 110 feet. 5c. Climb the crack to a niche, starting at a short overhung corner. Continue up the overhanging crack, peg, (crux) to a sloping ledge. Go up and right to the ledge directly above The Overlap. Escape right on easy ledges.

* **The Mind's Eye** 110 feet E4 (1980)
Start 13 feet left of The Overlap. Sparse protection.
1 110 feet. 6a. Pull over the bulge and immediately tiptoe traverse left to a rounded spike hold. Gain this with the feet to a small quartz ramp. Climb the ramp (crux) to a good hold at its top below a bulge. Step right (rest on No. 2 Friend) and go over the bulge leftwards to a spike. Climb another bulge direct to join The Overlap. Move right as for this route to ledges.

** **The Overlap** 110 feet E2 (1971)
The obvious overlap line trending left. A powerful line and a Tap Mawr classic.
1 110 feet. 5b. Climb the corner to a peg; traverse left and ascend (crux) to reach a good foothold below a crack. Ascend straight up on good holds to a bulge; pull over this on the right

and climb the wall above. Move out right above the last roof to a ledge, nut belays. Escape right on easy ledges.

* **Old Glory**   100 feet   E4   (1 rest pt.)   (1979)
Start as for The Overlap.
1   100 feet. 6a. From the shelf at the start of The Overlap traverse right at a low level. Ascend to the overhang and take the roof direct on good holds. Go up the ramp on the left past a peg and a wire, the latter used for a rest. Peg high up on the left. Difficult moves on awkwardly spaced holds allow the crux overhang to be breached. Climb the crack slanting right to a grassy ledge and belays.

China Shop   80 feet   Mild Very Severe   (1967)
Everything is concentrated in the first 25 feet. Start at the break in the overhangs directly below a small tree at 25 feet.
1   80 feet. 4b. Climb the steep wall on big holds moving left onto the lip of the overhang on the left. Take the steep crack above to the tree. Easier vegetated climbing in the same line leads to a large grass rake.

Wedgewood   85 feet   Hard Very Severe
Start beneath the inverted V-chimney.
1   85 feet. 5a. Strenuously go up the chimney until the angle relents at a good thread runner. Continue to a ledge below an overhang. Pull over the overhang moving right, then ascend a steep slab which becomes less steep then steepens again; move left at this point and finish up the grassy groove to small trees.

** **Bear Cage**   90 feet   E3   (1980)
A fine sustained pitch. Start 15 feet right of Wedgewood below a clean steep wall. Sparse protection.
1   90 feet. 5c. Pull over the initial overhang and climb a short faint groove to a good flake. Pull blindly over the bulge, (crux) to a ramp, peg. Make a move right up the ramp to another faint groove and climb this to a break. Make a long reach for a good jug and move right into the centre of the face. Follow a thin crack and edges to the large ledge with small trees.

Soldier   90 feet   E1   (1981)
Start 10 feet left of the corner of Delft below a vertical crack.
1   90 feet. 5b. Attain the crack and climb it using some good face holds in places to a niche. Foot-traverse left along the good ledge to a short ramp. Go up this to an overhang and pull over it rightwards. Climb right then go direct to the top on good holds.

Delft   70 feet   Hard Very Severe   (1973)
Start below a shallow corner topped by an overhanging block.
1   70 feet. 5a. Climb a crack directly under the corner to a sloping ledge at 10 feet. Climb the corner above to reach a

I. R. Tapley seconding Green Wall, E2 5c, Craig Cywarch.
Photo: John Sumner

Brian Dale on Strobe, E3 6a, Craig Cywarch.   *Photo: John Sumner*

second ledge at 40 feet. Keeping left of the crack, pull over the block to easy ground.

Flanker   100 feet   Very Difficult   (1966)
Start at the right-hand side of Tap Mawr, at a point where the grassy ramp below the face narrows and goes round an edge just before the gully. Block belay.
1   60 feet. Gain the top of the belay block and move up to the ledge above. Traverse first down left to a tree in a niche then go up to a ledge.
2   40 feet. Make a layback move up left and continue left again to gain a ledge. Traverse left to a group of trees on a grassy rake. Scramble off to the right.

UPPER TIER

The Steeple   205 feet   Mild Very Severe   (1975)
Start 20 feet right and above the large perched boulder above The Overlap.
1   20 feet. Ascend by a rising ledge to the left to gain a sloping ledge. This point can be reached by a traverse from the left. Stance in a corner with a smooth right wall and a cracked back wall, below and left of the prominent recess in the face.
2   120 feet. 4b. Climb the cracked wall and chimney to gain the top of a block on the left. Move up left and reach the bottom of a leftward leaning crack. Climb this to the top of the tower. Spike belay.
3   65 feet. Go up heather above the belay to finish up a wall to a grassy ledge. Belay on the tree 10 feet right.

Some 100 feet right of a large perched boulder, an obvious arête right of a tree in a corner gives **The Perishers**, 210 feet, Severe, a vegetated climb in 3 pitches.

OLD MAN OF CYWARCH

A little tower situated below the right-hand end of Tap Mawr and just left of the fence running up from the left-hand end of the plantation.

There are a number of short routes, ranging from Difficult to Very Severe (on the right). The longest on the front face is **Frontal Crack**, 25 feet, Very Difficult.

Ceunant Dwyren, (Little Gully), Difficult gives mainly steep vegetated scrambling with the odd jammed boulder.

TAP MAWR PELLA (SHEEP RUN BUTTRESS)

Well up Little Gully is a crag with an obvious horizontal vegetated ledge at mid-height. The lower section has a wall on the right with a tower on the left.

Barad D'ur 190 feet Severe
Start on the right of the Tower at a corner.
1 60 feet. Go up the right-hand corner of the Tower moving over a bulge then go left into the middle of the face. Climb directly upwards over an overhang block to a steep crack. Ascend this to good belays.
2 60 feet. Go up right over shattered pinnacles, then climb a short corner to a ledge.
3 70 feet. Climb an overhanging chimney then go up right below overhanging blocks. Move back left on them to gain the base of a chimney. Climb this to the top.

TAP-Y-GRAIG (SOUTH BUTTRESS)

This is the large buttress between Little Gully and Great Gully. Seen from the track above the first plantation, the most obvious feature is a shallow gully turning up diagonally from right to left starting above the chimney/cave pitch of Central Route. The left-hand edge of the shallow gully forms the right edge of a relatively clean triangular section of rock, giving some good climbs over 200 feet long.

To the right of the shallow gully the buttress is more vegetated though steep. A large heather terrace (known as Bed of The Yellow Policeman) cuts across this part of the buttress and it can be gained fairly easily from the Very Difficult Tower of Babel on the right. Ring Wraith and Quartzberg both start from the terrace.

The way down from the top of the buttress is by descending a sheep track left below Tap Dwyren (Upper South Buttress) then down into Little Gully and thence to the base of the crag.

The first 7 routes all start on the west-facing section of the buttress, overlooking the entrance to Little Gully.

Fritz the Cat, 100 feet, Very Difficult, (1976) starts 30 feet up to the left of Flu '69 below the last groove line before the descent gully. The groove leads to a tree (belay) then a corner with good holds.

Flu '69 150 feet Hard Severe (1969)
Start in the gully, level with a tree on the right.
1 50 feet. Traverse right to the tree, then climb the slab on the right to a slab and spike belay.

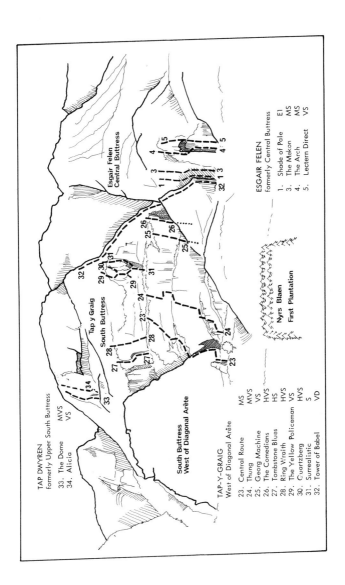

TAP DWYREN
formerly Upper South Buttress

33. The Dome   MVS
34. Alicia   VS

Esgair Felen
Central Buttress

ESGAIR FELEN
formerly Central Buttress

1. Shade of Pale   E1
3. The Mekon   MS
4. The Arch   MS
5. Lectern Direct   VS

Nyrs Blaen
First Plantation

Tap y Graig
South Buttress

South Buttress
West of Diagonal Arête

TAP-Y-GRAIG
West of Diagonal Arête

23. Central Route   MS
24. Thung   MVS
25. Georg Machine   VS
26. The Comedians   HVS
27. Tombstone Blues   HS
28. Ring Wraith   HVS
29. The Yellow Policeman VS
30. Cuartzberg   HVS
31. Surrealistic   S
32. Tower of Babel   VD

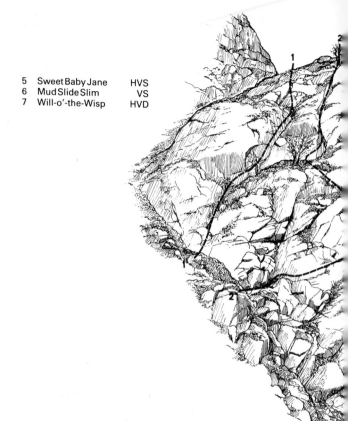

Tap-y-Graig
(South Buttress, West Face)

1	Fritz the Cat	VD
2	Flu '69	HS
3	Tappers Arête	VS
4	Porcupine	VS

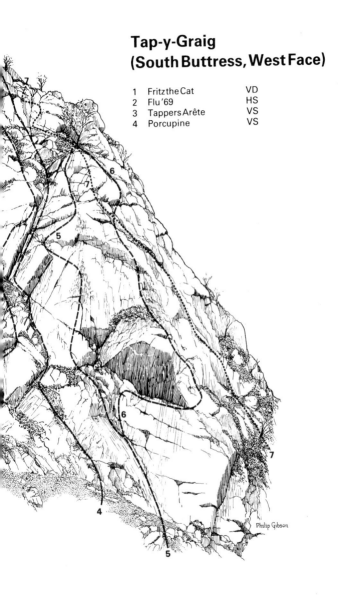

Philip Gibson

2 40 feet. 4b. Ascend the left wall of the corner moving left to a grassy ledge; climb the steep slab (awkward) to a tree.
3 60 feet. 4a. Follow the groove on the right, which trends left to a short steep wall with a tree above. Continue above the tree in the same line to the top.

Tappers Arête 175 feet Very Severe (1976)
The arête just to the left of Porcupine. Start 20 feet left of Porcupine, below a clean corner directly under the arête.
1 55 feet. 4a. Climb the right wall of the corner on good holds then continue up the steep wall above the corner to a ledge; move left to the ledge on Flu '69.
2 55 feet. 4c. Ascend the thin crack directly above a block to gain a good flake hold. Traverse right to the arête then slightly easier climbing up this leads to its top. Nut belay on the right.
3 65 feet. 4b. Move back left then go up vegetated rock to gain a small tree below a steep corner. Awkwardly finish up the corner.

Porcupine, 210 feet, Very Severe, (1970), starts 20 feet left of a large triangular overhang and makes for an obvious overhanging corner about 80 feet up.

** **Sweet Baby James** 140 feet Hard Very Severe (1976)
A delicate slab climb taking the cleaned overlapped wall between Porcupine and Mud Slide Slim. Start as for the latter at the ramp below the overhang.
1 140 feet. 5a. Go up the ramp with the white water mark on the right to a steepening (as for Mud Slide Slim). Pull left over the steepening to gain an upper short ramp, move left again to avoid an overhang and move up to the slab above. A delicate move up right gains a large hold. Continue delicately up to an overlap then go left via a ramp into the corner of Porcupine. Traverse out right between two overlaps to gain a groove. Ascend this more easily, finishing by a crack to the stance on Will-o'-the-Wisp with a tree belay.

* **Mud Slide Slim** 210 feet Very Severe (1972)
Start from the ramp under the large triangular overhang. There is a distinctive white water mark at its base.
1 60 feet. 4c. Climb the ramp trending left to a steeper section, move right and go up to gain the overhang. Traverse right under this to the arête. Move easily right to a small ledge, nut and spike belays.
2 70 feet. 4a. Move back left then go up diagonally left to the arête. Climb this to an overlap. Pull over on good holds to a slab and go up to the stance on Will-o'-the-Wisp beneath a steep wall.
3 80 feet. 4a. The steep wall above leads to a large tree. The wall above leads easily to the top.

Oread   295 feet   Very Severe   (1953)
Start at a large block with a short steep corner directly behind
20 feet down and to the right of the large triangular overhang.
1   50 feet. Ascend the steep corner behind the block to a ledge
below a small overhang. Climb the overhang by an awkward
wide crack, then a slab to a small stance.
2   75 feet. 4b. Traverse easily right to a spike after 15 feet. Go
up the wall above the spike for 10 feet, then traverse to the right
delicately into a groove and ascend this to a ledge.
3   50 feet. 4a. Move up and left to an obvious break in the steep
wall. Go up this for a few moves, then traverse left to a tree.
4   120 feet. 4a. Gain the rock ledge on the right and move right
again to the foot of a buttress. Climb a steep corner on the right
until it is possible to move round onto the face. Ascend this to
easier ground. Scramble up vegetation to the top.

Derwent   240 feet   Mild Very Severe   (1976)
Two vague crack-lines run up the centre of the buttress; this
route takes the left-hand one. Start beneath a lower vegetated
band, 50 feet below the foot of the crack-line.
1   55 feet. Ascend rock and heather to below a small overhang
at 45 feet. Traverse 3 feet left on vegetation, then go up to a
small stance below the crack-line.
2   55 feet. Follow the vague crack-line to a ledge on Will-o'-the
Wisp.
3   80 feet. 4b. Continue up the crack-line directly above, over a
bulge at 33 feet to a block below and left of a heather ramp. Gain
a small tree at the top of the ramp below the final tower of
Bluebell Babylon.
4   50 feet. Exit easily leftwards.

Electric Rail   150 feet   Hard Very Severe   (1980)
The wall sandwiched between Derwent and Raindrop.
1   40 feet. 4b. Start as for Raindrop but continue traversing to
the middle of the wall. Go up this in the centre.
2   110 feet. 5b. From a belay on Will-o'-the-Wisp climb the wall
20 feet left of Raindrop. Take the bulges direct, the last being the
hardest. Step left to a crack, avoid a block on the right and finish
up mixed ground.

* Raindrop   190 feet   Very Severe   (1979)
The crack-line to the right of Derwent. Start from the ledge below
pitch 2 of Bluebell Babylon, which is gained by doing the first
pitch of Will-o'-the-Wisp.
1   55 feet. 4b. Gain the crack by a move left from the left end
of the ledge and climb it to join Will-o'-the-Wisp just under its
second traverse ledge. Peg belay.
2   85 feet. 4c. Go directly up above the peg belay, following the
vague crack. Move awkwardly over a bulge and continue in the
same line to a ledge, then climb a crack direct to a small tree.
Belay below the final tower.

3 50 feet. 4c. In the centre of the tower is a thin crack-line. Climb this exiting left to the arête. Easy ground then leads to the top.

* **Bluebell Babylon** 260 feet Mild Very Severe   (1956)
The classic VS of the crag. Start as for Will-o'-the-Wisp.
1 90 feet. Make a rising traverse leftwards across the easy-angled wall towards a small tree and a large block. Climb diagonally back right up a slab (starting from the block) to a short wall (as for pitch 1, Will-o'-the-Wisp); climb this and move left to a stance under an overhanging wall.
2 50 feet. 4b. From a corner crack on the right climb diagonally up left over the overhanging wall on good holds, then take the delicate slab above to a ledge. From the ledge ascend direct and go delicately left into a corner. Small thread belay.
3 60 feet. 4b. Move onto the left edge of the corner and climb up to a ledge on a steeper section of wall. Gain the ledge by an awkward move then climb diagonally left. Move up to a sloping ledge and traverse right along this to a groove. Ascend this groove to a stance and belay.
4 60 feet. Above is the final tower. Climb its right-hand edge via a small tree until an escape left can be made to the edge. Go up over the large blocks to the top.

* **Pear Tree Blues** 180 feet Very Severe   (1978)
Pitch 1 takes a shallow groove just left of the obvious square-cut overhangs. Start from the first of the Tea Ledges on Will-o'-the-Wisp, i.e. top of pitch 2.
1 75 feet. 4c. Move left and climb the wall above to an overlap where it is at its narrowest (nut slot in the overlap). Pull over the overlap and gain a niche; climb the shallow groove above on good holds until a step out right to a big ledge can be made. Belay as for Touch of Class, 20 feet along the ledge.
2 105 feet. 4c. Climb the leftward-leaning ramp to the foot of a corner (as for Touch of Class). Climb the corner direct. Move out right beneath a bulge and gain a niche. Go awkwardly out left from the niche then ascend a steep groove to easy ground and the top.

Kathmandu Direct 70 feet E1   (1979)
Start from the nut slot on the first Will-o'-the-Wisp ledge.
1 70 feet. 5c. Go straight up the bulging wall until under the centre of the square overhang. Pull over this direct on widely spaced holds, then move left to a crack. Follow this to the terrace.

Kathmandu 220 feet Hard Very Severe   (1978)
Pitch 1 takes the right-hand corner of the obvious square-cut overhang above the start of the Will-o'-the-Wisp traverse. Start from the first Tea Ledge, Will-o'-the-Wisp (nut slot belay).

1 70 feet. 5a. Move 3 feet right from the belay and climb up to the steep overhung corner. Ascend this to the overhang pulling out right. Climb the wall above moving left to the large heather terrace.
2 70 feet. 4c. Move up Touch of Class to where the ramp starts, then traverse out right for 3 feet at a weakness in the right wall to a crack. Climb the steep slab above the crack to the traverse line of Touch of Class; move into the corner on the right.
3 80 feet. 4b. Ascend the steep groove directly above the stance on big holds then finish up heathery slabs.

** ** Will-o'-the-Wisp** 310 feet   Hard Very Difficult   (1972)
A popular route. A rising traverse left leads across the left-hand triangle of the buttress. Start at a weakness trending left in an easy-angled wall.
1 95 feet. Follow the weakness towards a small tree and a large block. Climb the rightward-slanting slab above the block, to a short wall; take this to a good stance on the right.
2 25 feet. Climb the short crack above to a bulge, then traverse right up a ramp to gain the big ledge above, (first Tea Ledge) nut slot belay.
3 50 feet. Go left along the ledge passing a small spike then continue left to gain a short ramp. Go up this easily to a good small nut slot then make a delicate traverse horizontally left across a slab to a crack. Climb this to another big ledge. (Second Tea Ledge.) Peg belay.
4 55 feet. Walk along the ledge and step across a gap to a ledge under a small overhang. Continue traversing horizontally left for 10 feet until a long stride left is made to a sloping foothold. Go left again and slightly down leading to good holds; finally move up to a ledge close to the arête under an overhanging wall.
5 25 feet. Move round the arête on the left then move up on good holds to a fine position on the arête. Move right at the top to a large tree.
6 60 feet. Gain the top of the large square block on the left. Climb the corner on its right to continue easily up to the right until a traverse left can be made to a small tree in a crack. Go up this to the top.

** * A Touch of Class** 255 feet   Very Difficult   (1978)
Tackles some improbable looking ground in its upper section. Start from the top of pitch 2, Will-o'-the-Wisp.
1 15 feet. Move right and go up to a small tree, flake belays.
2 45 feet. Move to the end of the ledge right of the flake belay and climb the wall above for 8 feet until a slightly rising traverse to the left can be made to a big spike. Swing left round the spike and climb up to the large heather terrace. Nut belay below a broken groove.
3 40 feet. Climb the groove to gain a ramp trending left. Follow the ramp to belay under a big corner.

Philip Gibson

Tap-y-Graig (South Buttress)

1	Sweet Baby James	HVS
2	Mud Slide Slim	VS
3	Oread	VS
4	Derwent	MVS
5	Electric Rail	HVS
6	Raindrop	VS

4 55 feet. Ascend the corner for 6 feet to gain ledges. Move right along these until a move can be made up the wall to gain a higher traversing line. Continue traversing right to a huge block in a corner. Make a move round the base of this to a stance with chockstone belay.

5 100 feet. Climb the steep corner above a spike for 6 feet then step right to a slab. Traverse the slab to a ramp on the right then follow the ramp to the arête. Finish up the arête.

Oh Calcutta   260 feet   Mild Very Severe   (1970)
A rather vegetated route but with some good rock. Start at the foot of a shallow chimney 30 feet left of a rowan tree.

1 75 feet. Climb the shallow chimney to a ledge. Move right and go up vegetation to reach a large heather ledge.

2 60 feet. Follow the vague chimney line then break back right. Move easily left to a large heather terrace and a small tree belay.

3 90 feet. 4a. Ascend delicately rightwards up slabs to the right of a square-cut overhang to reach a groove. Ascend this to an oak tree. Easily follow a ramp to belays.

4 35 feet. 4b. Gain the base of an overhanging chimney. Move onto its left arête then continue moving left to easier ground.

Elephant Walk   270 feet   Severe   (1971)
Sustained climbing higher up but with much vegetation between pitches. Start 30 feet right of Oh Calcutta.

1 90 feet. Move right to a little chimney then go right again to a slab above on the right. Ascend this to a heather ledge, move right into a little corner and climb the arête on the right. A slab leads to below an overhanging wall. Go up and left on heather into a corner.

2 60 feet. Ascend vegetation to a small tree below a clean left-leaning buttress bounded on its right by a diagonal arête and on its left by the ramp-line of Oh Calcutta.

3 120 feet. 4a. Climb out right by a line of holds, then go left under steepening rock to an arête on the left. Follow this to a small ledge. Move 6 feet left above a tree then go up diagonally left until a break can be taken onto the crest of Diagonal Arête.

Diagonal Arête, 325 feet, Difficult, (1953), is heavily vegetated and follows the arête on the left of the prominent shallow gully in the middle of the buttress (starting as for Oh Calcutta).

Baskerville   130 feet   Hard Very Severe   (1979)
A line on the smooth wall just left of the top of the large broken pinnacle (start of Central Route). Start about 130 feet right of Will-o'-the-Wisp on the left side of a huge boulder.

1 130 feet. 5a. Traverse 10 feet left then move up to the top of a flake. Move delicately right to a thin crack. Ascend this to a bracket. Gain the top of the bracket with difficulty and move delicately left to a scoop at the foot of the upper slab. Take a fairly direct line up this to an overhanging wall. Traverse right to a small tree. Finish straight up to a large tree. Abseil from the tree.

Dancing Man 100 feet Hard Very Severe (1979)
A vertical crack just right of Baskerville. Start from the huge boulder just right of Baskerville.
1 100 feet. 5b. Reach the crack by stepping off the top of the boulder; move up strenuously until good holds arrive above the steep section. Continue up the slab above to the large tree. Abseil from the tree.

The Fortifier 140 feet Very Severe (1979)
An obvious diagonal crack-line left of Central Route's diagonal chimney pitch. Start beneath slabs just right of the fallen pillar at the start of Central Route.
1 140 feet. 4c. Climb the cleaned slabs trending right to a small tree at the base of the diagonal crack. Climb the crack with difficulty at first until good footholds arrive and the climbing becomes less strenuous. Continue following the now vague crack-line to a small tree, then go up left to a cleaned corner which is taken to a big tree and ledges. Abseil from the tree.

The next two routes finish on the Central Terrace – known as Bed of the Yellow Policeman.

Central Route 220 feet Mild Severe (1952)
Sadly now very vegetated. At the right-hand extremity of the relatively clean triangular section of South Buttress is a large pinnacle which has broken into blocks and fallen against a steep wall. Start below the pinnacle.
1 30 feet. Gain the pinnacle by the crack on its right.
2 60 feet. A long traverse right leads to a ledge at the foot of a crack sloping up left. Move right and climb the corner to a cave.
3 40 feet. Climb the cave's left wall then a crack. Over the heathery edge move right to a stance in a small chasm.
4 90 feet. The next wall is over 20 feet back. Ascend a steep break to the right of small overhangs. Finish up slabs to trees on the Central Terrace. Escape down to the right into Great Gully.

Thung 290 feet Mild Very Severe (1956)
An experience in vegetation. Start 17 yards right of Central Route by a short chimney with a steep wall on the right.
1 60 feet. 4a. The 10-foot chimney leads to a grassy ledge on the right with a square block on its right. Go 12 feet right to a crack. Jam this to a large heather ledge. Recess belay.
2 50 feet. Trend right and go up to a small tree.
3 50 feet. The left edge of the recess then a steep slab lead to another large ledge between two small trees.

4   60 feet. Scramble right then trend up right to a steep buttress with a crack in a recess just right of a small tree. Spike 10 feet up a crack.
5   70 feet. 4b. 20 feet up the crack the wall bulges, then step left to a small ledge below an overhanging rib. The right of the rib is awkward until a delicate escape left. Mossy slabs lead to Central Terrace.

On the right-hand corner of the buttress close to the bottom of Great Gully is a steep wall. The wall itself is hidden from the valley by a small triangular-shaped buttress. Approach by a rightward slanting gully which joins Great Gully on to of the triangular-shaped buttress. The wall has the following six routes.

Bric-a-brac   135 feet   Very Severe   (1986)
On the left-hand side of the wall is a narrow cracked slab, the only real weakness to breach the lower section of the wall.
1   35 feet. Climb the cracked slab to ledges on the left-hand end of a line of overhangs.
2   100 feet. 4b. Climb directly up, peg, to an oak tree (crux). Traverse horizontally right on good foot ledges with increasing exposure to a groove. Go up this to an overhang then traverse right across a slab to a broken groove. Climb this to the top. Good nut belays a long way back.

* **Brick Wall**   120 feet   E1   (1986)
Takes a steep line up the overhanging wall left of Georg Machine to gain the obvious groove of Bric-a-brac. Start mid-way between The Comedians and the slab of Bric-a-brac, just right of a vegetated groove.
1   120 feet. 5b. Climb just to the right of an overhanging vegetated groove. Step left to a niche directly above the overhanging vegetated groove. Make a difficult move left to gain good holds and a peg below the exit groove. Move up into the groove (as for Bric-a-brac). From the top of this groove traverse right to a broken groove. Ascend this to a rounded block with a thread belay or continue up vegetation to good nut belays.

* **Georg Machine**   90 feet   Very Severe   (1981)
Start at a rib just above the boulder in the gully. The rib is also directly below a tree at the top of the wall. Sustained climbing.
1   90 feet. 4c. Ascend the rib to an overlap with an inverted V cut out. Move left over the overlap to some big holds. Step back right to gain a groove directly below the tree at the top of the wall. Climb the groove direct, over a bulge, to the tree.

* **The Comedians**   70 feet   Hard Very Severe   (1968)
The overhanging chimney just right of Georg Machine. Start beneath the overhanging arête on the right edge of the wall.

1 70 feet. 5a. Climb a little groove on the right-hand side of the edge for about 10 feet then move left onto the wall below the chimney line. Ascend the wall to a ledge beneath the overhanging chimney. Climb this to easier ground. Large block belay on the heather terrace above.

(1985)

* Second Foundation 75 feet E2
The overhanging arête right of The Comedians. Start right of the edge.
1 75 feet. 5c. Climb up into the corner below the first overlap and traverse left to the arête to an obvious sloping foothold. Make some very steep moves up the arête until it relents slightly. Continue up the arête to an obvious ledge.

(1985)

Auto-Man 75 feet Hard Very Severe †
1 75 feet. 5a. As for Second Foundation, up into the corner below the overlap. Go straight over the overlap to make some quite technical moves up a little slab and over the next overlap. Finish up a final short wall.

The next five routes all start from the large Central Terrace. (Bed of the Yellow Policeman.)

(1970)

Tombstone Blues 160 feet Hard Severe
From the tree stance above pitch 3 of Diagonal arête a clean groove can be seen high up on the right. The climb takes this groove and starts 40 feet below it from the left-hand side of the Central Terrace. Either scramble up vegetation or start up Central Route or Thung.
1 40 feet. Climb first left then right to gain a niche below the overhang. Climb the overhang and corner to a heather ledge.
2 70 feet. 4a. Ascend the groove then an arête on the right. After a move left across the smooth wall of the groove to a square-cut detached block ascend the arête. Heather ledge and spike belay.
3 50 feet. Finish up a steep little yellow wall.

(1968)

Ring Wraith 130 feet Hard Very Severe
At the left-hand end of Central Terrace are some smooth walls. The route takes a line up the walls following the thin obvious crack. Start in a groove beneath the crack.
1 80 feet. 5a. Climb the groove to a ledge at 20 feet. Climb the thin crack above (crux at the top) to a small ledge. Move into the groove left of a slight arête. Ascend this until it is possible to step right to a stance and belays.
2 50 feet. Ascend leftwards to easier ground.

(1971)

* The Yellow Policeman 175 feet Very Severe
High up on the right-hand side of South Buttress is a smooth slab above an overhanging wall. The climb takes the only

weakness in the smooth slab. Start beneath an overhang on the right-hand side of the wall.

1 30 feet. Move easily up a corner to the overhang then traverse left below it to a grassy ramp; scramble a few yards up this, passing a noticeable overhanging greeny-yellow groove.

2 30 feet. 4b. Climb the wall and steep groove above to a niche. Nut belays.

3 115 feet. 4c. Traverse three feet right and gain the slab above. Climb this taking a thin crack trending up right to a diagonal break going back left. Ascend this below a steep wall to an escape leftwards, then move easily up slabs to the top.

** **Quartzberg**   115 feet   Hard Very Severe   (1980)
A very fine pitch. Start in the greeny-yellow groove, just right of pitch 2 of The Yellow Policeman.

1 115 feet. 5a. Swing immediately out right across a steep wall to a thin crack. Go up this to a ledge and cleaned niche. Move diagonally left across the overhanging wall to a small ledge at the foot of a slab. Take a thin crack trending slightly right to a diagonal break; step right and pull over the overlap, then go up a quartzy crack above.

Surrealistic, 180 feet, Severe, (1969), a chimney line to the right of the overhanging wall of Yellow Policeman and Quartzberg gives three vegetated pitches.

* **Tower of Babel**   440 feet   Very Difficult   (1982)
The extreme right edge of South Buttress, overlooking Great Gully. Vegetated between pitches. Start at the lowest point of the buttress, just left of Great Gully, at a corner with a tree just to its right.

1 40 feet. Climb the crack in the left-hand side of the arête which is just left of the corner, to a ledge. Alternatively, climb the corner with an awkward chimney exit to the ledge.

2 40 feet. Climb the steep crack on the left to grassy ledges. Nut belay at the base of the arête above.

3 75 feet. The pleasant arête above to the top of a subsidiary buttress. Boulder belays. Walk across a saddle and move up to an undercut corner with a large quartz ledge on its right.

4 80 feet. Crux. From piled blocks make a difficult move up the corner and gain the quartz ledge on the right. Return left to some jammed flakes. Using these gain the tree above. Go up easily right to a quartzy corner crack. Nut belays.

5 80 feet. Climb a clean rib above to a tree on the left. Gain a ramp slanting leftwards and follow it to a short corner with a tree above. Ledge and nut belays above and to the left of the tree.

6 50 feet. A wall above has three cracks in it; gain the left-hand one and step into the centre crack. Climb this, then move left to a niche. Continue direct to finish at a large tree.

7 75 feet. Gain a groove on the right of the arête and follow it to a poised chockstone. Climb above the chockstone for a few yards then traverse left to the arête taking this to a vegetated groove and boulder belays.

Descent is made via a sheep track down to the left crossing a gully then traversing left over the top of the crag to the top of Will-o'-the-Wisp; then descend the gully as for that route.

TAP DWYREN (UPPER SOUTH BUTTRESS)

This is the dome-shaped buttress high above the left-hand end of South Buttress, overlooking Little Gully. A pleasant continuation to the climbs on South Buttress, especially as it gets most of the afternoon sun. The rock is good.

The Dome 90 feet Mild Very Severe (1970)
An obvious steep groove in the middle of the buttress. Start from a grassy ledge directly beneath the groove.
1 50 feet. 4b. Ascend the cracked overhanging wall to a ledge at 15 feet. Go diagonally up left to a large spike. Move 3 feet above the spike then traverse right on good holds into the groove. Ascend the groove to a stance on the left.
2 40 feet. 4a. On the right is a steep wall. Climb this on good holds moving right at the top.

* Alicia 130 feet Hard Very Severe (1983)
A sustained pitch which takes a direct line up the steep wall right of The Dome. Start 3 feet right of The Dome.
1 130 feet. 4c. Go rightwards up a ramp then back left to a large flake in the centre of the wall. Ascend directly up the wall, trending slightly left near the top.

Ceunant Brwnt (Great Gully) 500 feet Difficult
The gully is heavily vegetated but there are no serious difficulties and the pitches are short.

ESGAIR FELEN (CENTRAL BUTTRESS)

This buttress, lying between Great Gully and North Gully, is very broken and heavily vegetated. Except for an area of rock at the bottom left-hand corner at the start of Great Gully. Descent from Shade of Pale and Lone Ranger is down to the left into the gully, crossing this to a saddle on the left. Descent from The Arch, Mekon, etc. is by a sheep track to the right.

** Shade of Pale 175 feet E1 (1983)
A short distance up Great Gully is a light-coloured overhanging wall about 100 feet high. It dries quickly after wet weather. Start well down and to the right of the light-coloured wall, as for The

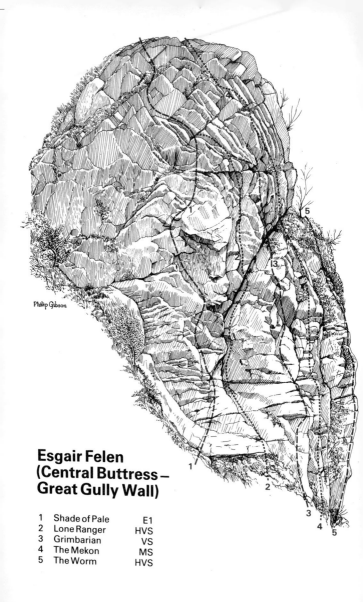

Esgair Felen
(Central Buttress –
Great Gully Wall)

1	Shade of Pale	E1
2	Lone Ranger	HVS
3	Grimbarian	VS
4	The Mekon	MS
5	The Worm	HVS

Philip Gibson

Mekon. A very good second pitch with good jug-pulling on a steep wall.

1   40 feet. Climb a short crack on the left, then traverse left up an obvious ramp until directly below the overhang wall. Old peg belay.

2   135 feet. 5b. Climb steeply just left of the peg to gain a niche. Go straight up on widely spaced jugs to reach a sloping ledge under an overhang. Move up to a thread in an undercut flake. Pull over this to the left to reach good holds. Step right onto the lip of the overhang to gain easier ground. Finish leftwards up easy rock.

Shade of Pale Right-Hand, E1,5c, (1981). Move down and right from the thread to gain a groove (peg in groove). Climb the groove to join Shade of Pale.

Lone Ranger   180 feet   Hard Very Severe   (1981)
The big curving groove just right of Shade of Pale. Start as for the latter.

1   140 feet. 5a. Climb a short crack on the left, then traverse left to beneath the groove line. Take this easily at first to a bulge, surmount the bulge and continue up the groove above until another groove on the overhanging left wall can be entered; follow this to join the easy section of Shade of Pale. Stance in a niche, good nut belays.

2   40 feet. An easy wall above. Tree belay well back.

Grimbarian   210 feet   Very Severe   (1984)
The arête left of The Mekon.

1   55 feet. 4b. Climb a crack to the top of a block (as for Shade of Pale) then move up to a small roof. Traverse right under this to the arête and climb this to a good ledge. Thread belay.

2   35 feet. 4b. Ascend the steep corner on the right to another ledge. Large block belay.

3   120 feet. 4b. Step out airily left and climb the broken arête to slabs: continue easily straight up to the top. Tree belay.

* The Mekon   170 feet   Mild Severe   (1972)
Left of a huge natural arch at the corner of Central Buttress and Great Gully, are two grooves with a tree at the bottom of the right-hand one. This route takes the left-hand groove. Ascend the gully for a short distance to the point where it meets the foot of the groove.

1   120 feet. Climb the corner of the groove for 10 feet then climb the slab on the right until it meets a ramp trending leftwards. Go along the ramp back into the corner and ascend this for about 15 feet, then move out onto the right-hand wall. Ascend for about 10 feet to a ledge which leads right to an arête. Gain this and follow it to the stance on a large ledge. Thread belay.

2   50 feet. Climb steeply behind the stance to gain a ledge at 10 feet. Move up left to below a small overhang, climb up to the right then go left to flakes and spikes. Ascend these to the top.

The Worm   80 feet   Hard Very Severe   (1983)
The left-hand edge of the clean pillar which makes the actual corner of Central Buttress and Great Gully. There is an overhang at 20 feet.
1   80 feet. 5b. Ascend the wall below the arête to a small tree under the overhang then move left to a ledge. Move back right to gain the arête directly above the overhang. Climb the arête to a small overhung groove and pull over this to the easier stepped arête above.

The Arch, 160 feet, Mild Severe, (1966) is a vegetated route which starts below the huge natural arch. After a crack, traverse left across a slab below the arch leads to another crack. Above this a break in the overhanging left wall leads to a holly bush. A traverse left across the wall leads to a corner and a final arête.

* **Lectern Direct**   150 feet   Very Severe   (Sustained)   (1967)
Start at a steep groove 15 feet right of The Arch.
1   150 feet. 4c. Climb the groove for 20 feet then make a move left onto the arête. Move up trending left then go straight up (oak tree in a corner on the left) to an arête. Climb the arête to another tree. Continue straight up vegetated slabs to a large ledge.

ESGAIR FELEN ISAF

A rather vegetated buttress but due to its easy angle and low position on the hillside makes an ideal beginner's crag.

Yggdrasil, 180 feet, Hard Difficult, (1968), is a vegetated route starting at the left-hand end of the crag to the right of the wall which runs up the north side of the first plantation. Follow a steep little nose of rock, partly hidden by a fallen tree, then various short walls above.

Peal   140 feet   Hard Severe   (1966)
Start on the left-hand side of the main buttress part way up a grassy ramp by a crack.
1   65 feet. Climb the crack and a slab then move right above the steep section and go up a crack on Recuperation to a grassy ledge in a corner. Move left to a tree below a rib.
2   75 feet. 4a. Climb the right-hand side of the rib for 20 feet, move left awkwardly and ascend the arête. Step right and finish up easier ground.

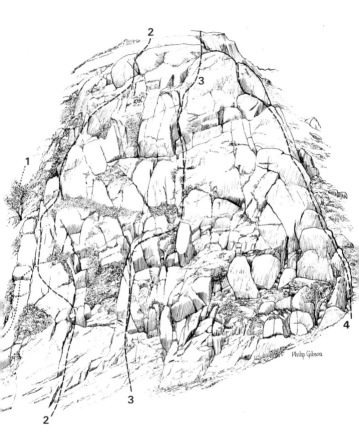

Esgair Felen Isaf

1	Peal	HS
2	Recuperation	D
3	Restoration	VD
4	First Anniversary	M

Recuperation   180 feet   Difficult   (1966)
Vegetated. Start at the lowest point of the crag below a vague
crack.
1   20 feet. Ascend easy-angled vegetated rock to a small ash
tree on the left.
2   70 feet. Move right to the crack, and climb it to where the
wall steepens. Make a slightly rising traverse left to a crack which
leads to a grassy ledge in a corner.
3   90 feet. Move right and go straight up to a small ash tree,
then to a hawthorn bush. Go behind the bush, then finish up a
short steep groove.

Restoration   160 feet   Very Difficult   (1968)
The best route on the crag, up the middle of the buttress, making
for a small inverted V-chimney. Start 20 right of the lowest point
of the crag.
1   80 feet. Easy slabs lead to the foot of a rib. Ascend the rib for
30 feet trending slightly left up a shallow chimney. Move right
to a huge wedged block belay.
2   80 feet. Move up left to the inverted V-chimney; take this
direct to a slab above. Step right and climb a short steep wall
on good holds to another slab and the top.

First Anniversary   105 feet   Moderate   (1956)
The arête on the right of the buttress. A good safe route for
starting the youngest of climbers. Start at the extreme
right-hand end.
1   30 feet. Climb the right-hand edge, moving first right then
left, to a big ledge and block belay.
2   60 feet. Go straight up the rib to another ledge. Thread belay
low down on the right.
3   15 feet. Finish up the steep corner. Steel spike belay.

The Archer   60 feet   Very Severe   (1970)
Above and to the right of the top of the arête of First Anniversary
are two small buttresses. The first is overhanging and has a
green watermark down it. Start at the bottom of a diagonal fault
on the left of the buttress.
1   60 feet. 4c. Pull up onto the fault-ramp and follow it to a niche.
Step down, go round the bulge on the right and climb up to a
tree. Step left to the top of the wall and finish at a good hold.
Poor protection at the top.

* **Lincoln Green**   60 feet   Very Severe   (1982)
Start directly below the greenish wall in the centre of the
buttress.
1   60 feet. 5a. Climb the greenish wall to a niche below an
overhanging groove. Ascend this, moving out left at the top.

Tap Isa Hafn Mawr (Lower North Gully Buttress)

1	Rolling Stone	S	3	Sickle Wall	S
2	Mother's Pride	HS	4	The Scythe	MVS

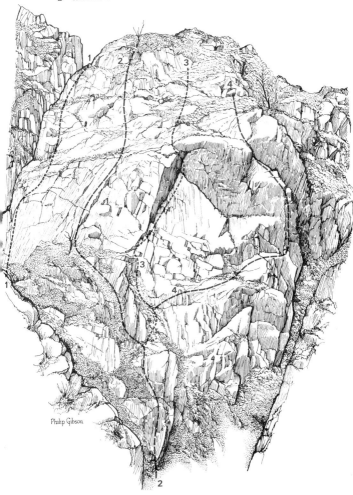

Philip Gibson

Inclination 65 feet Hard Severe   (1970)
The obvious arête on the small buttress to the right of Lincoln
Green buttress. Start at the base of the arête. Poor protection.
1 65 feet. Step up and move right onto the arête. Climb this on
big holds to a small tree. Continue up the arête, more broken,
to finish with a pull over a little overhang. Nut belays well back.
The arête direct can be avoided by moving right onto the face
forming the right-hand wall; this wall however takes some time
to dry out.

HAFN MAWR

North Gully 600 feet Hard Severe
Vegetated lower pitches can be avoided by scrambling to the
right or left. The gully only asserts itself at the tombstone pitch
where the walls converge some 220 feet up.
1 45 feet. Tombstone Pitch: The gully closes to form an
overhanging chimney. Awkward to start but the holds improve
and the left wall is climbed till its is possible to move right and
finish direct.
2 25 feet. Crux: A short pitch, undercut at the base. Awkwardly
struggle up the overhanging chimney. Scrambling leads to the
top.

On the right wall of North Gully are two short, steep and fairly
clean buttresses: Lower North Gully Buttress and Upper North
Gully Buttress. They lie roughly one above the other and are
separated by an upper right fork in North Gully. The Lower
Buttress, starting above the lower right fork has a smooth wall
on its left and large overhangs on the right.

TAP ISA HAFN MAWR (LOWER NORTH GULLY BUTTRESS)

Rolling Stone 160 feet Severe   (1967)
On the left edge of the smooth wall is a rightward leaning
chimney line. This can be gained by climbing vegetated rock at
about Difficult standard from the gully on the right. Start on the
left edge of the smooth wall, where it meets the gully.
1 60 feet. Ascend the steep edge then move right into the
chimney line; follow this then continue to the ridge.
2 20 feet. Traverse right easily along the ridge to a large flake
belay.
3 80 feet. Move left to the arête then finish up slabs.

Mother's Pride 250 feet Hard Severe   (1964)
A line up the middle of the smooth wall. Start at the lowest point
of the buttress, where the gully branches.
1 110 feet. Go over vegetated slabs to a small overhang, then
move right to a stance with a large spike belay.

2 30 feet. Move left, then go straight up vegetation to a wide terrace below the smooth wall.
3 60 feet. 4b. Crux. Ascend the wall by a steep crack just left of centre (the first few moves can be avoided by coming in from the right) then follow the line of weakness, trending right.
4 50 feet. Finish up easy vegetated slabs.

* **Sickle Wall** 185 feet Severe   (1968)
The striking rightward-ascending crack-line under the overhanging arête under a big roof. Start half-way up the lower right fork finishing at a corner with a cracked left wall.
1 35 feet. Move right and climb a steep little wall onto slabs above; move right then go left into a groove that leads to the ledge below the smooth wall.
2 40 feet. 4b. On the right of the smooth wall is an overhanging arête which finishes 12 feet above. A crack continues to the ground. Ascend the crack up rightwards to the big roof.
3 110 feet. Take the weakness out left from under the roof (easier than it looks) then finish straight up easy slabs.

** **The Scythe** 200 feet Mild Very Severe   (1970)
A way through the overhangs to the right of Sickle Wall. Poor protection on pitch 3. Start as for Sickle Wall.
1 85 feet. From the corner move right and climb the steep little wall onto slabs above, as for Sickle Wall. Ascend diagonally right up a ramp the right edge of which drops steeply into the gully, to a stance with a detached triangular block.
2 25 feet. 4a. Move right then climb the steep groove to a small stance beneath a roof. Nut belay.
3 40 feet. 4a. Ascend the slab on the left to below the roof (old peg) then traverse left over ribs and grooves to the slabs up to the left.
4 50 feet. Ascend straight up vegetated slabs to the top.

TAP UCHA HAFN MAWR (UPPER NORTH GULLY BUTTRESS)

A small buttress with a steep chimney line in the centre (taken by Apollo) and a ramp running up its right edge.

Apollo 120 feet Very Severe   (1969)
Start at the obvious vertical crack in a groove 3 feet to the left and below the steep chimney line.
1 60 feet. 4a. Layback up into the crack to good holds over the overhang. Continue up the crack to a big ledge and block belay.
2 60 feet. 4b. After moving right make an obvious rising traverse to good holds over the overhang and a ledge. Ascend the overhanging chimney with an awkward move to exit onto another ledge. The next overhanging chimney is difficult. Tree belay.

Half-Moon Crack   70 feet   Severe   (1968)
A variation start to Apollo. It is the steep curving crack finishing
on the right-hand end of the ledge under the steep chimney.
Start approximately 20 feet right from Apollo beside a man-sized
block.
1   70 feet. Move onto the block and climb the steep wall above
using big holds in a crack. Spike at 10 feet. Ascend to reach a
small flake then move round to the right into a corner crack
beneath the overhang. Climb the corner crack moving left to the
ledge at the top of pitch 1 of Apollo.

Relaxation   120 feet   Hard Very Difficult   (1956)
The easy-angled ramp on the right-hand edge of the buttress.
Start at the base of the ramp which is the lowest point of the
buttress.
1   60 feet. Move up the slab negotiating a bulge at 25 feet.
Stance with doubtful block belay.
2   60 feet. Ascend awkwardly up a steep section behind the
stance to the slab above; follow this to the top.

NORTH-NORTH-EAST TOWER

A short but distinct tower at the foot of the North East Buttress,
close to the bottom of North Gully, directly above the track to
North East Buttress.

South Face Crack   60 feet   Hard Severe   (1956)
Start on the left-hand edge at a crack.
1   60 feet. 4b. Ascend the crack then the left-hand edge of the
tower to a ledge below the final wall. Ascend the wall just left
of centre and finish at the highest point.

Bundu   70 feet   Mild Very Severe   (1958)
The best of three routes. Start on the north side of the tower
near the left-hand edge at a diagonal chimney.
1   70 feet. 4b. Climb the chimney to a grassy ledge and small
tree on the left. An open groove above leads to an overhang;
turn this on the right and gain the arête which provides the
finish.

Wig Walk, 70 feet, Hard Severe, 4a, (1957) takes the obvious
overhanging crack about 10 feet right of Bundu.

SAWDL Y GRAIG (NORTH EAST BUTTRESS)

North East Buttress is the fine steep nose of rock some 250 feet
high bounded on the left by the lower right fork of North Gully
and on the right by a line of vegetated terraces leading down to
the track beneath the crag.

The descent to the left is by the lower right fork of North Gully and to the right by the steep ramp known as Llwbyr Llewellyn, which descends over the top of North Buttress rightwards.

The two main features on the rock nose are the ramp line of Charon on the right and an inverted V-chimney of Hades on the left. Rock left of the steep nose, where the easier climbs go, is rather vegetated; the only prominent feature is the rightward slanting ramp of Lethe.

The first two routes start from the large heather terrace above and right of the lower scrappy pitches of North Gully; this is reached by easy scrambling just right of the gully.

Phoebus 240 feet   Very Difficult   (1969)
Start at the left-hand end of the heather terrace, where it reaches the gully at a small slab.
1 80 feet. Go up the slab to vegetation then to the start of another slab. Large block belay to the right.
2 80 feet. Crux. Traverse left across a slab to the edge overlooking the gully. Traverse back right to a break in the steep arête on the right. Move onto the arête and climb the steep wall directly above on good holds. Stance and belay on a heather ledge above.
3 80 feet. Finish straight up vegetated rock.

Lethe 230 feet   Difficult   (1969)
The obvious ramp line trending rightwards towards the top section of Styx. Start from the right-hand end of the heather terrace. Some vegetation.
1 40 feet. Ascend the corner until stopped by a bulge then traverse right to a ledge. Stance and belay.
2 20 feet. Climb the slab above to a stance below a groove leading to the ramp proper. Large spike belay high up on the right.
3 30 feet. Follow the groove to a tree; belay 3 feet past the tree below a slab.
4 50 feet. Take the slab trending up right to a small tree at the top. Go past the tree to vegetation and a large block belay below another slab.
5 15 feet. Ascend the slab to a ledge on the right; nut belay and a tree up to the left.
6 45 feet. Follow a groove up left to overhangs then move right to a stance in a groove. Spike belays.
7 30 feet. Pitch 4 of Styx. Ascend the steepening groove making an obvious traverse left to finish.

Directly below the main 250-foot nose of North East Buttress are two big trees below the trees is approximately 200 feet of vegetation. The trees mark the start of the climbs: Styx, Stygian

Sawdl y Graig (North East Buttress)

Philip Gibson

Wall, Hades, The Technician and Hell's Gate. The initial vegetation is started from a small bay beside a tree then scramble up first left then rightwards.

A.G.M.   275 feet   Hard Very Difficult   (1976)

A line parallel to that of Styx but at a lower level. Scramble up vegetation from the bay to the left for about 130 feet to an area of slabs. Tree belay. (The start of Styx, Hades, etc. continue up the vegetation to the right of the tree belay.)

1   50 feet. From the tree take the easiest line leftward up slabs to a steeper section; go up this on the left taking a small rib to a large stance, block belay.

2   65 feet. Traverse right then climb the overlapping slabs to a corner beneath a steep wall and ascend the corner moving out right to ledges. Gain the hanging slab on the left and climb this to a large heather ledge.

3   70 feet. Follow the short ramp on the right and continue up a groove then the awkward little wall above moving first right then left to a stance on Lethe.

4   90 feet. Follow the three last pitches of Lethe.

* Styx   215 feet   Mild Very Severe   (1956)

Start from the two big trees directly beneath the nose of the buttress.

1   50 feet. Ascend the slab trending left to a tree.

2   50 feet. 4a. Gain the next slab in the same line and follow this to a stance and belay at the foot of a short wall.

3   85 feet. 4b. Ascend the short wall then move left to the edge of a third slab. Continue up the edge until a traverse back right can be made. Move up the slab to its top. Belay in a groove.

4   30 feet. Climb the groove on big holds to an obvious exit out left.

The Technician   145 feet   E2   (1968)

The big groove between Styx and Hades. Start from the stance at the top of pitch 2 of Styx.

1   80 feet. 5c. Traverse diagonally right then left across a slab to below the groove. Climb the groove to an old peg then move left with difficulty to the arête, then go diagonally up left to a stance and belay.

2   65 feet. Ascend the easy slabs to a roof; move left round this and go up an arête to the top.

** Hades   150 feet   E1   (1959)

A compelling line which takes the prominent inverted V-chimney. Start from the stance at the top of pitch 1 of Styx.

1   80 feet. 5a. Go left and follow Styx for a few yards, then climb the steep groove above to a slab below the overhanging chimney. Ledge and belays below the chimney.

2 40 feet. 5b. Climb the overhanging groove to its top then make a difficult move left to enter an overhanging chimney. Ascend this to a ledge on the right.
3 30 feet. Finish more easily at an easy angle.

Hell's Gate 180 feet   E2   †   (1969)
Start from the tree stance at the top of pitch 1 of Styx.
1 90 feet. 5b. Follow Stygian Wall for a few yards then climb the steep groove above direct traversing out right near the top to join pitch 2 of Stygian Wall. Follow Stygian Wall to belay in the sentry box stance.
2 70 feet. 5b. Move left out of the sentry box then go diagonally up left to the next groove line right of Hades. Make some difficult moves up this to an old peg and some doubtful hanging blocks. Traverse right then go up to gain a heather ledge with a small tree.
3 20 feet. Steep vegetated scrambling leads to easier ground.

** **Stygian Wall**   225 feet   Very Severe   (1955)
The old classic of the buttress. Start from the stance at the top of pitch 1 of Styx.
1 60 feet. 4c. Climb just right of the overhung corner via a crack for 5 feet then take a slight weakness across the wall on the right to the arête. Move round this to the stance and belay in a corner.
2 40 feet. 4a. Climb a slab going up left to a ledge then follow a broken wall to a sentry-box stance. Old pegs.
3 90 feet. 4b. Pull out left of the sentry-box then step back right to gain a sloping ledge on the right with a doubtful quartz wall above. Follow the ledge to a niche. Ascend a crack on the right for a few yards then traverse right round an edge to a groove. Stance at the top of the groove.
4 35 feet. Climb the wall on the left to reach steep heathery rock.

*** **Strobe**   280 feet   E3   (1973)
A brilliant route, one of the best in the area. The line roughly follows the steep nose, first on its left then on the right. Start as for Styx, at the base of the nose by the two big trees. Using the thread runner on pitch 3 for aid the grade becomes E1, 5b.
1 105 feet. 5b. Go up the slab of Styx for a few yards to a brown water-stained slab on the right. Climb this to a big hold, then move up the wall to a niche. Go delicately right to the arête, then go right again to a groove. Ascend this moving right to the stance at the top of pitch 1 Stygian Wall.
2 60 feet. 5a. Climb the short ramp on the right. Move right across a slab to a rib. Continue right into a corner with a massive block.
3 75 feet. 6a. From the block move back left to the rib. Go up this to the steep wall (thread runner). Difficult moves follow to gain big jugs on the sloping ledge above. Continue straight up

the wall to a spike, then traverse left to where a weakness allows a groove above to be gained. Easier climbing up the groove leads to a stance and belays.

4   40 feet. Move easily out right then finish up vegetation.

Carrion   205 feet   E1   (1976)

Sparse protection on pitch 1. Start beneath an overhanging groove to the right and 20 feet above the two big trees at the start of Styx. Thread belay on the right arête of the groove.

1   70 feet. 5b. Move up the right wall of the groove, starting just left of the thread in the arête. Climb a short ramp diagonally up right, to gain a slab. Ascend this to the stance at the top of pitch 1 of Stygian Wall.

2   135 feet. 5a. The groove leads to the sentry-box as for pitch 2, Stygian Wall. Gain a footledge above the traverse of Stygian Wall to a steep slab, old peg. Ascend a groove just left of the peg to gain a niche above on the left. Step onto a spike on the left then pull over a bulge and move left into the top section of Hell's Gate. Go up this to a small tree, then ascend to a stance above.

** Trouble Maker   185 feet   E2   (1976)

The ramp line above the Charon ramp. All the quality is in pitch 2. Start a few yards up and to the right of the start of Carrion below a steep corner (normally wet).

1   70 feet. 5a. Climb the steep corner and ramp above to the massive wedged block at the top of pitch 2 of Strobe.

2   115 feet. 5c. Gain the rib on the left of the block and go up to the thread of Strobe. Move right to gain the start of the ramp; climb this to a peg. Climb the wall above the peg to a foothold beneath a good flake. Go awkwardly left to an obvious large spike then move left to easier ground with belays at the top of a groove.

Charon   190 feet   E1   (1967)

The obvious ramp trending rightwards across the very steep wall right of the nose of the buttress. Scramble up rightwards from the trees at the bottom of the slab of Styx to the wet corner at the start of Trouble Maker.

1   70 feet. Traverse right to avoid the steep wet corner, then go up to vegetation. Stance and belay below a steep little corner leading onto the ramp proper.

2   80 feet. 4a. Ascend the corner onto the ramp then go up this to huge detached blocks at the top.

3   40 feet. 5b. Climb the overhanging groove above.

Pluto   110 feet   E3   (1980)

The top pitch takes a big overhanging groove between Trouble Maker and Charon. Start below a cleaned line up the ivy-covered wall below the big ramp of Charon. It is best gained by a long

Bob Norris on Ice Man, Craig Rhwyddfor.   Photo: John Sumner

Alan Cooper on Lost Man, Craig y Llam.   Photo: John Sumner

vegetated traverse right starting about 50 feet down from the trees at the start of Styx.

1 50 feet. 5b. Climb the steep cleaned wall by cracks, making an awkward move to gain a ledge on the left. Ascend easily from the ledge to the ramp of Charon.

2 60 feet. 5c. The big groove line slanting leftwards is gained by some fingery moves to a doubtful flake on the right. Move left to a peg; continue up left to a thread and another doubtful flake; finish strenuously to the left.

Girdle Traverse 370 feet E1

A rightward traverse of the buttress from left to right with increasing difficulty. Start as for Styx.

1 50 feet. Pitch 1 of Styx.

2 50 feet. 4a. Pitch 2 of Styx.

3 65 feet. 4a. Traverse right as for The Technician; continue right to beneath the inverted V-chimney of Hades pitch 2. Continue right into the sentry-box stance of pitch 2 of Stygian Wall.

4 40 feet. 4a. Reverse pitch 2 of Stygian Wall.

5 75 feet. 5a. Climb the short ramp on the right then traverse right across a slab to a rib and go round this to a massive block (pitch 2 Strobe). Gain the ramp on the right and move up to a corner.

6 50 feet. 4a. Ascend the ramp on pitch 3 of Charon to huge detached blocks.

7 40 feet. 5b. Pitch 4 of Charon. Climb the overhanging groove.

CRAIG LLYWELYN (NORTH BUTTRESS)

North Buttress, gives the longest and probably best VS routes at Cywarch. It has a distinct rib and groove structure giving a different type of climbing to North East Buttress. Ways off are as for North East Buttress.

The outstanding feature of the buttress is a 400-foot rib going the full height. This is Acheron. The big curving groove to its right is taken by Doom. Right again the buttress deteriorates in vegetation for its first 200 feet. Above this point there is an overhanging black wall cut by the left-slanting crack of Northerner. The large corner to the right of this is The Big Cleft. Right again is a series of overlapping slabs capped by an overhanging rock barrier. The last obvious feature on the right side is a V-groove with a sharp-looking arête to its right. This is Jugs Groove.

At the extreme left-hand end of North Buttress is a vegetated section of rock which merges leftwards into large grassy terraces which divide North East and North Buttresses. Two routes brave

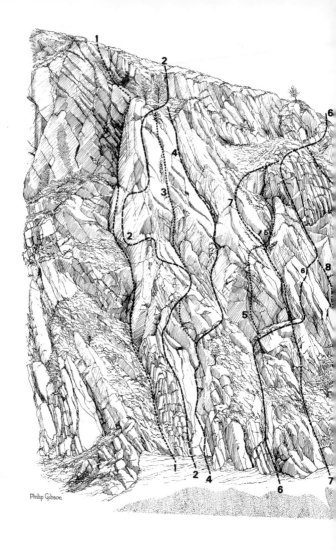

Philip Gibson

Craig Llywelyn (North Buttress)

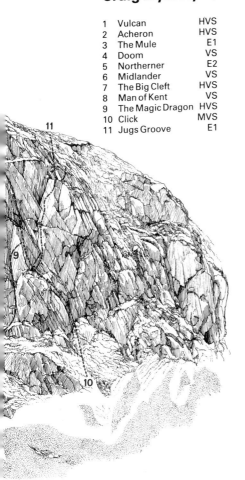

this section of rock. They both finish below the steep wall right of the nose of North East Buttress. Descent is down to the left to the trees under North East Buttress.

Trend, 340 feet, Mild Very Severe, 4a, 4a, 4b, (1964) starts on the extreme left-hand side of the buttress at a small slab at the foot of the largest rib. Pitch 1 has a steep corner and leads to two trees. A wall and rib lead to an overhang and another rib.

Troom, 360 feet, Hard Very Difficult, (1969) starts 75 feet left of Vulcan and follows a rib, a slab, an arête (junction with Vulcan) and an obvious ramp.

Vulcan   485 feet   Hard Very Severe   †   (1970)
The big corner just left of the prominent rib of Acheron. Vegetated between pitches. Start beneath the corner.
1   90 feet. Climb the vegetated corner direct to a stance above a small tree.
2   100 feet. Continue up vegetation to a large stance with a huge flake belay.
3   60 feet. 5a. Ascend the steep corner on the right and exit right. Climb a groove above to another big ledge.
4   75 feet. Move left from the stance and go up the vegetated corner to an easy-angled groove. Climb this and the steep corner above. Stance and large tree belay above.
5   80 feet. 5b. The groove behind the tree; move right into the steep corner under a line of overlaps. Climb the corner until a traverse right can be made to a small niche. Ascend the groove above for 35 feet to a ledge and tree belay on the right.
6   80 feet. Move back left into the groove and go up this leftwards to slabs leading to the top.

*** **Acheron**   480 feet   Hard Very Severe   (1956)
A magnificent mountaineering route finding its way up the huge rib on the left-hand side of the buttress. Start just left of the corner of Doom.
1   120 feet. 4a. Climb straight up for 60 feet to an overlap. Climb a left-slanting crack in the overlap to the left edge of the slab above. Ascend the arête to a ledge and belays.
2   90 feet. 4b. Climb the groove on the left to where it steepens (old pegs). Traverse right delicately to a nose. Ascend this to a narrow ledge. Traverse right again and go up to a stance and peg belay in a corner.
3   65 feet. 4b. Traverse 3 feet left and move up onto the slab then traverse left across the slab to the arête. Climb the steep groove just left of the arête (some doubtful flakes) to a ledge. Move diagonally down left to the gully.
4   60 feet. 4b. Climb a crack to an overhang and traverse right under this to the arête, then go up to blocks beneath a chimney.

5   90 feet. 5a. Climb the chimney awkwardly to a groove above. Ascend this to a small tree.
6   55 feet. 4a. Move right to a larger tree and climb the steep wall behind this to the top.

* **The Mule**   260 feet   E1   (1975)
Start at the top of pitch 1 of Doom.
1   75 feet. 4b. From the stance traverse 15 feet left to a groove and ascend this to vegetation and the corner stance on Acheron.
2   75 feet. 5b. Ascend the slab in the corner to an overhang. Go awkwardly up the right wall to a ledge on the right. Ascend into a niche at the base of a groove. Climb the groove until a move right can be made to easier ground. Belays above.
3   75 feet. 4b. Move left and go up to gain a slabby groove; climb this to a tree.
4   35 feet. Climb the steep wall behind the tree as for Acheron pitch 6.

*** **Doom**   370 feet   Very Severe   (1968)
A classic. The line follows the big slabby corner right of the rib of Acheron. Start just right of the huge rib beneath a big corner.
1   120 feet. 4b. Ascend the corner for 90 feet to where it starts to curve left, old peg; move up right to gain a slab in a corner, and climb this pulling out right over a block to a grassy ramp. Large stance and flake belay above.
2   100 feet. 4b. Make a slightly rising traverse right following a ledge to a small arête. Climb the slab above bearing right into the corner. Ascend this to an overhang then pull over the overhang to an eyrie-like stance below a big curving corner, peg belays.
3   120 feet. 4b. Ascend the corner for a few feet then step left to gain a small niche in the slab. Ascend the crack above making a traverse left at the top to a spike. Move up and right into the corner, climb this to below a smooth section then make a tricky move left across the slab to easier ground. Follow this up to a tree belay.
4   30 feet. 4a. Finish up the steep wall behind the tree.

Guillotine   175 feet   Very Severe   (1973)
The arête on the right of the 3rd pitch of Doom. Start from the corner stance at the top of pitch 2 of Doom.
1   35 feet. 4b. Traverse delicately right from the stance to the arête. Move right again to a stance.
2   100 feet. 4b. Move up the slab just right of the arête to a wide slanting chimney, gain this and climb the slab on its left. Move delicately over some hanging blocks to easy ground. Ascend an arête past trees to a belay on the left below an overhung corner.
3   40 feet. Ascend the arête and slab trending left from a vegetated groove.

Northerner   185 feet   E2   (3 pts. aid)   †   (1966)
Takes the leftward slanting crack in the black overhanging wall
between the corners of Doom and The Big Cleft. Start from the
top of pitch 1 of Midlander.
1   30 feet. 4b. Continue up the groove above to the overhanging
wall then move right to a rib. Block belay above.
2   75 feet. 5c. From the block go out left to an overhanging and
a leftward leaning crack. Ascend the crack to a resting place
(peg). Continue up the crack. Peg and nut for aid. Poor rock.
Move out right onto the slabs. Stance on the left below an
overhang. Old peg belays.
3   50 feet. 4c. Traverse a slab on the right then go up a little
wall to another slab. Belay below a very steep corner.
4   30 feet. 5b. Climb the steep corner using one point of aid.
Easier climbing leads to some protruding rocks then the
vegetated ramp up right.

* Midlander   370 feet   Very Severe   (1956)
A rather vegetated start leads to a good finish. Start at the next
groove right of Doom.
1   120 feet. 4a. Ascend the vegetated groove to a tree.
2   50 feet. 4a. Move rightwards from the tree over sloping
ledges to a cave. Stance and belay.
3   60 feet. 4c. Traverse horizontally right round the arête then
go up over a bulge to a short steep slab; ascend this then follow
a short traverse right to a small ledge. Thread belay.
4   70 feet. 4c. Move awkwardly right to gain a little steep slab
and move across this to a rib. Ascend the slab on the right-hand
side of the rib to an old ring peg. Move left and gain a small
ledge below a steep wall. Move back right above the peg, and
with difficulty gain a good spike on the right. Climb direct from
the spike on good holds to a ledge. Move left to a groove.
Stance.
5   70 feet. 4a. Climb the groove to a slab on the right and go up
this to easy ground; stance and belay on large detached blocks
on the right.

The Big Cleft   300 feet   Hard Very Severe   (1969)
Takes the big corner to the right of the corners of Doom. Start
approximately 20 yards right of Midlander with a corner directly
above.
1   150 feet. 4a. Climb a short section of rock then take a line up
vegetation and occasional rock to the cave stance on Midlander.
2   75 feet. 5a. Gain the base of the big corner and climb this
with difficulty to a slab above. Continue up a slabby groove first
left then right, to a flake under a steep crack. Left of this step
onto a slab and ascend diagonally left until easier climbing leads
to a belay below the steep corner on Northerner.
3   75 feet. Go up left then follow the vegetated ramp to the right.

** **Man of Kent**   300 feet   Very Severe   (1969)
A leftward-trending line over overlapping slabs with some vegetation on the lower pitches. Start at a hawthorn tree in a groove.
1   80 feet. Ascend the groove past the thorn tree for 30 feet moving out right onto easy-angled slabs. Ascend these to reach a large tree on the left.
2   70 feet. 4b. Work up easily above the tree to a corner, move right then gain a ledge below some overhangs. Move left to an undercut slab, and go up this for a few feet to a good ledge on the right. Stance.
3   80 feet. 4c. From the belay move out left onto a slab sloping left and climb this to an old ring peg then follow Midlander. Move left and gain a small ledge below a steep wall. Move back right above the ring peg, and with difficulty gain a good spike on the right. Climb direct from the spike on good holds to a ledge. Move left to a groove and a stance.
4   70 feet. As for pitch 5 of Midlander.

* **The Magic Dragon**   315 feet   Hard Very Severe   (1970)
A climb with some fine situations but there is some vegetation on the lower pitches. Pitch 2 is poorly protected. Start as for Man of Kent.
1   110 feet. 4a. As for pitch 1 of Man of Kent but do not go left towards the large tree, instead move up to a ledge on the right. Climb a short steep wall and move up to a ledge under a large blunt arête.
2   80 feet. 4c. Ascend a broken groove on the left to reach a ledge at 15 feet. Continue up the groove above with the blunt arête on your right to an old peg. Traverse delicately across the wall under the peg to obvious holds on the arête. Ascend the arête direct to easier ground; stance and belay.
3   40 feet. 4b. Ascend a steepish wall then move easily right to a rib which overlooks Jugs Groove. Old peg belay.
4   25 feet. 5a. Climb the weakness in the steep wall above (old peg) to a stance and belay.
5   60 feet. 5a. Climb a steep groove on the right making a thin move right to an exposed ledge. Finish up slabs.

* **Click**   320 feet   Mild Very Severe   (1969)
The leftward trending line of slabs on the right-hand side of the buttress. Poor protection on pitch 2. Some vegetation on the lower pitches. Start at a groove 90 feet right of the hawthorn tree.
1   70 feet. Go straight up the groove to a stance and belay under an overhanging wall.

2   110 feet. 4a. Move right and go up an easy slab to a small tree. Climb the steeper slab above to join the top of the arête. Nut belays.
3   40 feet. 4b. Move easily up right to the base of a leftward trending slab. Ascend this with the crux half-way, and a delicate step left to the edge. A short wall at the top leads to the large ledge with a tree belay.
4   60 feet. The slabby wall on the left leads to some large detached blocks on the right. Escape to the right.

** **Jugs Groove**   120 feet   E1   (1971)
The groove immediately left of a striking sharp overhanging arête. Start from the small tree of pitch 2 of Click. Move a few yards up and right to a small stance. Poor protection at the start of pitch 1.
1   50 feet. 5b. Ascend the overhanging wall on the right to enter the groove, then follow the groove to the overhang. Gain the right arête and climb this for a few feet. Move back left and go up to a large ledge.
2   70 feet. 5b. Move right to gain the arête then follow it moving right at the top to a grassy ledge. Steep vegetated scrambling leads to the top.

Girdle Traverse   670 feet   Hard Very Severe
A lengthy expedition with some good pitches. Start as for Click.
1   70 feet. Follow pitch 1 of Click.
2   110 feet. 4a. As for pitch 2 of Click.
3   70 feet 4c. From the left-hand end of the belay ledge descend slightly then make a long horizontal traverse for 60 feet to the left, crossing Man of Kent. Reverse the awkward first section of pitch 4 of Midlander to the small ledge. Thread belay.
4   60 feet. 4c. Reverse pitch 3 of Midlander.
5   65 feet. 5a. As for pitch 3 of The Big Cleft for 25 feet, then go diagonally left up a slab to a flake, then go horizontally left to small ledges and a stance below an overhang. As for the top of pitch 2 of Northerner.
6   40 feet. 4b. Go up diagonally left to the arête; ascend this for 20 feet to a ledge then make a traverse left to the stance and peg belay at the top of pitch 2 of Doom.
7   85 feet. 5a. Step down and traverse 20 feet left to the lower extremity of the prominent overlap (exposed). Move onto the slab and climb diagonally left up the slab past a high flake runner (stance on The Mule). Continue traversing left and do down slightly to a stance below pitch 5 of Acheron.
8   90 feet. 5a. As for pitch 5 of Acheron.
9   80 feet. Traverse left into a groove and ascend this moving up left to a slab below an overhang. Move left to finish.

FFENESTR Y GRAIG (NORTH FACE)

The steep area of rock above and to the right of North Buttress which extends from the steep rake (descent ramp from the top of North Buttress) to a vegetated gully on the right which contains the tower of Dinas Llywelyn.

The descent is not obvious; first traverse left past all steep rock then descend bilberry ledges to gain a huge rightward descending ramp (also descent from North Buttress) to the bottom of the crag.

The first five routes all start from the top of a very wet gully coming down from the big quartz wall, an obvious feature of the face. This gully develops a few feet right of the lowest point of the huge ramp.

Hope Street 140 feet Severe (1955)
Exposed with some unsound rock. From the top of the wet evil gully below the big quartz wall ascend the grass slope on the left to its top. Start at a short chimney right of some blocks.
1 20 feet. Climb the chimney to a belay block.
2 80 feet. 4a. Right of the belay block make an awkward step onto a perched block then traverse right below an overhang with a wide crack. Surmount the crack and steepish rock above moving left at the top to a belay block in a small niche.
3 40 feet. Go up left then right to a grassy ledge. Scrambling then leads to the top of the crag.

Hopsit 260 feet Hard Severe (1956)
A vegetated route with some doubtful rock, which takes the obvious chimney crack in the corner to the left of the big quartz wall. Start directly below the corner.
1 30 feet. Ascend the wall immediately to the right of the evil wet corner. Move right to a corner with a spike belay.
2 80 feet. 4b. Enter the corner by a grassy ramp up left, old peg. Awkwardly ascend the wide corner crack to the vegetated rake on the left.
3 90 feet. 4b. On the right wall is a tree growing out at right-angles. Gain this via a crack. Ascend a grassy ramp rightwards to a corner. Gain the top of a pedestal and move up then right to steep heather which leads to a corner. Stance and belays.
4 60 feet. Ascend a vegetated groove to a grassy rake on the left. Follow this to the top. Chockstone belay.

The Whisper 270 feet Hard Very Severe (1969)
Very poor rock on pitch 1. Start as for Hopsit.
1 75 feet. 5a. Follow Hopsit to a good spike runner/belays. Climb the groove above, poor rock, to an old peg. Gain a ramp

Philip Gibson

Ffenestr y Graig (North Face)

1	Hope Street	S
2	Hopsit	HS
3	The Whisper	HVS
4	Quartz Wall	E1
5	First Visit	HVS
6	Quartz Buttress	HVS
7	Powder Monkey	E2
8	Hard Rain	E2
9	Plankwalk	HVS
10	Keel Haul	E1
11	Sybarite	HVS/A1
12	Heretic	E2
13	Spartan	E2
14	Quartz Vein	VS

Dinas Llywelyn
15	King Edward's Army	HVS

rising leftwards, then ascend steep grass to a good stance in a corner.
2   75 feet. 5a. Move right to the arête, step right round the arête and make an airy rising traverse across the wall to the small stance and peg belay on Quartz Buttress.
3   70 feet. 5a. Ascend the chimney crack to a quartz overhang. Pull over this and immediately move right for 10 feet to an old peg below a quartz corner. Ascend the quartz corner to a good ledge and belay below an overhanging corner.
4   50 feet. 4c. Take the right arête of the corner to a grassy ramp, which leads to the top.

Quartz Wall   320 feet   E1   (1978)

The obvious diagonal weakness onto the big quartz wall from the corner on the right. Start at the big corner pitch of First Visit.
1   70 feet. 5a. The corner groove is gained by a steep entry from the right. Ascend the groove until the right wall steepens, then make a difficult move left onto a ledge. Good nut belays.
2   55 feet. 5a. A wide corner crack above is followed until a line leftwards across the big quartz wall can be gained. Follow this to a small stance on The Whisper traverse. Nut belays.
3   115 feet. 5c. Make a slightly rising traverse left to the arête. Move round into a groove climbing the good rock on its right edge, to a ledge where the arête steepens. To the right is a scoop in the wall. Gain this then make a difficult move over a bulge above the scoop. Easier ground follows finishing left of a chimney/crack. Stance in a corner on the right.
4   80 feet. Go left to a groove and climb this to the top.

First Visit   280 feet   Hard Very Severe   (1955)

The obvious corner immediately right of the big quartz wall. Start as for The Whisper and Hopsit.
1   70 feet. Follow Hopsit to a good spike runner in a corner then make a vegetated traverse slanting down right below the steep quartz wall to the corner.
2   100 feet. 5a. The corner groove is gained by a steep entry from the right. Ascend the groove until the right wall steepens then make a difficult move left onto a ledge. Climb the chimney above the ledge, overhanging at first, to a large grassy ledge on the right.
3   80 feet. Follow vegetated ledges to their right extremity. Stance shared with Plankwalk and Keel Haul.
4   30 feet. Go up right taking the line of least resistance to the arête.

The following seven routes start roughly level with the start of Hopsit, The Whisper, etc but from a large grass ledge on the right of the evil wet gully. The ledge is approached from the right up steep vegetated terraces starting in the gully which contains the striking tower of Dinas Llywelyn. The ledge is identified by a large cave-like opening just above it.

* Cat o' Nine Tails   110 feet   E2   (1979)
The arête immediately right of First Visit. Start at the left-hand extremity of the grassy ledge from which Quartz Buttress, Plankwalk, etc start.
1   110 feet. 5c. Climb the wall 6 feet right from the arête, to a niche with a peg in place. The arête is gained with difficulty in 10 feet via a ledge. Go up left to another ledge then still with difficulty traverse right round a bulge then go up slabs to a final hard move up the arête. Finish as for Quartz Wall or Quartz Buttress.

Quartz Buttress   240 feet   Hard Very Severe   (1966)
Some doubtful rock. Start from the grassy terrace 25 feet left of the cave.
1   40 feet. Climb diagonally up right to a grassy bay. Belay at the top of the bay.
2   50 feet. 4c. Ascend the left edge of the bay then go up the wall above to a large grassy ledge.
3   30 feet. 5a. From the left end of the ledge step left and climb the steep wall to a quartz corner. Go up this to a small stance and old pegs.
4   70 feet. 4c. Ascend the chimney crack above, over a quartz overhang, and follow in the same line up a ramp to below a steep crack, nut belays.
5   50 feet. 4c. Climb the crack above to easy ground.

* Powder Monkey   230 feet   E2   (1978)
Left of Plankwalk pitch 1, an obvious crack slants leftwards. Pitch 2 (only fair protection) is a corner topped by a small overhang below the crux of Plankwalk. Start as for Plankwalk.
1   105 feet. 5b. Climb the ramp right of the cave continuing up the groove above to below an overhang (part of Plankwalk's first pitch). Move left to a ledge below the crack slanting left. Ascend the crack with difficulty to a sloping ledge; continue to an awkward exit. Belay on the grassy terrace above on the left below two steep corners.
2   125 feet. 5c. Go up the left-hand corner to a peg (out of sight from below). Difficult moves follow to gain the slab on the left. Continue with steep sustained climbing up the wall above to the block on Plankwalk, then as for Plankwalk via the fingery wall diagonally up left to the gully on the left.

** Hard Rain   260 feet   E2   (1978)
Takes the fine finishing wall between Plankwalk and Keel Haul. Start as for Plankwalk.
1   110 feet. 5a. Ascend to below the overhang (as for Plankwalk). Follow the steep groove continuation through the overhang to a big terrace. Move left to the foot of two steep corners.

2 55 feet. 4c. Climb the right-hand corner until it fades; move right and go up to a ledge at the foot of the awkward ramp on pitch 2 of Keel Haul. Good spike belay.
3 95 feet. 5c. Move left onto the block of Plankwalk then gain a thin crack in the wall above. Follow this to a peg below an overhang. Gain a shallow niche above; move out left with difficulty to easier ground.

** **Plankwalk** 240 feet   Hard Very Severe   (1966)
Takes the line of least resistance across the big smooth wall. An outstanding feature of the North Face. Start just right of the cave at a ramp formed by a huge flake.
1 110 feet. 4c. Ascend the ramp then climb the continuation groove above which slants right beneath an overhang. Follow this to a grassy ledge then go up easy vegetated ground to a sloping terrace.
2 130 feet. 5b. Take a weakness on the right, then go up left until a long slightly rising traverse left can be made to a noticeable small squarish block in the centre of the wall. Gain this and make some delicate moves left and up then left again to reach the left edge of the wall. Go left then up an easy gully/groove to the top.

*** **Keel Haul** 230 feet   E1   (1969)
A superb line through the overhangs right of Plankwalk. Start at an arête a few feet right of the start of Plankwalk.
1 100 feet. 5b. Move just right of the arête then climb a crack slanting up to the left, to a ledge on the arête. Climb the steep arête above to gain a shallow groove, and follow this to the large grassy terrace common with Plankwalk.
2 130 feet. 5b. Take a weakness on the right then go up left until a slightly rising traverse left can be made to a good spike runner beneath a short rightwards-slanting ramp (15 feet to the right of the noticeable squarish block of Plankwalk). Awkwardly go up the ramp to a little corner beneath the small roof. Swing out right beneath the roof to some old pegs. Make a long reach to the spike above the overhang. Climb for 6 feet above this then move left to a good nut runner. Ascend directly up the wall above to a ledge. Climb up to a big block overhang. Traverse up left to the arête

Gornik 130 feet   Severe   (1969)
A poor climb whose second pitch is the easiest escape from the big sloping grassy terrace. Start beneath a corner to the right of the arête of Keel Haul.
1 100 feet. 4a. Go easily up grass to a steep ramp which forms the left wall of the corner. Ascend the ramp to a grass ledge at the top. Move a few yards right and continue up the wall above to reach the big sloping terrace. Stance.
2 30 feet. 4a. As for pitch 4 of First Visit. Take the weakness on the right, up a slab, to exit right onto the arête.

About 60 yards above and to the right of the previous routes is another wall marked with bands of white quartz. Left of this wall is a corner with overhangs above. This corner is reached by steep scrambling with the odd V. Diff move to the right of Gornik. The corner can be quitted easily by moving out left above Keel Haul etc. This escape is known as Highway. The corner marks a starting point for the next four routes.

Ceramic Chimney 70 feet Severe   (1957)
An obvious chimney on the left of the corner, formed by a precariously balanced tower of blocks.
1 40 feet. Ascend the chimney to a stance.
2 30 feet. Move up right until clear of the overhang, then follow easy rocks above.

Sybarite 130 feet Hard Very Severe (5 pts. aid) † (1974)
The overlapping corner to the left of Spartan. Start below the corner just left of the start of Spartan.
1 130 feet. Climb the corner using two pegs, then go up free into a niche with a downward pointing flake on the right. Use a sling to place a small thread on the right-hand rib, and use this to gain the chimney groove on the right. Ascend the groove to stepped overhangs (peg in place) go over the first step and traverse left to a ledge on the left arête. Climb up the wall to the top (sling used to rest near the top).

* **Spartan** 150 feet E2   (1966)
A strenuous and technical line up the reddish wall beneath a roof a few feet right of the corner.
1 90 feet. 5c. Awkward moves lead upwards and right to a corner under the left-hand side of the roof. Traverse right under the roof to its end then move up with difficulty to a small ledge. Old peg. Traverse delicately right to a spike runner. Go right again and move over a bulge to gain a chimney.
2 60 feet. 4c. Climb the chimney to the top.

* **Heretic** 140 feet E2   (1978)
Start below the Spartan overhang.
1 75 feet. 5c. From a belay under Spartan overhang traverse right below the overhangs (loose) to the arête. Climb the arête (difficult) then follow a groove diagonally up leftwards to a footledge just below the slab on Spartan.
2 65 feet. 5c. Up to the left is a blank groove with a sideways spike in it. Ascend the groove and the overhang above moving right to finish up a crack.

Quartz Vein 130 feet Very Severe   (1969)
A climb which breaches the large quartz band to the right of Spartan. The rock in places is appalling. Start about 30 yards down and to the right of Spartan. Large block below an overhang chimney on the right.

1   40 feet. 4b. Climb right past the chimney then go up and back left to beneath a steep groove.
2   90 feet. 4c. Ascend the steep groove, then move across right to a small ledge. Go up steeply for about 10 feet then move left to gain a grassy ramp. The ramp leads to a small cave then follow the groove on the right finishing up a chimney.

DINAS LLYWELYN

A striking tower in the gully between the North Face and Far North Buttress.

King Edward's Army   150 feet   Hard Very Severe   (3 pts. aid) †   (1975)
A line up the front edge. Start at a smooth slab below the tower. Often wet.
1   75 feet. From a point 10 feet right of the slab base, traverse up left to the arête. Ascend this via a grassy ledge to an old peg. Continue straight up to the top of the slab using a peg for resting. Boulder ledge above.
2   75 feet. Take the overhanging wall above using two aid pegs. Go up left to a quartz rib then ascend the overhanging rock above, moving right to a chimney. Ascend this to the top.

CREIGIAU SAWDL EFA (FAR NORTH BUTTRESS)
An area of short steep walls to the right of the tower of Dinas Llywelyn. Bubble Wall follows the highest of the steep walls, on a level with the Dinas Llywelyn Tower. A noticeable horizontal grassy ledge runs under this wall.

Bubble Wall   80 feet   Hard Severe   (1956)
Start from the horizontal grass ledge on its extreme left.
1   80 feet. 4b. Ascend the wall trending up right to a break.

From the large boulder on the right of the horizontal grassy ledge. A corner leads up to the top. This is **Ronkle Boot Chimney**, 30 feet, Difficult.

The lowest of the steep walls, near to the stream, has a very prominent large overhanging section of rock, forming a huge cavern. A rib and chimney line to the left of this is taken by:

The Little Red Helmet   220 feet   Severe   (1970)
A vegetated route 200 feet left of the huge cavern. To the left is an open grassy gully. On the right of the rib is a slab that the route takes to the bilberry terrace above. Above this the route takes a chimney and an arête line to the top.

Phil Gibson on Bear Cage.

Photo: John Sumner

Andy Grondowski on Meisterspringer,
Craig-y-Mwn.

Photo: John Sumner

Where Eagles Dare   100 feet   Hard Very Severe   (1970)
An obvious groove with a small tree at the top, immediately right of the large overhanging section of rock. Start from the stance at the top of pitch 1 of Whirligig.
1   60 feet. 5a. Climb to an arête starting from the left-hand end of the ledge, then make a rising traverse left to below the obvious groove guarded by a bulge. Move awkwardly over the bulge and climb the groove above to the tree.
2   40 feet. 4c. Climb up left to the base of a steep crack and finish up this.

Whirligig   205 feet   Severe   (1969)
Takes the obvious weakness round the front of the buttress. Start at the lowest point of the buttress, on the right of a grassy ramp that goes up to the overhangs.
1   70 feet. Ascend trending right at 30 feet, then return left to a ledge below the overhangs; good spike belay.
2   75 feet. 4a. Gain the arête on the right then traverse right to a grassy bay. Move down to the base of a grassy ramp on the right and make a tricky move onto a slab. Continue moving right to vegetation, then go up left to a small stance in a niche.
3   60 feet. Climb the steep corner behind the belay; move right to avoid bad rocks, then climb direct up a chimney to the top of the buttress via a chimney crack.

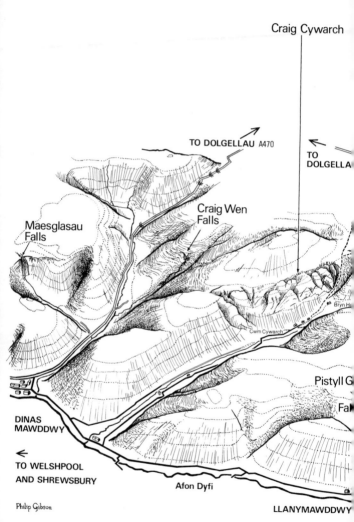

Craig Cywarch

TO DOLGELLAU A470

TO
DOLGELLA

Craig Wen
Falls

Maesglasau
Falls

Bryn H

Cwm Cywarch

Pistyll G

Fa

DINAS
MAWDDWY

←
TO WELSHPOOL
AND SHREWSBURY

Afon Dyfi

Philip Gibson

LLANYMAWDDWY

The Arans and Surrounding Areas

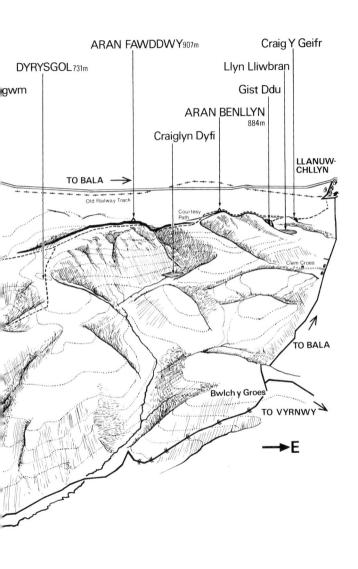

DYRYSGOL 731m

ARAN FAWDDWY 907m

Craig Y Geifr

Llyn Lliwbran

gwm

Gist Ddu

ARAN BENLLYN
884m

Craiglyn Dyfi

LLANUW-
CHLLYN

TO BALA →

Old Railway Track

Courtesy
Path

Cwm Croes

TO BALA

Bwlch y Groes

TO VYRNWY

→ E

THE ARANS

Approach
There is no direct access to the crags on Aran Fawddwy or Aran Benllyn and climbers must **NOT** try to approach the crags directly from below. Climbers have in the past gone down from the summits but even this approach is liable to offend the local farmers. Please do nothing to aggravate the current situation.

Aran Fawddwy

There is one recorded route which is quite good and entertaining. Ascend the East Face overlooking Craiglyn Dyfi. The route takes a line up the best of the broken buttresses directly beneath the summit of the mountain.

* **Christmas Retreat**   530 feet   Very Difficult   (1965)
At the base of the most continuous buttress is a large overhang approximately 200 feet above the south end of the Llyn. Start just to the right of the overhang.
1   100 feet. Follow the easiest line onto the slab on the right. Climb up the right edge of the slab, tricky move at the top, to a grassy stance with block belay.
2   80 feet. Ascend right to blocks go over these to take a stance between two massive boulders.
3   90 feet. Go over a hole on the left, then work across diagonally left over easy ground to below a steep tower.
4   90 feet. Climb a crack on the right edge of the tower, then move left to the top of the tower. Go up right to a wide crack in yet another tower above.
5   50 feet. The crack is taken with increasing difficulty to a grassy ledge with a spike belay below a slab.
6   120 feet. Climb the left edge of the slab, then ascend easy ground to the top of the buttress.

Aran Benllyn

On the east face directly below the summit is a fine compact-looking wall, a lonely sentinel in this rather remote area. The route below takes this wall.

* The Grey Citadel 350 feet Hard Very Severe (1969)
The last pitch takes the wall itself. The climbing beneath this is
much easier and is just a pleasant way up to the wall using the
best of the rock available . Start approximately 200 feet beneath
the wall from a huge grassy terrace. Small cairn.
1 60 feet. Climb a small rib, then go diagonally right over
vegetation to a grassy ledge with a spike belay.
2 50 feet. Above on the right are two corners. Climb the first
one exiting right at the top then climb up to a grassy ledge.
3 50 feet. A steep pleasant wall leads to a flake belay.
4 70 feet. Follow a steep little wall and a wide chimney to
beneath the wall itself. Belays on the left.
5 120 feet. 5a. Climb a few feet up left to a ledge. Work back
right taking the obvious traverse line to a short crack. Ascend
this to a good pocket, and make a difficult move right then go
up to better holds. Continue direct to a vague horizontal ledge.
Go right along this to a niche on the arête. Ascend the crack
above the niche to a ledge then continue up a groove to the top.

Gist Ddu
O.S. ref. SH 873255

Approach
Access from the Cwm Croes road is strictly forbidden. Only the
courtesy path along the Aran ridge route may be used. This is
fully described in the introduction to the Aran Range near the
front of the guide. The shortest approach is from the north end
from Llanuwchllyn on the B4403. Approximately 3 miles. When
level with the crag below, descend keeping well clear of the
steep areas to the foot of the crag.

Character and Topography
A high mountain crag facing east which overlooks Llyn Lliwbran.
It is vegetated in places and takes some time to dry out but the
rock is the best in Mid-wales. The crag has a remote feel to it
and will appeal to the climber who wants to get away from the
crowds, but still wants to enjoy routes of great quality. The main
central section of the crag has impressive corners and arêtes on
the right finishing with the huge clean arête of Aardvark. To the
left are quite distinct leftward-slanting grooves and slabs
finishing with the deep Souwester Gully.

To the left and right of the Central Buttress are vegetated areas
of rock which are named the Left and Right Wings.

Descent
Ways off Central Buttress are not obvious. The safest is by
traversing left until a descent into Souwester Gully can be made,

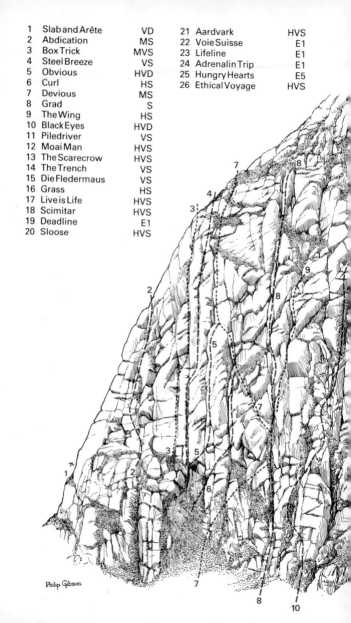

Philip Gibson.

Gist Ddu

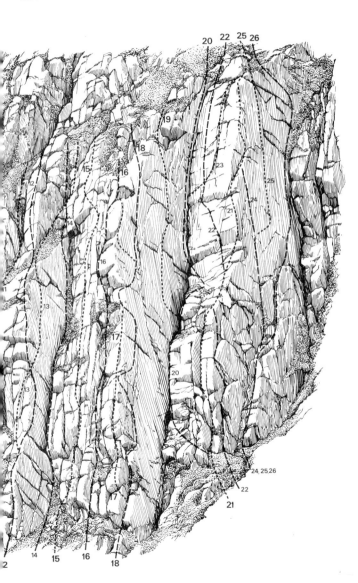

crossing this above its first hard pitches to vegetated ledges on the left, which lead to the bottom of the crag.

A possibility on the right side of the buttress, and only recommended when the crag is very dry, is to make two 150-foot abseils down Sloose; the first from the tree at its top, and the second from the jammed boulder; dubious abseil tapes are usually found under the boulder.

LEFT WING

In a wide gully, the next one left of Souwester Gully, is a very noticeable sharp-looking rib. This is Monolith. Beyond this forming the right wall of the gully are several slabs, the first is grassy but the rib at its left edge is clean and gives the line of High and Dry. The next slab is taken by Jambiri which follows it on its right just left of the grassy corner chimney.

Stiff Lower Lip   180 feet   Very Difficult   (1976)
Start at the left-hand end of the slab taken by Jambiri, below a large block.
1   150 feet. Ascend a groove starting on the right then on the left. Move right passing to the right of the block to gain a ledge. Go up and leftwards to gain a rib and ascend this to the top. A slab leads to a ledge and belay.
2   30 feet. Large blocks lead up to easy ground.

Stiff Upper Lip   150 feet   Severe   (1976)
A line up the centre of the slab. Start just left of the start of Jambiri.
1   150 feet. Gain the right end of the small overhang above by zig-zagging up the centre of the slab. Move left then go up climbing a groove in a steeper wall above to finish.

Jambiri   150 feet   Severe   (1972)
Start at the right-hand end of the slab just left off the grassy corner chimney.
1   50 feet. Ascend slabs left of the vegetated corner making a move right over a block back in the corner to gain a large ledge and belays.
2   50 feet. Go up slabs left of the corner then move up left to a cleaned area through vegetation. Belays back in the corner.
3   50 feet. Trend up the slabs and the ramp below an overhang to gain a cracked corner. Move back right taking the slab above the overhang to finish.

High and Dry   170 feet   Severe   (1972)
Start by the rib at the right of the main slab.
1   65 feet. Ascend the rib to the overhang, move right then go up to vegetation. Just above this is a ledge with belays.

2 65 feet. Take the slabby rib on the right. The small overhang is climbed direct. Pinnacle belays.
3 40 feet. The overhang with a crack in it has good holds. Finish easily.

Monolith Direct   180 feet   Hard Severe   (1976)
Above the sharp arête which is the start of Monolith are two ribs. Monolith Direct takes the right-hand rib. Start below the rib.
1 110 feet. Take the easiest line upwards to a slot on the ridge. Make an awkward move left to the rib. Ascend this to a ledge.
2 70 feet. The slab is followed then go up the right edge of The Monolith, followed by the crack and slab above.

Monolith   275 feet   Difficult   (1970)
Takes the striking knife-edge arête rising out of the base of the next gully left of Souwester Gully. Start on the left at the bottom of the arête.
1 110 feet. Ascend trending rightwards along a break to an arête. Follow this to its top passing a small tree.
2 75 feet. Climb the broken wall on the left trending left to a big pinnacle. Ascend a huge flake on its right then go up to a wide ledge. Flake belay.
3 90 feet. Move 20 feet left to a huge detached block. Ascend this by its right-hand side then follow a groove above which overlooks the gully. Belays above. The easiest way down is by the gully on the left.

CENTRAL BUTTRESS

Souwester Gully   300 feet   Severe   (1941)
The vegetated gully bounding the left side of Central Buttress usually has a small stream down it and difficulties are mainly near the bottom.

Slab and arête   200 feet   Very Difficult   (1941)
Steep vegetation just right of the gully bed leads up to a wall with a crack in it.
1 35 feet. Work awkwardly up the crack to a stance and belay.
2 55 feet. Diagonally up to the left is a big tree. Move up to the tree then go right to the base of an arête; stance and belay in a crevice.
3 90 feet. Climb the arête to a grassy ledge.
4 20 feet. Finish up the arête.

Abdication   200 feet   Mild Severe   (1960)
On the left-hand side of the buttress is a large horizontal terrace. It can be gained from either end by steep scrambling. At its centre there is a slight change in level. Start at a groove just right of this.
1 45 feet. The groove leads to a small overhang; cross a slab on the left and ascend the corner to a grassy ledge above.

2   45 feet. Take the slab in the corner then go left to the start of a short chimney. Climb the left wall of the chimney then follow vegetation to a tree.
3   80 feet. Crux. Gain the niche in the wall behind the tree. The niche has a large prominent flake, ascend the niche for a few feet then make a rising traverse left to the arête.
4   30 feet. Go straight up the arête, as for Slab and arête.

* Box Trick   180 feet   Mild Very Severe   (1970)
A vague crack-line slanting leftwards to the left-hand side of a scoop under a large overhang. Start about 6 yards right of the groove of Abdication.
1   50 feet. Climb the wall, following the indefinite crack-line to a ledge with a triangular wedged block.
2   70 feet. 4b. Move up then go delicately right across the scoopy slab beneath the overhang to the corner. Climb this pulling awkwardly over an overhang then go up in the same line to a second overhang which is surmounted with the aid of a small spike. Good ledges and belays above.
3   30 feet. Climb a steep groove behind the ledge to another ledge with a tree belay.
4   30 feet. Follow the corner above the tree to finish.

Steel Breeze   180 feet   Very Severe   †   (1980)
Start 20 feet right of Box Trick.
1   50 feet. 4a. Ascend the slabs direct on good incuts, past a clean V-niche, to a belay in a slanting groove-line 15 feet below the overhang on Box Trick.
2   130 feet. 4b. Swing right across the right-hand wall and make an awkward move up the slabs. Move left and climb the increasingly obvious thin crack trending diagonally up and left to a ledge. Step right up a short groove and scramble to the niche and belay.

** Obvious   220 feet   Hard Very Difficult   (1970)
Takes a long leftward-slanting groove on the left-hand side of the buttress. Start from a tree on the right-hand end of the horizontal terrace.
1   20 feet. Traverse right from the tree just above a large overhang to gain the base of the groove.
2   50 feet. Climb the groove (good holds keep appearing on the right wall) to a small ledge with good nut belays.
3   60 feet. Continue up the groove, negotiating two overhangs to a good ledge; a ramp comes into it from the right. Stance shared with Devious.
4   90 feet. 4a. Then, as for Devious, continue up the groove-line which becomes more of a chimney. Finish up the short wall above.

Curl 220 feet Hard Severe (1965)
A natural line starting at the foot of a clean slab below an overhang, near the top of a steep vegetated ramp slanting up left to the horizontal terrace on the left-hand side of the buttress.
1 40 feet. Ascend the steepening slab, working up right to a large flake belay.
2 80 feet. 4a. Move up to a chimney then climb this with a difficult initial move to the grassy ledge of Devious.
3 100 feet. Finish as for pitches 4, 5 and 6 of Devious.

Devious 230 feet Mild Severe (1941)
Belays difficult to find. Start a few feet right of Curl.
1 75 feet. Ascend right by ledges until under a light coloured overhang. Gain the base of the chimney on the right by a delicate traverse. Ascend the chimney to a grassy ledge on the left. Old peg belay.
2 15 feet. Climb the slab above or follow the wide crack on the right, to a chimney. Stance above.
3 40 feet. Go left along the terrace then move up to gain an open groove.
4 40 feet. The groove leads up until a descending ramp goes down leftwards to a chimney.
5 30 feet. Ascend the chimney to a stance.
6 30 feet. Go up the wall above on good holds, then scramble off to finish.

Grad 350 feet Severe (1964)
A vegetated groove-line running the full height of the crag. Start down and to the right of Devious below the groove-line.
1 50 feet. Ascend the groove to a stance on the right.
2 90 feet. Go up on the right of a large block to its top, and move left into a niche. Ascend to the foot of the chimney forming part of Devious and climb this to a stance on the left. Old peg.
3 15 feet. Climb the slab then a short chimney with a stance above. Pitch 2 of Devious.
4 95 feet. Continue up the groove-line to an overhang. A move up to the right gains a grassy slab under another overhang. Climb the narrow chimney on its left. There is a grassy stance.
5 70 feet. Move 3 feet left then go straight up to a grass bay.
6 30 feet. Scrambling leads to the finish.

* **The Wing** 130 feet Hard Severe (1963)
A climb with some exciting moves through an overhang. Start from the stance at the top of Devious pitch 1.
1 100 feet. 4b. Ascend the slab above on the right, as for Devious, then traverse right following a ledge until below a hanging edge of rock. Climb the corner to just below the hanging edge then take the narrow chimney on its right to a ledge. Finish up the chimney above, moving left on a large grassy ledge.
2 30 feet. Ascend in the same line to easier ground.

Black Eyes   390 feet   Hard Very Difficult   (1973)
A devious line following a weakness between The Wing and
Piledriver. Some vegetation. Start at the base of the steep
vegetated ramp that leads up to Devious, Curl etc where a
cleaned rib juts out of the vegetation, which is directly below the
weakness between the steep upper sections of The Wing and
Piledriver.
1   130 feet. The rib leads to a large vegetated ledge, spike belay
above under the overhangs.
2   70 feet. Traverse 25 feet left to a crack going diagonally left.
Ascend the crack and the groove above to a small ledge with
nut belays.
3   45 feet. Ascend 3 feet up the groove then move right then go
down to gain a corner. Move right again to a small ledge. Climb
a short wall to a good belay ledge in a groove.
4   60 feet. Ascend the groove then move right onto the face.
Follow a line first right then left then go up to a belay ledge under
on overhang.
5   85 feet. Move right for a few feet then go straight up to a
steep wall. Awkward moves left up a short groove to gain a slab
follow (crux). Climb the slab to easier ground above. Finish up
a little wall to the top. Jammed block belay.

Piledriver   260 feet   Very Severe   (1963)
Scramble leftwards up vegetated ledges from the base of
Sloose, until two corners can be seen above a vegetated wall.
The right-hand corner is immediately left of the clean arête of
Moai Man. Start below and just left of the left-hand corner.
1   60 feet. Ascend the vegetated wall to below the left-hand
corner. Thread belay in the corner.
2   50 feet. 4b. Ascend the left-hand corner moving onto the left
edge after a few feet. After a move up the edge go back into the
corner again. Ascend this to a flake belay on the left.
3   50 feet. 4c. Return right to an undercut groove then go up
this to a grassy ledge.
4   100 feet. Ascend the corner above to finish.

** **Moai Man**   240 feet   Hard Very Severe   (1972)
A good climb up the left arête of The Trench. Start directly below
the arête.
1   40 feet. 4a. Follow the arête to a ledge and good nut belay in
an horizontal crack.
2   140 feet. 5a. Go directly up the slab above to a small ledge
on the arête. Move right round the arête and make an awkward
move up to gain a small ledge. Old pegs. Move up a crack
trending back left to a ledge on the arête, good runner. Above
is a wall; climb this with difficulty trending slightly left. Continue
up the arête with the odd awkward bulge to a large vegetated
ledge. Old peg belays high up in the corner.
3   60 feet. 4b. Reach the arête left of the corner and climb its
left wall to the top.

** **The Scarecrow**   240 feet   Hard Very Severe   (1984)
Excellent climbing. Start as for Moai Man.
1   40 feet. 4a. Follow the crest to a ledge and good nut belay in a horizontal crack.
2   65 feet. 5a. Go up and left to climb a steep groove to a ledge on the arête. Climb a short steep wall directly above the ledge (crux of Moai Man) then step down right to a large flake.
3   65 feet. 5a. Directly above the flake is a thin crack. Climb this first gaining it by an awkward move from the left. Follow the crack to a big vegetated ledge above.
4   70 feet. Ascend the vegetated corner moving out right then back left.

The Trench   260 feet   Very Severe   (1963)
A vegetated route in the big corner left of Sloose. Note: If vegetation runs up the length of the first pitch the grade would be much harder. Start by scrambling up grassy ledges to the base of the corner.
1   70 feet. 4c. Ascend the undercut base of the corner crack. Continue up the corner crack until it disappears. Make awkward moves on doubtful flakes, pulling over a final bulge using a pocket hold above. Move up to a ledge and belay.
2   90 feet. 4b. Continue up the vegetated corner crack via two large overhanging blocks. At the top of the corner traverse out left to a large vegetated ledge.
3   100 feet. Ascend vegetation to an overhanging corner. Go up this on the right to belay above.

* **Die Fledermaus**   300 feet   Very Severe   (1985)
The big groove-line on the right wall of The Trench. Start a few yards right of the corner where scrambling leads up to the right into a corner below the right-hand of two chimney lines. Huge flake belay.
1   115 feet. 4b. Climb the steep right-hand chimney on big holds to its top then step left to gain the left wall of the groove-line. Ascend this to a small ledge under an overhanging block.
2   70 feet. 4c. Go over the block to gain a ledge under an overhanging wall. From the left end of the ledge climb a crack for a few feet to a loose block and move out right to a rightwards-slanting groove going through an overhang. Pull awkwardly up this and move up to a good ledge.
3   115 feet. 4b. Continue up the broken chimney-line above to a niche. Traverse left to the centre of the clean wall, climb this with a difficult move over a bulge then move left at the top. Scramble up heather to good belays.

Grass   290 feet   Hard Severe   (1963)
A fairly direct line with some vegetation, although not as bad as it sounds, up the buttress between The Trench and Sloose. Start below a small corner above some steep heather, 20 feet left of the start of Scimitar.

1   30 feet. 4b. Climb the corner, awkward, to gain a groove on the right, and ascend this to a stance above vegetation. Steep corner above. Thread belay.
2   70 feet. 4a. Move left round the corner and ascend to a grassy ledge below a steep wall. Step right onto a large foothold then go up to a slab on the left, climb this, and continue direct to a stance below a corner; nut belay.
3   80 feet. Ascend the corner to vegetation; traverse right easily then return left to a stance and large spike belay in a corner below an overhang.
4   60 feet. 4a. Move to the left of the spike, then go up and left again, to a vegetated crack; climb this to a stance with a spike belay.
5   50 feet. 4a. Move right then ascend to a ledge. Climb the steep little wall above to heather ledges. Scramble up these to a good nut belay beneath a little wall.

Live is Life   305 feet   Hard Very Severe   (1985)
Start as for Scimitar below the overhung corner on the arête.
1   130 feet. 5a. Go up the corner for a few yards then climb the left wall to some large flakes below a short undercut arête. Gain the arête with difficulty then follow a crack-line up the left-hand side of the main arête to a ledge. Climb the bulging arête above to sloping ledges. Good nut belay crack.
2   90 feet. 5a. Continue up the arête for a few yards to the roof, move onto the right wall and climb to an old peg below the start of the curving flake of Scimitar. Traverse left to gain a small ramp (with the feet) on the arête. Ascend the arête for 3 feet to small ledges and nut belays.
3   85 feet. 4c. Continue up the steep arête above to a sloping ledge then move left and climb a steep little wall to vegetation. Finish up this to a ledge and belays.

** **Scimitar**   270 feet   Hard Very Severe   (1970)
A fine route with an extremely fine 4th pitch (when dry). It takes the huge slabby wall left of Sloose. Start at the bottom left edge of the huge slabby wall below an overhung groove.
1   20 feet. Climb the groove to a stance and belay below the roof.
2   90 feet. 4b. Ascend to the roof then move right and climb a vague crack-line up the wall trending left at the top to a ledge on the arête.
3   30 feet. 4c. Step back down right onto the wall and gain a crack. Climb this until it is possible to move back left onto the arête. Belay on sloping ledges.
4   110 feet. 5a. Continue up the arête to the overhang. Step right round the arête to a crack in the wall. The crack soon disappears and a line of weakness is followed to the base of a curving flake. Climb just right of the flake to a small ledge. Move up with difficulty to gain the big ledge above.

5   20 feet. 4a. Move up a ramp to the right and so to the top of the wall.

* **Deadline**   120 feet   E1   (1972)
A fine thin crack in the impressive wall between the upper sections of Sloose and Scimitar. Start from the huge jammed boulder in Sloose.
1   120 feet. 5b. From the top of the boulder gain the thin crack-line in the wall on the left and climb this over two small overlaps. Slightly easier climbing follows continuing in the same line to the roof at the top of the wall. Originally done at the same grade by escaping left after the second overlap.

** **Sloose**   240 feet   Hard Very Severe   (1963)
A route of quality and its final pitch when dry must rate as one of the great corner pitches of Wales. Avoid the initial very wet 60-foot gutter by coming in from the right beneath an overhang by some jammed boulders.
1   90 feet. 4a. Gain the chimney in the corner by traversing left under the overhang. Climb the chimney to the huge jammed boulder. Move up behind this to a ledge on the right.
2   150 feet. 5a. Make an easy rising traverse up left into the chimney in the corner. Ascend this over a bulge (doubtful blocks) to the corner crack above. Climb this on good holds to where the crack becomes an awkward width and holds diminish. Persevere with the crack to better holds on the right wall. Continue up the corner with slightly easier climbing to the tree at the top.

Lifeline   150 feet   E1   (1976)
Start below the top pitch of Sloose.
1   150 feet. Follow Sloose top pitch to just above doubtful blocks then take a traversing line out right to a groove and crack-line in the middle of the wall. Follow this to the top.

*** **Voie Suisse**   270 feet   E1   (1984)
A brilliant route whose top pitch takes the fine clean wall between Aardvark and Sloose.
1   120 feet. 4c. Climb the stepped groove/arête a few yards right of the start of Aardvark to the big ledge.
2   150 feet. 5b. Move up the slab to the break in the first overlap, pull over this to the left, trend slightly left, and go up to a peg. Make some delicate moves again slightly up left to reach good holds beneath the second overlap. Step left (10 feet from the corner of Sloose) and pull over the second overlap to the right through a weakness, then move up to a flake/block. Move up 3 feet from the block then step left to gain a thin crack-line. Climb this to the top.

*** **Aardvark**   270 feet   Hard Very Severe   (1966)
A superb route, a Mid-wales classic taking the great arête right of Sloose. Start from some jammed blocks under an overhang as for the start of Sloose above its initial wet gutter. This is reached by scrambling up steep grass on the right then steeply leftwards up vegetation to the jammed blocks.
1   120 feet. 5a. Gain the niche on the right using a small wedged block as a foothold. Make some difficult moves up the steep crack above to gain a sloping ledge. Move left to the base of a groove, and climb this moving right at its top then go up to the large grassy ledge.
2   100 feet. 5a. Ascend the slabs trending right to a spike on the arête under the big overlap. Move right round the arête and climb an awkward crack moving back onto the arête at a small ledge under a bulge. Climb the bulge and the groove above to perched blocks.
3   50 feet. Move leftwards and finish up the arête.

** **Adrenalin Trip**   160 feet   E1   (1980)
A direct line up the left-hand side of the big wall to the right of Aardvark. Protection is rather poor on the upper section of pitch 1. Start from the top of pitch 1 of Ethical Voyage, below a cleaned area of wall.
1   110 feet. 5a. Climb the wall with increasing difficulty following a vague weakness which gradually gets closer to the arête. Finally finishing up the last few feet of Aardvark's 2nd pitch.
2   50 feet. Ascend the arête as for Aardvark, pitch 3.

*** **Hungry Hearts**   150 feet   E5   (1984)
A superb wall pitch which starts as for Adrenalin Trip.
1   150 feet. 6a. Climb the first 40 feet of Adrenalin Trip then make a rising traverse right to the centre of the wall (thread and peg). Climb the wall direct to a ledge then continue to finish up easier ground.

Ethical Voyage   455 feet   Hard Very Severe   †   (1978)
The crack on the right-hand side of the big wall to the right of Aardvark. Start at the base of a vegetated stepped ramp rising rightwards just round the arête from Aardvark.
1   135 feet. Ascend the stepped ramp to a good ledge beneath a steep corner.
2   70 feet. Start in the corner then climb its right edge to a ledge in the middle of the wall. Go right along the ledge to belay in a cave.
3   100 feet. 5a. Move back left to the foot of a crack in the wall above; climb this to another cave belay.
4   150 feet. Go back to the wall then ascend the gully until a traverse left can be made to the abseil tree above Sloose.

A girdle traverse of the main crag has been done at HVS. Its main interest is in the section crossing the Scimitar Slab and Sloose. The rest is of a much easier standard with a fair bit of vegetation.

RIGHT WING

Looked at from below the big arête Aardvark a clean arête stands out from the steep vegetation and slabby walls which go to make the Right Wing. Tambourlaine takes the clean arête.

Tambourlaine 255 feet   Hard Severe   (1970)
Gain waterworn slabs leading up to the arête which is undercut at its base.
1   70 feet. Ascend wet slabs to a clean steep crack. Follow the crack to a grassy ledge on the left.
2   45 feet. Ascend a rib for 20 feet to a corner. Traverse right to a break in the arête. Move round this to a grassy cave.
3   110 feet. 4b. Move back left to the arête. Ascend the steep rock on good holds for about 30 feet, then gain the left flank of the arête via a weakness using holds on the left of the rock. Climb the arête to the top.

CRAIG-Y-GEIFR   OS ref. SH 874270

An east facing crag lying on the north end of the Benllyn Ridge. It does not exceed 100 feet in height but is of sound compact rock with strangely little vegetation. The crag is approached as for Gist Ddu (q.v.), descending the main ridge track after 1½ miles. Access from the Cwm Croes road is strictly forbidden.

Tilt 60 feet Severe   (1971)
On the left side of the crag is a horizontal ledge above which is a very steep smooth wall. Start under the right-hand end of the ledge.
1   60 feet. An awkward scoop on the right leads to the ledge. Move left along this to the ramp-like corner. Ascend the ramp to finish.

The Nest 40 feet Severe   (1971)
The hanging slab on the right of the horizontal ledge at a large flake.
1   40 feet. Gain the top of the flake then the ledge on the right. The smooth slab above leads to the arête.

Left-Hand Break   70 feet   Very Difficult   (1971)
The first obvious weakness to the right of The Nest.
1   40 feet. Climb over the undercut base then go up to a stance
and belay below an overhanging block.
2   30 feet. Move left below the overhanging block until an
escape can be made.

Thin Man   130 feet   Difficult   (1971)
A worthwhile climb, taking the next easy break right of Left-hand
Break. Start by some massive jammed blocks.
1   40 feet. About 20 feet up is a vertical chimney in a corner.
Climb easily up to this and ascend it, chockstone runner at its
base. Gain a ledge with a boulder belay.
2   30 feet. Move right along a ledge to another boulder belay
on a ledge.
3   50 feet. Gain a wide horizontal crack in the slab on the left
and follow this to the top.

Grit   50 feet   Hard Very Severe   (1971)
On the right-hand end of the crag are three impelling crack-lines
in a steep wall. Start at the middle one.
1   50 feet. 5b. The crack is followed direct, strenuous, with the
crux in the middle.

DOLGELLAU AREA

Bird Rock (Craig yr Aderyn)   O.S. ref. SH 643069

Bird Rock rises dramatically out of the flat Dysynni Valley only 7 miles from the seaside town of Tywyn. Approaching from the inland side via Welshpool or Dolgellau make for the junction at the Cross Foxes Inn and go down the A487 then the B4405 to Tal-y-Llyn. A mile downstream from the Llyn take a minor road marked to Llanegryn which follows the river Dysynni to the crag.

Character and Topography
Although very low lying being only a few feet above sea-level it has a northerly aspect and can be cold to climb on in winter. However the main attraction The Diamond Wall dries very quickly making it an obvious choice when most other crags are wet.

The rather vegetated big north-east facing crag above the quarry is a cormorants' nesting site. Apparently the crag used to be an old sea cliff. Much lower down and practically next to the road is the main attraction, The Bastion, which has The Diamond Wall. Between these two is a section of rock with prow-like overhangs. This is known as Central Buttress.

EASTERN FACE

The Eastern Face, the largest of the Bird Rock crags lying above a quarry, is a bird sanctuary and climbing is forbidden during the nesting season. There is a notice beneath the crag to this effect. The crag is heavily vegetated in places with some doubtful rock. The start of most of the routes can be gained by approaching from the right. Only Safe as Sausages is approached from the left.

Safe as Sausages   140 feet   Hard Very Severe   (1983)
On the extreme left-hand side of the Eastern Face is a slim pillar with an obvious groove-line up its centre. It has some dubious rock. Start at the lowest point of the pillar directly below the groove-line.
1   140 feet. 4c. Ascend the pillar for 35 feet then step left into a groove. Climb this to a large spike runner. Step left again to enter another groove and follow this to a ledge on the left. Finish up the easier continuation groove.

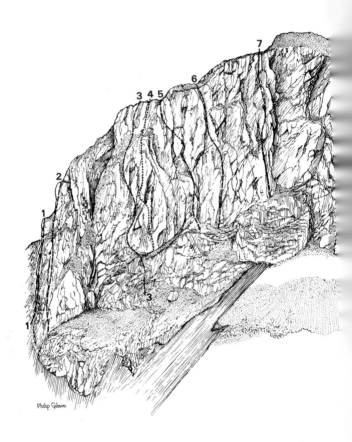

Philip Gibson

Bird Rock (Eastern Face & Central Buttress)

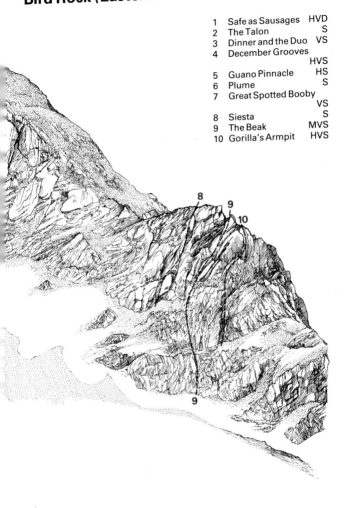

The Talon   290 feet   Severe   (1964)
Takes the pinnacle on the left-hand side of the face (the pillar of
Safe as Sausages is round to the left of this pinnacle). Some
doubtful rock. Start at a crack gained from the right by traversing
above the quarry.
1   130 feet. Ascend the crack to grass at 15 feet. The crack
continues above; climb the wall to the right of this moving right
near the top. Continue more easily above to a ledge in a grassy
gully.
2   30 feet. Move left across the gully and gain the top of a
pinnacle on the left.
3   60 feet. Take the easiest line, up the wall above first left to
an old peg then go right to the arête at some blocks. Ascend the
pinnacle to its top on the left.
4   70 feet. Step down from the left end of the ledge. Move round
an arête then go left again to another arête. Ascend this to the
top of the pinnacle.

Dinner and the Duo   305 feet   Very Severe   (1975)
A fairly direct line up the centre of the large buttress to the left
of Guano Pinnacle. Start at a weakness slanting left in a lower
wall situated directly below the large buttress.
1   65 feet. Start easily up a vague crack trending left for a few
feet. Move left on grass and go up a short wall to a grassy
terrace. There is an ivy-covered wall up to the right. Spike belay
on the left.
2   120 feet. 4b. Gain the wall above and move up between two
overhangs. Ascend steeply up right above the right-hand
overhang to easier ground. Move up right to a poor ledge on
the edge of the wall then go left to below a corner crack; avoid
this and move up right to the top of a huge spike.
3   75 feet. Take the easiest line left to ledges then go directly
up on easy ground to a steep wall with a crack in it. Stance on
the right.
4   45 feet. 4b. Gain the top of a big spike on the left then ascend
the steep crack above to a niche. Climb awkwardly from the
niche to the top.

* **December Grooves**   250 feet   Hard Very Severe   (1975)
The big groove to the right of Dinner and The Duo. Poor
protection on pitch 3. Start from the top of pitch 1 Dinner and
The Duo. Move right to a groove just right of an ivy-covered wall.
Large spike belay.
1   45 feet. 4c. From a ledge climb the groove, moving left at the
top to a ledge.
2   65 feet. 4b. Continue up the groove to the overhangs; move
left round an edge and climb to a huge spike.
3   100 feet. 4c. From the top of the spike step right onto an
exposed wall and ascend this on big well-spaced holds to

ledges. Continue to a notch between a pinnacle and the wall above.

4 40 feet. 4b. Finish up the steep groove above.

Guano Pinnacle 310 feet Hard Severe (1959)

A mountaineering route, with some interesting situations. The route makes for a large conspicuous pinnacle (cormorants favourite roosting ground) in the middle of the crag. Some doubtful rock. Protection rather poor on pitch 3. Start below the conspicuous pinnacle at a broken groove/chimney line coming down from the right-hand side of the pinnacle.

1 120 feet. Ascend a short wall then go up a grassy ramp moving leftwards. Continue up vegetation to a corner on the right. Ascend this until a move left can be made to more vegetation which leads to a steep corner beneath the chimney line from the pinnacle.

2 80 feet. 4a. Ascend the arête on the left for a few feet to a ledge. Climb the steep wall above on good holds moving right to a ledge above the steep corner. Go up the broken wall above, some doubtful rock, to easy ground leading to the base of the chimney.·

3 110 feet. 4a. Ascend the chimney to evil ledges between the face and the pinnacle. Large spike on the right. Gain a foot-ledge above on the face behind the pinnacle which is followed left beyond the pinnacle to a groove. An awkward move across this leads to easier but rather unstable ground and the top.

Plume 320 feet Severe (1974)

The next crack-line to the right of Guano Pinnacle. A similar mountaineering route to Guano Pinnacle. 30 feet right of the Guano Pinnacle start is a cleaned rib. It leads up directly to large flakes and spikes at the start of the long traversing section into an upper groove-line.

1 120 feet. Ascend the rib then take a fairly direct line up cracks and short walls to the large flakes.

2 90 feet. Traverse left to more spikes and flakes, then ascend the highest and biggest of these. Move left and make a delicate step down to gain a grassy ramp on the left. Follow the ramp to a slab leading to a small stance in a little corner. A broken spike forms the left wall of the corner.

3 110 feet. Ascend the little corner to the top of the broken spike and traverse left into a steep corner; continue up this to an overhang (steep crack above) then move left to the edge and ascend on big doubtful holds. Go back right above the overhang and ascend the broken crack above to the top.

Great Spotted Booby 230 feet Very Severe (1974)

To the right of the crag centre where it is highest a large wet corner cuts the entire face. The route takes a series of grooves in the arête on the left of this big corner. Some unstable rock.

Start below a clean steep groove (old peg at its foot) about 150 feet up the vegetated lower section of the face. Ascend the lower section first by taking a large grassy ramp on the right then a little wall followed by more vegetation to a rock niche on the right. Go up left of the niche to another wall then zig-zag up vegetated ramps to the groove.

1   110 feet. 4c. Climb the groove negotiating a small overhang half-way (crux). Step left at the top to the arête, ascend vegetation, passing some doubtful blocks to gain a large pinnacle.

2   80 feet. 4b. Right of the belay is a groove. Climb this to the second of two small ledges. Go left avoiding two pinnacles ahead on the right to a chimney behind the last one. Go up this to belay on the left below an overhanging block.

3   40 feet. 4c. Climb up to the right of the overhanging block (loose rock on the left) and gain a slab moving right to ledges on the arête. Finish easily.

CENTRAL BUTTRESS

The buttress has an upper and lower tier. Prow-like overhangs dominate the upper tier. Above the lower tier is a track which comes in from the left ending below the final pitch of The Beak.

Siesta   110 feet   Severe   (1962)
A favourite with the Aberdovey outward bound school. Poor protection on the crux slab section. The line takes a slanting groove on the upper tier, 16 yards left of the prow-like overhang of the final pitch of The Beak. Start from the track about 17 yards past a fence just before a huge block with a rectangular block lying across the top of it.

1   110 feet. 4a. Climb a crack on the left then climb right to a small cave (pitch could be split here). Make a traverse to the right for about 10 feet to the edge of a slab. Go delicately up the edge then follow an easier section to a jammed block overhang; surmount this to easy ground and the top.

The Beak   200 feet   Mild Very Severe   (1964)
On the lower tier, directly below the prow – a prominent feature of Central Buttress. The first pitch follows the lower tier at its highest section. There is a shallow corner to its left and a vague groove to its right. Pitch 2 is merely scrambling. Start at the cleanest section of rock.

1   70 feet. 4b. Move straight up the buttress front, stepping right at 40 feet to a ledge and dubious spike; climb on good holds above the spike to grass; block belay above on the right.

2   80 feet. Scrambling up over broken rock and grass, to a large niche just above the track. Above are the grooves which slant down from the prow.

3 50 feet. 4b. Climb the cracks slanting up right negotiating small bulges until below the final roof. Either move out right onto the edge of the prow (exposed) then go up this to the top, or surmount the overhang direct.

** **Gorilla's Armpit**   125 feet   Hard Very Severe   (1975)
The obvious overhanging groove right of The Beak. Start at a steep crack in a wall a few feet below the end of the track that comes in from the left above the lower tier.
1 90 feet. 4c. Climb the crack to a ledge. Step right and climb a steep cracked ramp to a ledge directly below the overhanging groove.
2 35 feet. 5a. Finish up the groove.

THE BASTION

The most popular of the Bird Rock crags. It has two faces, north and west, divided by The Buttress route. The rock on the North Face is clean but is doubtful in places. The West Face is much scrappier with some vegetation. The main feature of the North Face is The Diamond Wall slightly overhanging for most of its 150 feet.

* **The Gizzard**   60 feet   Hard Severe   (1964)
To the left of The Diamond Wall the rock diminishes in height. The first definite feature on the left is a groove with a small narrow slab rising leftwards below it.
1 60 feet. 4b. Climb the leftward slanting narrow slab to enter the groove with difficulty; good hold at the base of the groove. Ascend the groove to its top moving out left to a grassy slope. Scramble up this to the descent track where metal belay spikes will be found.

The Jug   110 feet   Severe   (1967)
Start a few feet right of The Gizzard, taking the easiest line to a steep obvious corner to the left of the pedestal on Pedestal Route.
1 110 feet. 4a. Go easily up to a ledge which is just left and level with the large pedestal (possible belay). Go left up a ramp to an overhanging corner, old peg. Climb the steep wall diagonally up right to a ledge. (Then as for Pedestal Route.) Go along the ledge up left to broken rocks. Belay on metal spikes by the track.

Pedestal Route   110 feet   Hard Severe   (1962)
Rather poor protection on the steep little wall above the pedestal. Start below the pedestal.
1 110 feet. 4b. Climb steeply to a niche below the pedestal, then move right and go up to the top of the pedestal (possible belay).

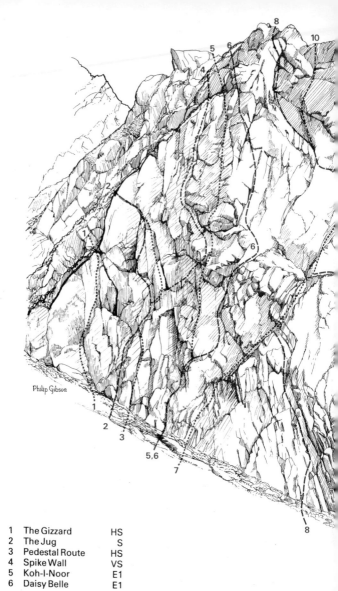

Philip Gibson

1	The Gizzard	HS
2	The Jug	S
3	Pedestal Route	HS
4	Spike Wall	VS
5	Koh-I-Noor	E1
6	Daisy Belle	E1

Bird Rock (The Bastion)

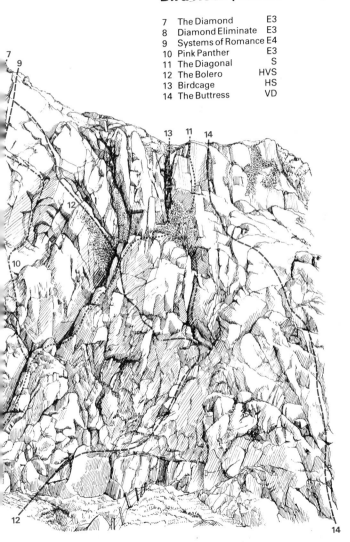

Ascend the steep little wall above the pedestal, crux, to gain a ledge on the left and follow this up left to grass and broken rocks. Belay on the track.

* Spike Wall   130 feet   Very Severe
A line up the left edge of The Diamond Wall. Start below the pedestal. Holds on the steep upper section are better than they look.
1   130 feet. 4c. As for Pedestal route until just right of the pedestal, then traverse right, passing an old peg. Climb steeply up to gain a slab beneath an overhang (old peg and good nut). Go up left via a crack to a large spike; above is a groove. Gain this by pulling over a bulge. Climb the groove to the top and belay on the track above.

* Koh-I-Noor   130 feet   E1   (1978)
A vague groove-line between Spike Wall and Daisy Belle. Start as for Daisy Belle, at the large boulder.
1   130 feet. 5c. From the boulder step 3 feet right then continue straight up the slight groove to join Spike Wall at the peg. Go steeply up right to the slab below the overhang (as for Spike Wall) then pull out rightwards on layaways to reach a flat-topped spike. Continue straight up the groove using holds on the left. Move right at the top to a slab. Junction with Daisy Belle and finish leftwards as for Daisy Belle.

** Daisy Belle   130 feet   E1   (1964)
Takes the easiest and most obvious line up The Diamond Wall. Exhilarating climbing. The first pitch gains the left end of the central ledge in The Diamond Wall while the second is the obvious groove system above the left end of the ledge. Start from the large boulder below the pedestal on Pedestal Route.
1   60 feet. 5a. Step up from the boulder and traverse right, then go up and right again to a groove with a peg in it. Climb the groove, exiting right to the ledge.
2   70 feet. 5b. Climb strenuously up the overhanging groove above the left end of the ledge (old pegs) to a niche. Ascend this to a small overhang then move out left onto a slab . Go up this moving left to finish.

** The Diamond   150 feet   E3   (1976)
A fine route but with poor protection at the crux on pitch 2. It takes a ramp-line rising rightwards (dark rock) to the central ledge, then a steeper rightward-trending ramp-line on the upper wall. Start just right of Daisy Belle, about 6 feet right of the large boulder.
1   70 feet. 5b. Climb up rightwards to a shallow groove with an old peg (not seen from below). Move up and traverse right across the steep wall then go up to a belay niche on the central ledge.

2 80 feet. 5c. Just right of the belay niche climb a shallow groove to its end. Move up with difficulty (poor in situ nut) to a resting place below an obvious slanting slab. Ascend the slanting slab to a ledge and continue up the short wall above to the top.

** **Diamond Eliminate**   150 feet   E3   (1978)
Poor protection at the crux on pitch 2. Start at the foot of The Diagonal, from the lowest point of the wall. The objective is the large central niche in the upper wall. Sensational climbing up the centre of the wall.
1 80 feet. 5b. Go up diagonally left for 25 feet, then up again for 6 feet to a spike. Ascend the obvious leftward-slanting crack into the first pitch of The Diamond, then follow this to the belay ledge.
2 70 feet. 5c. Follow The Diamond taking its unprotected crux to the resting place below the slanting slab. Then delicately traverse left until below the central niche. Move into this then ascend its left-hand slab and arête to finish.

** **Systems of Romance**   185 feet   E4   (1979)
An excellent first pitch. The rest is rather contrived. Start at the foot of The Diagonal.
1 75 feet. 6a. Climb The Diagonal for 10 feet, then go strenuously out left over a bulge to a spike. Go right to a horizontal ragged crack (doubtful spike runners) then gain a diagonal ramp up right (peg) and climb this to a ledge. Nut and spike belay.
2 35 feet. Go easily left along the central ledge to the niche belay (peg).
3 75 feet. 5c. Go back right and up a groove, past an old in situ nut, to the resting place below the slanting slab (pitch 2 of The Diamond). Move down right and round the corner (Pink Panther in reverse) to below two thin cracks. Go up these and a steep wall to the top.

** **Pink Panther**   195 feet   E3   (1978)
Excellent sustained and technical climbing. Start as for The Diagonal.
1 80 feet. 5b. Climb The Diagonal for 35 feet until under a scoop. Gain the scoop then move out right onto a steep wall. Follow this to a ledge.
2 35 feet. 5c. Move right to a groove/slab and climb this to its top. Go up the steep wall above to a hanging belay on a spike.
3 80 feet. 5c. Hand-traverse to the left on ledges until a few hard moves lead to the resting place on The Diamond, then continue as for Diamond Eliminate into the central niche but climb the wall out to the right.

The Great Mogul 185 feet E2 (1979)
A high-level traverse of the Diamond Wall. Start as for Pedestal Route.
1 35 feet. Climb easily to belay just right of the Pedestal.
2 150 feet. Follow Spike Wall right go and up into its final groove, until standing on a sloping ledge. Traverse right with difficulty until a good edge enables a resting place in Daisy Belle to be reached. Step down 6 feet and traverse right to the bottom of the niche. Reverse the traverse of Diamond Eliminate and finish up the slab of The Diamond.

The Diagonal 120 feet Severe (1964)
The prominent diagonal crack slanting up right from the base of the steep diamond wall. Adequate protection except for the first 30 feet; normally a peg is in place. Start at the base of the crack.
1 85 feet. Take a line just below the crack on good rock to a ledge. Climb more in the crack-line with an awkward final move to a large ledge, boulder and tree belay.
2 35 feet. Move easily right to a stance on the buttress then ascend a clean-cut groove on the left to the top.

** The Bolero 120 feet Hard Very Severe (1974)
Start at the top of pitch 1 of Birdcage, just beneath the black cleft. Its top pitch gives a good introduction to the exposure of The Diamond Wall and also allows an inspection of the harder routes.
1 50 feet. 5a. Take Birdcage for 3 feet to where it overhangs, then traverse left on good holds making an awkward move to gain the top of a pedestal. Go up left from the pedestal with difficulty to good holds. Make a move up then go diagonally up left to reach the ramp of The Diagonal. Ascend this for a few feet to the big ledge.
2 70 feet. 5a. Step back down left across an ivy groove to reach a steep ramp; climb this to its top. Ascend the steep wall above until just above a good spike runner then traverse out left along good footledges making some steep moves up to a ledge on the left. Ascend the final steep little wall to the top.

Birdcage 110 feet Hard Severe (1967)
Makes for the deep black cleft below the big ledge with the tree on The Diagonal. Only the wall above the cleft is of interest. Start a few feet right of the fence below a slab slanting up right.
1 40 feet. Climb the slab then go up easily into the cleft.
2 40 feet. 4b. Move up into the cleft then swing out left and climb steeply on wide spaced jugs to the tree.
3 30 feet. Finish up the vegetated groove above.

* The Buttress 135 feet Very Difficult
The obvious line of the buttress can be climbed as 2, 3 or 4 pitches with several variations. Protection is rather difficult to find. Start at the lowest point of the buttress.

1   40 feet. Ascend the left-hand wall of the buttress to a large ledge; spike belay on the left.
2   70 feet. Go up to the left of a bulge then ascend fairly directly to easy ground. Metal spike under the final steep wall.
3   25 feet. Climb steeply up the wall on good holds; scrambling above leads to metal spike belays.

To the right of The Buttress route the climbs face west thus forming the dividing line between the two faces. The following routes are on the West Face.

Rockerfeller   70 feet   Hard Severe
Good rock, following a rather artificial line. Poor protection on the lower section.
1   70 feet. 4b. Takes a direct line up the right flank of The Buttress to the right end of a large platform beneath the last pitch of The Buttress. Finish as for The Diagonal.

* North Face Girdle   300 feet   Hard Very Severe
Has some good independent climbing. Start as for Rockerfeller.
1   80 feet. Ascend Rockerfeller for 25 feet then move left to a ledge on the arête; traverse left to the black cleft on Birdcage.
2   60 feet. 5a. As for The Bolero. Go up Birdcage to where it overhangs, then traverse left to a pedestal. Go awkwardly up left to join The Diagonal then descend The Diagonal for a few feet to a ledge.
3   60 feet. 5b. Climb strenuously up the overhanging left wall diagonally up left to a good spike; two old pegs in place. Traverse left to gain the central ledge with a niche stance and peg belay.
4   100 feet. 4c. Go to the left end of Central Ledge and move left on good handholds to a slab. Move left to a crack, then continue as for Spike Wall; go up the crack to a steep wall, pull over this to a groove and follow this to the top.

Chouca Rib   200 feet   Very Difficult   (1974)
Takes the first rib to the right of The Buttress. Interesting climbing although escapable at several places.
1   60 feet. The rib leads to a ledge; continue up a steeper section above on good holds. Belay round the pinnacle.
2   40 feet. Make an awkward move to gain a ledge on the right then traverse right round an edge to a corner. Climb the corner to easier ground. Belay to a large prominent spike on the right.
3   70 feet. From the spike make an ascending traverse right to the edge. Move back left up a ramp above a steep wall until a long stride can be made across a slab to easy ground. Ascend slabs to a large ledge. Belay in a shallow chimney on the left.
4   30 feet. Climb a steep wall on the right of the chimney.

Picket Line 195 feet Hard Severe (1974)
A series of short steep walls to the right of Chouca Rib; pitch 2 is a noticeable wide crack in one of the walls. Pleasant climbing though rather artificial. Start about 50 feet right of Chouca Rib, at a small vertical corner beside a small black hole.
1 55 feet. 4b. Climb the corner to a good foothold. Move left and go up to some spikes; step back right and climb a short slab above to a grassy ledge. Climb the wall just right of the ledge to a corner on the left. Stance. Wide crack in the steep wall above.
2 40 feet. Climb the crack, moving left at the top to finish directly up a short tower; large grassy terraces above.
3 100 feet. Take the clean wall above on the right, moving right at the top. Ascend easy slabs to finish.

* **Curly Fringe Frown** 130 feet Very Severe (1974)
Interesting climbing taking the best of the rock hereabouts. The second pitch takes the obvious leftward-slanting clean arête. Beneath this is a black overhang cut by a crack. Start beneath the crack.
1 50 feet. 5a. Climb up to the crack in the overhang; surmount this by a little rib just left of the crack, stepping back right above the overhang. Then, as for The Rockery, go up the wall above on big holds to a ledge (small flake belay) below the arête.
2 80 feet. 4c. Climb 10 feet up a short slab directly above the belay, just left of the arête (good nut in crack on the left). Traverse right to a good small spike on the arête. Ascend the wall right of the arête following a leftward line up the edge to the top. Ascend more easily to a sloping grassy ledge and a large block belay.

The Rockery 170 feet Severe (1966)
A meandering line, aiming for the clean section of rock to the right of an oak tree. Start 3 feet up left of the huge block at the start of Goat Walk; black overhang on the left.
1 40 feet. 4a. Climb the weakness leading leftwards over the overhangs to a spike, then ascend directly up the wall on good holds to a ledge (small flake belay) below a steep arête.
2 80 feet. 4a. Go easily right to a corner, move up this for 10 feet then make a move left and go up the steep wall. Easier climbing above leads to a large sloping grassy ledge and a large block belay.
3 50 feet. On the left is a wall with a niche in it. Gain the niche, moving out right over steps to broken rock and the top.

Goat Walk 140 feet Moderate
The rib to the right of The Rockery. Start by a huge block beneath the rib.
1 70 feet. Ascend the slabby edge of the rib above to a ledge on the left; block belay above.

Dave Shepherd on The Girdle of Gist Ddu. *Photo: John Sumner*

Andy Grondowski on the 1st ascent of The Floater, Barmouth Quarry.
Photo: Wendy Grondowski

2 70 feet. Surmount the wall directly behind the belay on big holds to a ledge. Climb the left edge of the smooth wall above to grass and a spike belay above.

Craig y Llam
O.S. ref. SH 755135

Approach
From the Cross Foxes Hotel, follow the A487 Corris-Machynlleth road for 2 miles to the pass where the crag appears above.

Character and Topography
Craig-y-Llam is approximately 300 feet high and faces north-north-west looking out over the slopes of Cader Idris. Its lower 150 feet is heavily vegetated and most routes start above this vegetated band. The routes Judge and Two Convicts, Bomber and Tyburn Gate are best gained by climbing the initial section of White Rock (VS), then traversing right. Gate of the Winds is probably best gained from the top of the crag and descending to it from the right.

The most obvious feature is a huge green ramp cutting across the crag from right to left. This is the line taken by Gate of the Winds. To its left is a very steep wall undercut at the base. To the right of the ramp the crag is more scrappy although the top is guarded by a band of overhangs.

Descent
From the top of the crag descend the ridge to the north cutting down one of the easy gullies to the road.

White Rock   300 feet   Very Severe   (1980)
Takes the white slab which bounds the left-hand side of the crag. The rock is doubtful in places. Start at a tree on the left-hand side of the buttress.
1 150 feet. 4a. Ascend up to the right to the foot of an arête with a corner on its left-hand side. Move right to reach the arête and climb steeply to the white slab in a good position. Continue more easily and belay on the left where the rock steepens.
2 80 feet. 4b. Climb rightwards to the foot of a flake crack. Follow this until one can move right to an overhung stance, nut belays.
3 70 feet. 4a. Return left then follow the slabs to the top, finishing on the left at the final tower.

Craig y Llam

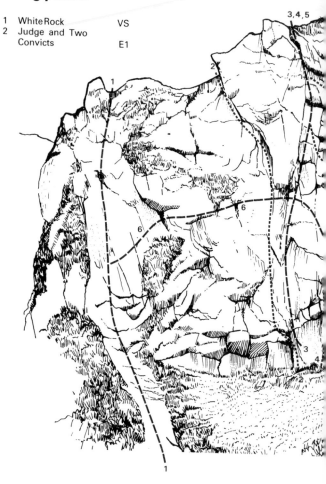

Philip Gibson

3	Bomber	E3
4	Tyburn Gate	E2
5	Gate of the Winds	HVS
6	Roumagaou	E2

* Judge and Two Convicts   120 feet   E1   (1980)
The big groove at the left-hand side of the crag, starting just left
of Bomber. Approach via White Rock, making a long traverse
right after the first pitch. Start from the stance as for Tyburn Gate
and Bomber.
1   120 feet. 5b. Climb the leftward-slanting groove 3 feet left of
the groove of Bomber to a peg. Make some awkward moves,
passing a second peg, to exit on a slab on the left (Girdle
crosses). Continue straight up a short steep wall to ledges. Climb
the corner above on good holds to the top.

* Bomber   120 feet   E3   (1980)
The vertical wide crack running the full height of the crag, from
just left of the quartz coffin block at the start of Tyburn Gate.
Some poor rock. Start as for Tyburn Gate.
1   120 feet. 5c. Go up to the coffin block. Stretch left and climb
with difficulty to the base of a chimney. Ascend this and the
groove above until a step right can be made to a ledge. Take the
steep crack above to the top.

*** Tyburn Gate   150 feet   E2   (1980)
A groove-line up the steep undercut wall just left of the
prominent green ramp of Gate of the Winds. Start by climbing
the first pitch of White Rock then make a long traverse right to
the side of a pinnacle which almost reaches the lip of the roof.
The pinnacle is topped by a quartz coffin-shaped block. To the
right of this block is a cantilevered block.
1   150 feet. 5c. Reach the quartz coffin block by a traverse in
from the left. Above is a 3-foot roof; pull over this (peg) and
traverse right on the lip of the overhang to good holds in a niche.
Move up right and climb the obvious groove (peg) to a slab on
the left. Traverse left across the slab to a hanging rib, gain the
rib and climb this to the top.

* Gate of the Winds   135 feet   Hard Very Severe   (1980)
Follows the obvious green leftward-trending ramp which is the
main feature of the crag. Start at the foot of the ramp, best
reached from the top of the crag by descending steep heather
slopes to the right until an easy terrace left can be taken to the
start.
1   135 feet. 5a. Climb the chimney on the right of the slab to an
overhang. Traverse left to the edge and climb the steep wall
(crux), trending left to attain the upper ramp. Continue left in the
obvious line to finish up a short groove to the top.

** Roumagaou   260 feet   E2   (1980)
The girdle of the crag. Only fair protection on pitch 3. Start from
the overhung stance of pitch 2 White Rock.

1 110 feet. 5b. Step down and move right round an edge, then follow the cleaned slabs to the steep groove of Bomber. Make a few moves up Bomber to the obvious exposed ledge on the right arête. Using this as a handhold move right to a peg, and continue moving right and go down to the niche above the overhang on Tyburn Gate.

2 90 feet. 5b. Step up and traverse right between the overlaps to a ledge. Go up the short steep wall above and move right to a spike. Continue moving right round an arête into Gate of the Winds. Climb the right-hand overhung retaining wall to gain a ramp. Good stance at the bottom of the ramp.

3 60 feet. 5c. Move right onto a rib then climb the steep wall trending back slightly left to a groove; climb this, then traverse right to a grassy groove. Belay well back.

** **Lost Man**   110 feet   Hard Very Severe   (1980)
To the right of the main crag above the quarry is a striking arête. Lost Man takes the right edge of this. Approach by a traverse in from the left above the quarry. The route dries quickly and gets the afternoon sun. Start below a crack on the right of the arête.

1 110 feet. 5a. Climb the crack to the edge of the arête. Continue just right of the edge on good holds to the final steep section. Make some difficult moves up and left to gain the top of the arête.

Buzzards Groove   160 feet   Severe   (1980)
The groove to the left of Lost Man arête and the wall above. Start 6 feet to the left of Lost Man arête at the foot of the obvious groove.

1 110 feet. Climb the groove until a small ledge on the left can be gained. Continue up the slabs on the right and belay at the top of Lost Man..

2 50 feet. Climb the small groove on the left of the continuation arête for 15 feet until a traverse right to a small bay in a fine position on the arête itself. Exit up the left-hand wall and the arête to reach the top.

Right Little Lady   110 feet   Very Severe   (1980)
The ribbed undercut wall immediately above Lost Man. Start at the lowest point of the rib descending to the right of a cave.

1 110 feet. 4b. Climb diagonally leftwards to gain the prominent slab. Traverse right (crux) to gain the rib and follow this to the top.

CADER IDRIS

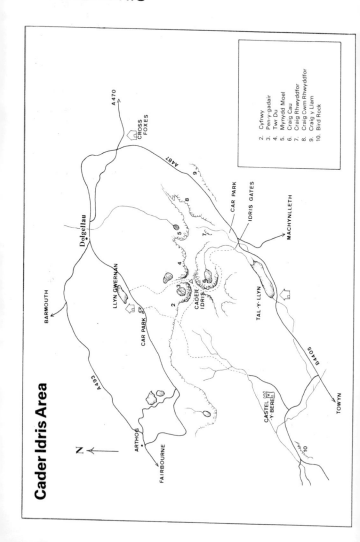

Cader Idris Area

2. Cyfrwy
3. Pen-y-gadair
4. Twr Du
5. Mynydd Moel
6. Craig Cau
7. Craig Rhwydfor
8. Craig Cwm Rhwydfor
9. Craig y Llam
10. Bird Rock

Craig Rhwyddfor

O.S. ref. SH 734122

Approach
Turn off the A487 Corris-Machynlleth road at the layby a quarter of a mile north of the junction with the B4405. Take the short road down to the Cwmrhwyddfor farm (good camping facilities) and gain the track which ascends the hillside diagonally up left to the small Cwm Rhwyddfor and the crag. Good relations with the farmer exist at present. Courtesy and good behaviour are requested to maintain this situation.

Character and Topography
This low-level crag facing east is about 110 feet high. It is steep with an undercut base, rather squarish in appearance, and the rock on the whole is good. The main features are overhangs, the most obvious one being a large butterfly overhang at the base. Just right of this is the only weakness in the very steep base, giving access to a slight ramp line crossing the wall to the right. This is taken by the easiest route on the crag, Blatch's Folly.

Descent
To the left (Ice Man Direct) side of the crag, take a gully line back down to the foot of the crag.

* Ice Man Direct   110 feet   E2   (1979)
The big central groove directly above the centre of the butterfly overhang at the base of the crag. A 6-foot roof bars entrance to the groove.
1   110 feet. 5c. Ascend an easy vegetated wall to the roof. Pull over this with difficulty, peg, to the base of the groove, then strenuously work up this to a resting place. Continue up the groove with a final tricky move to join Ice Man. Then as for Ice Man go up and left to a slab and finish by a steep groove to a tree.

* Loki   110 feet   E1   (1980)
Takes the next groove to the right of Ice Man Direct. A small tree growing out of the base of the crag is just right of the base of the groove. The groove is barred by a small overhang. Start below the groove which is gained from the right above the tree (nut runner can be arranged high in a crack on the right to safeguard the initial moves over the overhang).
1   110 feet. 5b. Pull over the overhang on big but doubtful holds and climb steeply up the groove to a peg. Continue up the steep groove, moving out right to a resting place. Move up to the roof and traverse up left for 3 feet onto a sloping ledge. Climb directly up to a large spike and make an awkward move up right to gain a steep ramp. Continue straight up on good holds, finishing airily out left.

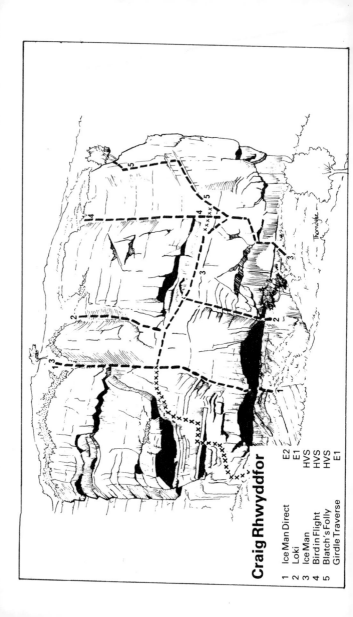

Craig Rhwyddfor

1	Ice Man Direct	E2
2	Loki	E1
3	Ice Man	HVS
4	Birdin Flight	HVS
5	Blatch's Folly	HVS
	Girdle Traverse	E1

** **Ice Man**   130 feet   Hard Very Severe   (1979)
Good sustained climbing up the steep central section of the crag,
starting at the only weakness in the undercut base, above a big
tree. The line then traverses leftwards below a line of small roofs
which increase in size, finally taking a steep groove to a tree at
the top. Gain the open groove the only weakness in the undercut
base from the left.
1 130 feet. 5a. Go up the open groove for a few feet then make
some difficult moves right to small ledges. Move up left to the
line of small roofs and traverse horizontally left below these to
a bulge. Pull left over the bulge and go left to a groove. Make a
move up the groove then go left again to a slab. Climb up the
steep groove above on big holds to a tree belay at the top of the
crag.

* **Bird in Flight**   110 feet   Hard Very Severe   (1980)
A direct line up the crag above the big tree at the bottom. Start
as for Ice Man, then continue directly, following a line of light
coloured rock.
1 110 feet. 5a. Climb the open groove for a few feet then
traverse right with difficulty to small ledges (as for Ice Man).
Move up and go slightly left to a small roof, pull over this on
good holds and go up steeply to a niche. Move steeply leftwards
out of the niche, using big underpulls and reach a small groove
topped by a small triangular overhang. Move right then upwards
on big holds; move back left to reach easy ground.

Blatch's Folly   135 feet   Hard Very Severe   (1979)
A rightward slanting line across the wall on the right-hand side
of the crag. The first moves are much harder than anything else
on the route. Start as for Ice Man.
1 100 feet. 5a. Climb the open groove for a few feet then
traverse right with difficulty to small ledges. Move up right
following the obvious diagonal line across the wall to the edge.
Ascend this for a few feet then traverse right to a big tree.
2 35 feet. Go easily right then left to the top.

** **Girdle Traverse**   175 feet   E1   (1980)
Follows a line between the roofs, starting on the left. Go up easy
rock on the left of the crag to a vegetated ledge with a tree and
a gorse bush. Level with this ledge a short horizontal ramp cuts
into the very steep undercut wall on the right.
1 65 feet. 5b. Traverse right along the short ramp then make a
long reach up to holds above an overhang; pull over this and
move up to a larger horizontal ramp-line with a big roof above
(peg). Traverse right along the ramp then move up to a small
ledge (nut and spike belays).
2 110 feet. 5a. Climb down 10 feet then traverse right under a
line of small roofs (Ice Man in reverse) to small ledges. Continue
the rising traverse right following a weakness, then move up and
right again to a large tree just under the top of the crag.

Craig Cwm Rhwyddfor

The line of broken buttresses on the south-eastern slopes of Cader Idris, running parallel with the pass road down to Tal-y-Llyn. The only recorded routes lie on the buttress closest to the road directly above the farm of Cwm Rhwyddfor and on a section about ⅓ of the way along the escarpment, called the Central Area. The buttress above the farm has a large shield-like face with a descent gully. Close proximity to Craig Rhwyddfor allows for somewhat easier optional climbing. Approach as for Craig Rhwyddfor. Gwth o' Wynt and Trick in the Tail are on the shield-like face above the farm.

Gwth o' Wynt   130 feet   Hard Very Severe   (1982)
Follows a ramp up the centre of the wall. Start 6 feet left of the lowest point of the wall.
1 130 feet. 5a. Climb a short steep section to gain the obvious ramp running diagonally up right across the wall. Climb this to a peg below a ragged crack. Take the crack to the top. Large boulder belay well back.

Trick in the Tail   120 feet   Very Severe   (1982)
A light coloured groove on the right-hand side of the wall, with a small holly tree at the top. The first 30 feet are rather artificial. Start directly under the groove.
1 120 feet. 4c. Climb the slabs directly below the groove for 30 feet then make a step left to gain the groove. Climb this with an awkward move over the final overhang to gain the holly. Large boulder belay well back.

CENTRAL AREA

This section of crag is probably the most significant of the long escarpment crags of Craig Cwm Rhwyddfor. Some 150 feet high by 300 feet long, the most outstanding feature being an arête starting halfway up the crag. Descent from this crag is down a gully on the left when facing the crag.

Tri-Grainian   100 feet   Very Severe   (1986)
Takes the crack in the mossy slab to overhangs, left of the big arête line.
1 100 feet. 4c. Climb the crack on the right-hand side of the slab to a niche under the overhangs. Traverse left to a ledge on the left-hand side of the slab. Move up then go left to tree belays. Abseil from trees.

* Giotto 150 feet Hard Very Severe (1986)
Takes the main arête line. Start to the left of the arête-line below
a chimney leading up to overhangs. The left-hand side of the
chimney forms the right-hand side of the slab of Tri-Grainian.
1 80 feet. 4c. Ascend the chimney to the overhangs, some
doubtful rocks, then traverse right to a hanging slab. Climb the
slab diagonally right to the arête, go up this a short way then
make a traverse left to a stance below the arête.
2 70 feet. 5a. Move up to the bulging arête on the right, peg.
Step right and climb its steep right edge on good holds to a
ledge. Continue directly up the arête above to easier ground. Peg
belay in a slab well back.

Craig Cau
O.S. ref. SH 712122

Approach from the Tal-y-Llyn (south) side of the mountain. Take
the track from Idris Gates up through woodlands, following the
stream which comes down from Llyn Cau. The track leaves the
trees and in about ¾ of a mile reaches the Llyn. The crag rises
on the far side and is best gained from a small track on the
left-hand side of the Llyn.

Character and Topography
The crag having a north-easterly aspect lies below the summit
of Mynydd Pencoed. It is a very large complex crag about 800
feet high which unfortunately is heavily vegetated. It is seamed
with terraces and due to this makes it probably the longest of
all the Mid-wales crags to dry out. However all is not gloom as
some of the upper sections not overhung by vegetation have
some brilliant routes on good rock.

The outstanding feature of the crag is undoubtedly the Pencoed
Pillar with its tremendous great gully side-wall dropping
vertically for over 200 feet. To the right of the pillar very steep
vegetation takes over separated by walls with no distinctive
features until a rib roughly coming down from the summit is
seen – this is Central Rib. Right again very steep but very wet
vegetated walls continue until another feature stands out a
200-foot chimney/crack-line in a cleanish-looking wall. This is
Crack of Cau. Right of this the upper wall greatly decreases in
height and vegetation takes over again.

Descent
From the Pencoed Pillar routes and routes finishing in this area
descend the main track south-east down the ridge passing the
tops of East Gully and Little Gully. Descend the next gully along

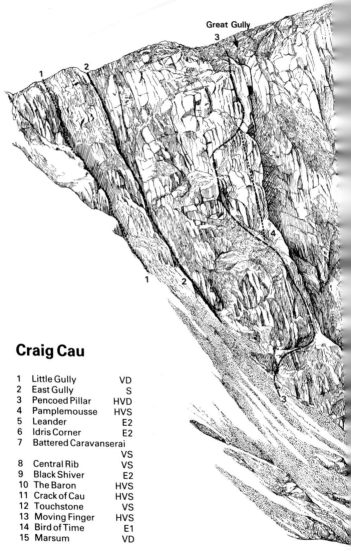

Great Gully

Craig Cau

Philip G

which has a wide bilberry funnel exit, keeping to the slopes on its left (when looking down). Descend to a sheep track and the base of the crag.

For the routes, Crack of Cau, Bird of Time, etc. gain the ridge and descend towards the col between Mynydd Pencoed and Penygadair. Before reaching the col the ridge flattens out. Descend here following an easy grassy ramp, cross a shallow gully then follow a sheep track to below two small pinnacles; follow this round to the foot of the climbs.

Little Gully   450 feet   Very Difficult

The next gully to the left of East Gully. The final overhanging chimney pitch is normally avoided and if climbed direct the grade would be Hard Severe.

1   150 feet. Scramble up the gully bed to the first obstacle, a huge wedged block.
2   30 feet. A tight chimney on the left of the block is climbed to vegetation.
3   150 feet. Vegetation leads up to an overhanging chimney.
4   120 feet. Take an easy groove at the start of the overhanging chimney until just below a large chockstone. Move out left to a small grassy bay on the left wall and follow this to a large spike on the left. A move down from the spike then a long stride left leads to a big foothold. Continue traversing left to easier ground.

East Gully   600 feet   Severe   (1985)

The gully immediately to the left of Pencoed Pillar. It is very wet and vegetated in its lower section, but improves towards the top.

1   100 feet. Scramble up grass on the left to enter the gully then go up a short steep section by grass on the right wall.
2   150 feet. The gully continuation is normally wet so ascend a chimney on the left, traverse right at the top, back into the gully, then climb a wet gutter to where the gully narrows.
3   150 feet. Ascend the groove above then climb a mossy slab followed by a jammed rock. Continue easily to below a clean groove.
4   100 feet. Crux. Ascend the groove, with three steep sections, until an easy traverse right, crossing an arête, leads to a shallow vegetated groove.
5   100 feet. Go straight up the groove to the top.

PENCOED PILLAR

A huge tapering pillar, though heavily vegetated on two of its three faces. The east face taken by the Pencoed Pillar route is the least formidable of the three; East Gully forms its left boundary. The north or front face is slightly less vegetated but has a lot of poor rock. In complete contrast the west face, forming the left wall of Great Gully in its upper section, is made up of good compact rock which is steep and having an undercut base.

** Pencoed Pillar 740 feet Hard Very Difficult (1903)

A very good mountaineering route of considerable character. The upper part of the pillar has good stances and belays with adequate protection; the lower vegetated section less so. The route takes the easiest line up the left-hand side of the pillar, finishing directly to the narrow summit. The initial vegetated slabs will deter the non-mountaineer. Start from the top of the second pitch of Great Gully; this is best reached by scrambling in from the left via a large vegetated ramp. A rock with white quartz indicates the start below some wet slabs.

1 120 feet. The initial slabs. First trend 12 feet right to some vegetation, then step left and climb the slabs above on good holds to more vegetation. Ascend this directly to a doubtful spike, then trend right to a small rowan tree. Nut belay.

2 200 feet. Wander up vegetation to the left passing beneath a steep grey wall on the right until a broad chimney is reached.

3 120 feet. Climb the broad chimney and the short wall above, moving out left to more vegetation. Above is the pillar proper. Move right and gain the base of a groove, slanting left, with some chockstones wedged in a crack near its top. Belay beneath the groove.

4 50 feet. Climb the groove with the aid of the chockstone; exit left and ascend more easily straight up to a stance and fine thread belay on the right.

5 50 feet. Go up the wall on the right taking a rising traverse line on big holds to a good stance and huge block belay on the arête.

6 110 feet. Ascend directly up the wall above on good holds, keeping just left of the arête, gaining a long narrow vegetated ledge under a steep wall. Nut belay in a crack in a little corner on the left.

7 70 feet. Take the little corner on the left then go up a short ramp on the right to a wall (chimney on the left). Climb the wall slanting right making a final awkward move to a hidden hold on the edge. Move easily right and go up to a ledge. Good nut and spike belay.

8 20 feet. Go up a short groove on the left then brief scrambling leads to the narrow summit of the pillar.

Pamplemousse 430 feet Hard Very Severe (1973)

A line up the front of Pencoed Pillar, making for an obvious groove at about one-third height. The upper section goes under the large overhangs at the top of the pillar, giving an exposed finish. Rather poor protection on pitch 1. Start from part-way up the second pitch of Pencoed Pillar. Scramble up a vegetated groove (steep grey wall on the left) which leads to the base of a ramp rising diagonally left to the bottom of the groove.

1   75 feet. 5a. Climb the left-hand slanting ramp (peg) to a small quartz cave; thread in quartz. Move awkwardly over the bulge above the cave (peg) to a slab beneath the groove. Peg on slab to the right of the bulge.
2   55 feet. 4c. Climb the groove to a big grassy ledge.
3   40 feet. Continue in the line of weakness diagonally up left to a huge block.
4   160 feet. 5a. From the block move up for a few feet then go up a grassy ramp on the right. Climb a slab to an overhang formed by a large wedged flake. Go over this moving right to a good crack. Climb up this until just below the roofs. Move round an arête to belay above a bottomless groove.
5   100 feet. 4c. Traverse right beneath the overhangs to the obvious weakness through them. Take this moving slightly right then step back left and ascend the slab to the top of the pillar.

***   **Darker Angel**   435 feet   E3   (1974)
A magnificent route destined to become one of the great Welsh classics. Takes the only real weakness in the superb west wall of Pencoed Pillar which drops into Great Gully. Start at the bottom left-hand end of the wall below the arête, which forms the dividing line between the north and west faces. This is best gained by ascending the V. Diff Pencoed Pillar until part way up its second pitch, before reaching the steep grey wall. Go up a vegetated groove on the right, continue right up vegetation to beneath an obvious ramp rising up to the right.
1   150 feet. 5a. Climb the ramp leading rightwards. Traverse right for 20 feet, move up and continue rightwards until an obvious traverse back left guarded by a block, can be taken. Traverse to the base of a groove and climb this to a spike belay below a small fang of rock.
2   30 feet. Move right along a grassy ramp to its end.
3   35 feet. 5a. Traverse right across a slab to a bulge with an obvious projecting foothold. Go right round the bulge to a small stance.
4   80 feet. 5c. Climb up to the right-hand end of the overhang, then take an obvious ramp up right until it peters out. Climb the continuation crack with increasing difficulty (peg) to a small ledge beneath a roof.
5   50 feet. 5c. Climb up to the roof. Traverse up left across the slab to gain a rib. Easier climbing left of the rib leads to a stance under a large roof.
6   90 feet. 4c. As for Pamplemousse, go back right for 10 feet and climb through the roofs to gain a slab. Finish up the slab.

The Gods Themselves   180 feet   E2   (1 pt. aid)   †   (1974)
Takes the bottomless groove on the left edge of the wall. Start from the stance at the end of pitch 3 of Darker Angel.

John Codling on Sundog, E2, Mynydd Moel. *Photo: John Sumner*

Jill Sumner on King of Maybe, VS 4c, Craig Rhiwarth.

Photo: John Sumner

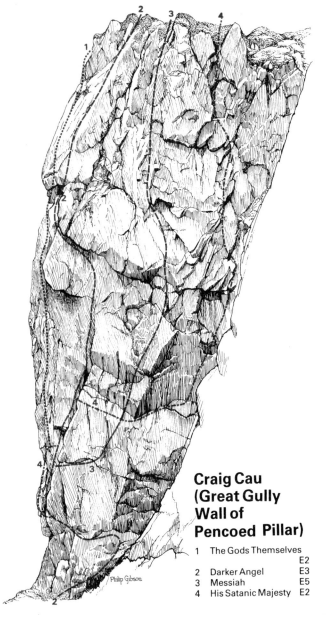

**Craig Cau
(Great Gully
Wall of
Pencoed Pillar)**

1 The Gods Themselves
E2

2 Darker Angel   E3
3 Messiah   E5
4 His Satanic Majesty   E2

Philip Gibson.

1   110 feet. 5c. Climb above the stance as for Darker Angel then go diagonally left to a little corner below the overhangs. Move 10 feet left to a fault-line which is taken up to the groove (some doubtful rock). Ascend the groove to the stance below the roof at the end of pitch 5 of Darker Angel.
2   70 feet. 5c. Move left under the roof to its narrowest point. Pull over this using a peg (in situ) to gain the slab above. Climb directly up the slab to a bulge, traverse left to the arête and continue to the top.

*** **Messiah**   190 feet   E5   (1980)
A tremendous pitch. Start at the stance at the end of pitch 3 of Darker Angel.
1   150 feet. 6a. Traverse right for about 20 feet. Climb up 3 feet on small holds until some difficult moves lead rightwards to a small ledge near the arête. Continue up the crack above to its end. Holds above and to the right enable good holds on the left to be gained. Climb onto a slab, moving rightwards. The moves between the two overlaps above are the crux and involve a difficult move for an undercut (2 pegs). Using layaways to the right then small face holds gain the steep slab above; continue directly up this until a foothold is gained below an overhang. Take the overhang on the left and continue with relative ease up the leftward-slanting crack to a grassy ledge and belays.
2   40 feet. Traverse left and finish up easy slabs as for Darker Angel.

His Satanic Majesty   290 feet   E2   †   (1974)
A girdle of the wall. Start from the end of pitch 2 of Darker Angel, at the downward-pointing spike.
1   50 feet. Climb up trending slightly left from the belay to a bulge at 25 feet. Traverse right until a move up can be made onto a slab. Move left to a poor stance in a shallow depression, old peg belay (in place).
2   60 feet. Move back right into a groove and continue onto a small slab (wire sling in place). Follow this line into The Gods Themselves. Reverse part of pitch 1 of The Gods Themselves to a stance at the base of the ramp on Darker Angel.
3   60 feet. Ascend Darker Angel for 20 feet then take a slab line right and go down slightly. This leads onto a larger slab near the gully. Move diagonally to a small stance (peg belay).
4   30 feet. Broken rocks lead to a peg belay below a square chockstone.
5   90 feet. Pull over the chockstone and go up to a steep wall. Follow cracks to the left over bulges until a move right can be made to a good ledge. Go up and left to finish.

In the upper section of Great Gully, on the left wall, are the following routes which take a long time to dry.

Demian 325 feet Very Severe † (1975)
Start in Great Gully just below where the gully almost closes, some 75 feet below Abraxus.
1 115 feet. Go left to a shallow corner. Ascend this for 40 feet, then traverse delicately right to a narrow corner. Go up to a wide crack then move out right at the top of the crack on a flat ledge to the rib on the right. Climb straight up to a ledge some 40 feet below an overhang with a half round break in it.
2 70 feet. Climb up cracks, then gain a slab beneath an overhang on the right. Ascend a break in the overhang then move left across ledges to below a rib. Peg belays.
3 140 feet. Take the groove in the right of the rib, move left 30 feet and climb up the rib to reach easy ground. A tower with a deep crack can be climbed to reach the top.

Bassillades 235 feet Very Severe (1975)
About 220 feet down from the top of Great Gully is a steep corner pointing up to a chimney which is formed by a large flake. Start level with the foot of the corner.
1 100 feet. Go left from the base of the first corner to gain a slabby ledge. Ascend the wall above until an obvious weakness trending up left can be taken. Go up this until a move can be made into a groove. Ascend the groove, exiting left at the top to a ledge.
2 60 feet. Move back right and take a crack on the right, then go up slabs and ledges to a small stance.
3 75 feet. Ascend a crack system close to the left edge of the steep upper wall. Climb the cracks to the top.

Here Comes The Sun 235 feet E2 † (1977)
A Direct on Bassillades. The first pitch is the crux. Start as for Abraxus and Bassillades.
1 150 feet. Go 20 feet left from the foot of Abraxus corner, as for Bassillades. Directly above is an overhanging corner, leaning leftwards at the top. Climb this (crux at the top) then go straight up easier rocks and ledges to a large spike belay below the clean-cut upper wall.
2 85 feet. Ascend to the foot of the wall. Take the centre of the wall directly to the top.

Abraxus 225 feet Hard Very Severe † (1975)
Start as for Bassillades and Here Comes The Sun. The climb takes the corner and the chimney above. Start level with the foot of the corner.
1 130 feet. Ascend the corner then go up slabs trending right to avoid two bulges in the corner. Traverse back left to the foot of a chimney formed by a flake. The chimney and more broken ground above lead to a poor stance below a short corner.
2 95 feet. Go up the corner then move right to the base of a steep shallow chimney in the wall above. Climb this, go over the overhang above it, and finish up the wall.

Deadpan   200 feet   Hard Very Severe   †   (1975)
About 160 feet down from the top of Great Gully is a 25-foot chimney in the gully bed. Just below and left of this is a chimney/groove with a chockstone at 25 feet. Start below the groove.
1   110 feet. Climb the chimney and onto the chockstone. Go up for 10 feet then move left across a series of ribs and grooves (peg) until a small slab below a prominent roof can be gained. Cross this and climb up to the left of the overhang to a ledge and belays.
2   90 feet. Ascend left then go back right to a shattered groove immediately right of the big overhang above. Ascend this for 10 feet then go up and left above a smaller overhang to reach a corner system. Finish up this.

Great Gully   980 feet   Hard Severe   (1895)
The big gully to the right of Pencoed Pillar. Normally wet, loose and vegetated it is not a good summer route. Start at the base of the gully above grass and scree slopes.
1   40 feet. A double chockstone pitch taken on the right.
2   140 feet. Another chockstone pitch is passed on either side, then scrambling leads up the gully to a wet cave pitch. Avoid this by moving out left up vegetation to a large grassy ramp coming in from the left.
3   130 feet. Cross the gully and scramble up vegetation on the right to avoid another wet cave pitch. Move back left up more vegetation to some rock. Nut belay.
4   120 feet. Continue traversing left to gain the bed of the gully. Ascend this taking a huge chockstone on the right. Stance and belay above on the right wall.
5   100 feet. The gully becomes narrower; climb the vegetated chimney above to a grassy bay on the right; nut belay.
6   130 feet. Go over a chockstone on the left then move up to another chockstone which is taken on the right. Nut belay on the right.
7   140 feet. The converging walls pitch is above. Go up a groove crossing the gully from right to left; move right out of the groove then continue straight up the gully to ledges. Nut belays. The rock on this pitch is very loose.
8   80 feet. Above climb the narrowing chimney pitch on the left then go easily to a chockstone which is taken on the right. Belay under a steep short little chimney pitch.
9   100 feet. Avoid the steep chimney by traversing out right up a grassy ramp, then return left to the top of the gully.

MAIN CRAG

White Lady   180 feet   Hard Very Severe   (1 pt. aid)   †   (1974)
About 35 feet left of Dawn's Left-Hand is a grassy ledge at 20 feet. Start beneath the right-hand end of this.

1 120 feet. Climb up to the ledge and go left along it to the groove at the end. Climb the groove until it peters out. Go up left to a short crack. Using a peg for aid move up then traverse right below the overhang to easier ground leading to a grassy ledge.

2 60 feet. Scramble 35 feet up to the right up grass to an easy groove leading to easy ground.

* Dawn's Left-Hand 170 feet Hard Very Severe (1974)

Near the top of the crag across Great Gully from the Pencoed Pillar is a fairly clean triangular buttress. It is best reached by abseil. Start at a groove at the bottom right-hand end of the grassy ledge below the buttress.

1 110 feet. 5a. Go straight up the cracks to a corner with a wide crack in the back. Move up the corner then go out left to the arête. Move up the arête and go back into the corner. Continue to a grassy stance beneath an overhang.

2 60 feet. 4b. Climb up right on vegetation to below a small overhang then traverse right to a groove. Go up this, exiting out left at the top.

Terraneai Rib 180 feet Hard Severe † (1974)

The rib about halfway between Central Rib and Great Gully. On the left of the rib is a large block which forms a wide crack. Some vegetation and doubtful rock.

1 100 feet. 4b. Climb on the left of the rib then take a crack in the right wall. Ascend this to a small ledge with a little overhang above. Go over the overhang to a block belay.

2 40 feet. Go up the rib to a spike belay.

3 40 feet. 4a. Move up and left and climb a crack in the wall.

Beneath Terraneai Rib, but above the huge vegetated ramp coming out of Great Gully, is a large clean wall. The next two routes take this wall.

Snodgrass Diversification Company 320 feet Hard Severe (1975)

The wall above the left part of the huge grass ramp leading right out of Great Gully above the lower tier. Scramble up about 220 feet from where Great Gully is crossed. There is a triangular overhang at 220 feet. Start at a rib of rock directly under this.

1 50 feet. 4a. Climb the rib, then follow grass above slanting right to reach rock again. Spike belays.

2 70 feet. 4b. Ascend then move slightly left until a short left traverse leads to a ledge and belays at the start of a conspicuous diagonal groove/chimney.

3 130 feet. 4a. Go up the groove/chimney diagonally left to a grassy ledge. Nut belays.

4 70 feet. Climb the wall above onto steep grass then traverse right to a belay (The start of Terraneai Rib is some 75 feet above).

* Snodgrass Diversification Company Direct   130 feet
Very Severe
The obvious groove just right of the triangular overhang above the second pitch of Snodgrass Diversification Company.
1   130 feet. 4c. Climb the groove direct to its top. Continue up a more broken groove then up grass to good nut belays in a corner on the right.

The next three routes lie on the lower tier beneath the huge vegetated ramp leading right out of Great Gully.

* Leander   165 feet   E2   (1983)
To the left of Idris Corner are two arêtes. Leander takes the left-hand one. Sparse protection on pitch 2. Start directly below the arête by a long thin flake.
1   50 feet. 5c. Step right from the flake and climb a short wall to easy ground. Move up to a steep corner below overhangs. Ascend the corner (2 pegs), exiting left via an awkward slab. Nut belays above and to the right.
2   115 feet. 5a. Above the belay gain a small ledge and climb straight up the blunt arête to a ledge. Continue just left of the blunt arête for 30 feet then step right onto the arête and go up this via a flake. Step right from the top of the flake, then go back left. Finish easily up to a good stance and belays.

** Idris Corner   100 feet   E2   (1982)
The obvious open book corner on the lower tier. Start by scrambling up 100 feet of vegetated rock to the base of the corner. Huge spike.
1   100 feet. 5b. Climb the corner crack mainly by layback to an in situ bong. Continue with more difficulty up the more restricted crack to the top.

Battered Caravanserai   325 feet   Very Severe   (1974)
At the right-hand end of the lower tier is a rib of rock with a weakness in it and wet slabs below it.
1   80 feet. 4b. Follow the weakness up and curving left, then move rightwards to gain a grassy chute. Belay at the top of this.
2   50 feet. 4b. Traverse 20 feet left over slabs then move up to a short square chimney. Exit right from the top of this onto a grassy ledge and climb a short vegetated groove to a flake belay and stance.
3   25 feet. 4a. Ascend the corner above to a ledge.
4   40 feet. 5a. Continue up the corner, moving out left to a grassy ledge.
5   90 feet. 4b. Go diagonally right up vegetated rock for 10 feet until the main groove on the right can be gained. Climb this for about 20 feet to reach the right wall then go up this to heather. Go left and climb a short crack to a ledge.
6   40 feet. Ascend the corner above gaining a ledge and peg belays on the edge of the diagonal grassy ramp.

Central Rib 400 feet Very Severe (1974)
The prominent rib dropping from the summit of Mynydd Pencoed to the huge vegetated ramp leading right out of Great Gully. The tower forming the second pitch is a prominent feature, with an overhang on the left wall. Reach the foot by scrambling up the grassy ramp out of Great Gully; or better, climb Battered Caravanserai which finishes at the base of the rib. Start by ascending grass just right of a short bottom step to a ledge behind it. Some bad rock.
1 70 feet. 4c. Ascend the groove on the right-hand side of the wall until a move right can be made. Slant right up the wall to gain the arête and grass at the top. Go up grass for 20 feet to a stance below the next wall.
2 80 feet. 4c. Above is The tower. Go up a system of cracks in the arête to a narrow grassy ledge. Traverse left below a small overhang then ascend up leftwards to the top. Thread belay.
3 130 feet. 4b. Climb the next step by the right-hand arête (rock loose in places).
4 70 feet. Scramble up to the final wall.
5 50 feet. 4b. There is a groove farther to the right of the rib line with overhangs at its base. Climb over the overhang at its right-hand end. Step left into the groove and ascend it to the top, finishing about 20 feet from the summit.

The next six routes are on Black Shiver Buttress. This is the name given to the area of steep wet walls and overhangs between Central Rib and Crack of Cau.

Tremor 460 feet Hard Very Severe † (1974)
On the left-hand side of Black Shiver Buttress is a short groove leading to uninviting grassy rocks. The route provides an access to The Gulch.
1 85 feet. Climb the groove to grassy rocks and an earthy chimney. Ascend this to a stance and peg belay.
2 75 feet. Go up left then back right just above the stance to a groove. Ascend the groove moving left to a flake crack. Go back right to reach a slab, then climb this to its top left edge and a small stance.
3 85 feet. Traverse right below an overhang to gain the foot of an overhanging chimney. Continue traversing for 15 feet then move up to a grassy niche (peg). Go diagonally right until easier ground close to the top of Black Shiver pitch 3 can be gained. Climb up to the ledge and spike belays of Black Shiver.
4 65 feet. Ascend the groove on the left.
5 100 feet. Move right onto a slabby buttress. Ascend this slanting left to reach a large grassy bay. Belays at the top left of this below a deep crack.
6 50 feet. Ascend the crack followed by a bulge to reach easy ground. Scrambling to finish.

The Gulch   350 feet   Hard Very Severe   †   (1975)
The obvious steep chimney/gully at the left end of Black Shiver
Buttress just right of Central Rib. Usually wet. Start from the top
of the second pitch of Tremor.
1   75 feet. Move down left then traverse left to just above the
base of the corner. Ascend a flake on the left wall to the bulging
corner. Go over the bulge to a small ledge and old peg belays
on the left.
2   125 feet. Go up the corner taking an overhanging section to
climb a final chimney to a large ledge.
3   150 feet. Climb the left corner to gain easy ground. Belays
are eventually reached on the right.

Mere Gill   430 feet   E1   †   (1975)
Just below the start of Black Shiver, go up left across steep
vegetation above a small wet wall to two grooves.
1   115 feet. Climb the left-hand groove and go up the slab
above, slanting right to an overhung corner. Climb this moving
right to the stance at the end of pitch 2 of Black Shiver. Old peg
belays.
2   100 feet. Go up the cracks straight above the stance then
move left for 15 feet to a leaning corner and thin flake on the
right wall. Slant right onto a rib and right again into a corner.
The corner leads to the grassy halfway ledge. Spike belays. 45
feet of scrambling on grass trending right leads to a peg belay
just right of a left-slanting slab.
3   70 feet. Climb the slab to its top, then go left to a very small
incut ledge. Go left again across a bulge to gain an easy groove.
Ascend this to a spike belay.
4   145 feet. Climb up grass on the right then go back left to the
gully. Ascend the gully to easy ground.

Tatham Wife   525 feet   E1   †   (1975)
Start at the groove just right of Mere Gill. All the difficulty is in
pitch 2.
1   65 feet. Ascend the groove then move up to a small stance
where a traverse line goes right.
2   85 feet. 5c. Move right to a small flat ledge, and make a very
difficult move right to reach holds on the rib. Go up into the
groove above and ascend this to its top (junction with Black
Shiver). Move right onto a rib and ascend this moving right to
vegetation and belays.
3   65 feet. Go back left into a corner and climb to its top. Move
left across the left wall, then go up and left again to a rib. Work
up to grass and spike belays on the midway ledge (junction with
Mere Gill).
4   85 feet. Grass scrambling up to the right leads to a ledge and
belays.
5   85 feet. Take the groove which is just below and left of the
stance, slanting right to a stance.
6   140 feet. Scrambling remains.

** **Black Shiver**   350 feet   E2   (1974)
Start at the base of a line of slabs and grooves trending leftwards
100 feet left and slightly lower down than the start of Crack of
Cau.
1   70 feet. 4c. Ascend a short corner to a slab, then go left and
climb up to a block wedged behind a fang of rock. Traverse left
round this and go up the groove and slab to a small stance.
2   50 feet. 5a. Move into a groove up to the left. Climb this until
a slab can be crossed on the left to a rib. Go round the rib and
traverse the next slab. Move down to a stance in a groove.
3   70 feet. 5c. Above the stance climb direct over a bulge.
Traverse left for about 12 feet and use an undercut flake on the
right to gain a rib; step right across a slab into an overhung
corner, and go up this to vegetation and spike belays on the
terrace.
4   70 feet. 5b. Go left along the terrace to below a slabby
groove. Take the slabby groove to just below the overhang.
Ascend rightwards into a niche beneath the right-hand end of
the overhang. Move out right and climb into the groove above
with a good hold on the lip. Continue up the groove to an
awkward stance below the next overhang.
5   90 feet. 5a. Go right round the overhang to continue up the
groove. Move left at the next overhang then go back right to
steep grass. Ascend the grass to a stance and nut belays. Easily
move right to a grassy gully, then 200 feet of easy climbing and
scrambling lead to the top.

The Baron   290 feet   Hard Very Severe   (1 pt. aid)   †   (1974)
Start 100 feet left of Crack of Cau at a large waterworn groove
below a big roof.
1   50 feet. There is a bulge in the centre of the groove. Take a
diagonal line on waterworn rock on the left of the bulge to a
block on the right.
2   40 feet. Follow the groove to a slab below the large roof.
Traverse below the roof. Peg belay removed.
3   40 feet. Go left onto the left edge of a slab. Climb the slab
with an aid peg to reach a grassy terrace.
4   40 feet. Scramble down to the left along the terrace to its end.
5   120 feet. Ascend the groove on the left of the overhang and
continue up the gully until scrambling remains.

The next three routes take the large, steep cleanish wall high on
the right-hand side of the crag. It has a noticeable crack-line
splitting it. The wall faces north-east and the rock on the whole
is good.

The wall is best gained by ascending the huge vegetated ramp
just left of Whale Back Buttress until above the base of the wall.
A long traverse is then taken to the left descending slightly to
beneath the wall.

Gotterdamerung   335 feet   E2   †   (1975)
A line up the left wall of Crack of Cau. Start at the top of pitch 2 of Crack of Cau.
1   130 feet. Traverse out left for 15 feet and go up the obvious line to a small undercut overhang. Move up left of this for 10 feet, then traverse right to reach a line trending up left. Ascend this to a block on a vague arête then traverse left to a wide crack at the back of a large detached flake. Climb to the top of the flake.
2   70 feet. 5c. Move right from the flake and make a move up a shallow groove to reach a horizontal crack (peg in place); traverse right for 6 feet. Ascend to reach a shallow groove. Climb this for 3 feet then move down right onto a traverse line level with the base of the groove. Go right round a rib, and traverse across a smooth groove to a very small ledge 6 feet left of Crack of Cau. Nut belays high up to the left.
3   70 feet. Ascend slightly left to a groove with a large projecting block. Move past this then slant left to reach easy ground. Go up grassy ledges to a sharp arête and spike belays.
4   65 feet. An easy arête leads to the top.

** **Crack of Cau**   240 feet   Hard Very Severe   (1973)
The great chimney crack splitting the large steep wall high on the right-hand side of the crag. Start just to the right and about 40 feet under the base of the crack at a cracked wall.
1   40 feet. Ascend the left edge of the wall, then follow grass to the chimney.
2   40 feet. The chimney leads to a grassy stance on the right.
3   80 feet. 5a. Continue up the chimney and take the steep groove above, following a crack slanting slightly left to a good resting place. The crack, difficult at first, leads to good holds then a wide crack in an overhang. Climb this to a small stance with good belays.
4   80 feet. 5a. Ascend the groove above with three steep sections, finishing just right of a large projecting overhang.

* **Touchstone**   280 feet   Very Severe   (1973)
Start at a chimney slanting left and cutting the steep wall 40 feet right of the start of Crack of Cau and 12 feet above it, where a ledge comes in from the right.
1   40 feet. 4c. Go up the cracked slab which forms the left wall of the chimney to a good spike; continue more easily to reach a grass ledge on the left with a large belay flake.
2   70 feet. 4c. 10 feet right of the belay climb to a thread under a big detached spike. From the spike traverse right round a sharp edge, gaining a good foothold. Move right to a corner, and go up this via a crack on good jams to a ledge and large block belay.
3   70 feet. 4b. Start a few feet left of the belay and climb a scoop slanting slightly left to where it steepens. Make a long step across to the right then go up steeply on big holds slanting right to the right arête of the buttress.

4 100 feet. The final tower is above. Climb a broken corner on the right moving back left onto the arête. Gain a wide crack above with a slab on its left to reach a cave. Chimney out to gain a foothold on the right (thread runner); then go more easily up the chimney to a big flake belay. Take the grassy gully with an awkward finish.

The next three routes follow the fairly clean section of rock to the right of the Crack of Cau. The right-hand side of this section of rock is bounded by an outstanding clean arête.

** **Bird of Time**   180 feet   E1   (1974)
A quality route but with poor protection on pitch 2. Start at a short chimney below and just left of the clean arête.
1 40 feet. 4a. Climb the chimney and ledges above to a long grassy ledge. Belay in the centre of this.
2 90 feet. 5b. From the centre of the ledge climb a crack to a small ledge. From the right-hand end of the ledge climb down rightwards then ascend right to a groove set in the arête. Take this to a ledge. From its right-hand end move right and ascend the arête to an overhang. Belay on the right below the roof.
3 50 feet. 4b. Go right and up into a chimney. Climb this by an inside route, exiting through a hole at the top.

Moving Finger   180 feet   Hard Very Severe   (1974)
A line up from the left-hand end of the ledge at the top of pitch 1 of Bird of Time. Poor protection on pitch 3. Start at a chimney.
1 50 feet. 4a. Ascend the chimney, move left and go up to a grassy ledge (as for Bird of Time).
2 20 feet. 4c. Climb the groove from the left-hand end of the ledge to a small stance under an overhang.
3 50 feet. 5a. Move round the edge on the left and climb the small ramp delicately to its end, move left and gain the large vegetated ledge above.
4 60 feet. Easier climbing leads to the top.

The Sufri   200 feet   Very Severe   (1974)
Not a good route owing to poor protection and some bad rock. Start 35 feet left of Moving Finger, at a cracked corner.
1 50 feet. 4b. Ascend the crack to a grass ledge, with a block belay at its left-hand end.
2 40 feet. 4c. Climb the obvious line above, reaching a leftward leaning groove, and follow this to a ledge.
3 50 feet. 4b. Hand-traverse left along the block above then take a line trending left to a grassy ledge below bulging rock. Belay at the left-hand end.
4 60 feet. 4c. Traverse left for 10 feet then go steeply upwards trending slightly left to the top.

WHALE BACK BUTTRESS

An area of smooth clean slabs low down on the right-hand side
of the crag only 150 feet above the Llyn.

* **Marsum**   370 feet   Very Difficult   (1973)
Begins well but becomes rather artificial; the rock on the whole
is good. Start on the far right-hand side of the undercut slabs,
where a weakness leads to a groove.
1   130 feet. Climb the groove and the short wall above to a slab
then slant left taking the easiest line to where it steepens. Move
right to a vegetated ledge with a good nut belay on the wall
above.
2   90 feet. Go up a chimney in the corner and traverse left then
climb a rib above to a large block belay.
3   80 feet. Move off the top of the block and climb the rib to
vegetation. Go left and climb another rib to a stance and belay.
4   70 feet. Climb straight up behind the belay to a rounded
arête. Move left onto a slab and continue up the arête to the top.

Mynydd Moel   O.S. ref. SH 728138

Approach
Take a minor road out of Dolgellau alongside the Afon Aran to
Maes-Coch O.S. ref. SH 744158. A walk of approximately 2
miles, still following the Afon Aran, then leads to its source Llyn
Aran. Scramble up rock scree and heather slopes above to the
crag.

Character and Topography
The crag which lies just below the summit of Mynydd Moel faces
north-east and is about 200 feet high. The quality of the rock is
good. Immediately left of the crag is a large easy-angled gully
which gives the best means of descent. The crag on the right is
bounded by a pinnacle ridge and just left of this is the largest
section of the crag its main feature being a central band of
overhangs which forms the cruxes of most of the routes which
break through it. Probably the most obvious lines are two
grooves which go up to the overhangs; the left-hand one is taken
by The Bee.

* **The Sketch Man**   180 feet   Hard Very Severe   (1981)
Takes the first section of Sundog, then the groove topped by an
overhang on the left.
1   130 feet. 5a. From the base of the pillar climb to a bulge at
40 feet, take this on the right via a crack, then traverse left above
an overhang to a rounded crack (all this as for Sundog). Step

left onto a small ledge and climb the left edge of the groove to the left-hand side of the overhangs. Make a sensational traverse left on downward-pointing spikes to easier ground. Trend right to a good stance.
2   50 feet. 4b. Step right onto an arête and climb this to ledges.

** Sundog   165 feet   E2   (1981)
The slim pillar just left of The Bee.
1   120 feet. 5c. From the pillar base climb up to a bulge at 40 feet, take this on the right via a crack, then traverse left above an overhang to a rounded crack. Ascend this, avoid a ledge on the left, and move right to climb a wall to a ledge. Make a delicate rising traverse left to reach a jug below a peg. Move back right using a diagonal crack to below an overhang; pull over this to a groove and go up this to a ledge. Nut belays.
2   45 feet. 4c. The groove directly above leads to easier ground and belays.

The Bee   200 feet   E1   (1974)
The left-hand groove to the overhangs, breaking through these on the left. Go up the first 15 feet of broken rock to a ledge with a big leaning pinnacle immediately right of the groove.
1   50 feet. Gain the top of the pinnacle then go left into the groove. Ascend this on big holds to a grassy stance below an overhang.
2   100 feet. 5c. Go up to a peg under the overhang on the left and with difficulty gain a large spike on the left under a second overhang. Move left and go up through the break, following the groove to a ledge. Go straight up from the ledge, keeping to the rock on the left to a ledge below an undercut crack.
3   50 feet. Ascend the crack above to the top.

* Twist Grip   220 feet   Hard Very Severe   (1975)
A route which weaves its way through the overhangs between Route Central and The Bee and finishes up the wall left of Ritander. Rather poor protection on pitch 2. Start below the central groove 10 feet right of the pinnacle at the start of The Bee.
1   65 feet. 4a. Climb easily up the central groove to the large recess. Take the obvious traverse line out left to the stance and belay at the top of pitch 1 The Bee.
2   80 feet. 5a. Move up right onto the top of a large spike to a weakness in the overhangs. Reach a good little spike which enables the wall above to be gained. Go up to an overhang made of downward-pointing flakes then move right under the overhang to gain a groove on the right. Go up this for 3 feet to gain easier rock on the right. Good spike belay a few feet up to the right.

3   75 feet. 4c. Move right along a small ramp then go up to the right of some large doubtful blocks. Climb a steep groove directly above the blocks then go right and follow an easier groove to the top.

* **Route Central**   230 feet   Hard Very Severe   (1959)
Start below the largest of the overhangs, at the base of a vegetated terrace trending up right.
1   50 feet. Ascend an easy short groove and the vegetated terrace above to a large flake belay.
2   80 feet. 5b. Move left and climb a diagonal crack to the overhangs. Move right to avoid these and climb a steep groove for about 20 feet, then make difficult moves up left to a ledge. Nut belays.
3   100 feet. 4b. Climb trending leftwards taking the easiest line to the top.

* **Rabble Rouser**   150 feet   E5   (1981)
A testing pitch through the overlaps just right of Route Central. Start from the top of pitch 1 of Ritander.
1   85 feet. 6b. Move leftwards up a ramp to gain a groove and then a niche. Continue over the overlap above, moving slightly leftwards and make a sustained series of moves past a hammered nut and a knifeblade to gain a steep groove. Exit left.
2   65, feet. 4c. Traverse right along a ledge and go up a wall and chimney. Step left onto a nose and go over blocks to finish.

Ritander   170 feet   Very Severe   (1960)
Start from the top of the vegetated terrace up right of the top of pitch 1 of Route Central.
1   50 feet. 4a. Ascend the pillar and go up the wall to a grass ledge on the right.
2   120 feet. 4c. Trend left up the grassy groove and traverse left below the overhang into a steep groove. Move up to the right then go back left into a niche. Go up the groove above to the top.

* **Morning Crescent**   165 feet   Hard Very Severe   (1974)
Traverses the crag, but with rather poor protection. Start from the foot of the grassy rake on the left-hand side of the crag.
1   60 feet. 4b. Traverse horizontally right passing an obvious spike, to gain the first pitch of The Bee at roughly half-height. Ascend to the stance under the overhangs of The Bee.
2   35 feet. 4c. Move right passing a large spike, then traverse across a scoop on the right (delicate) to some jammed blocks; continue right to the stance below the big overhang on Route Central.
3   70 feet. 5a. Step down and gain a ledge under a small overhang then make an awkward move right to join Ritander's first pitch. Go easily up the last few move of this and finish up that route or scramble off to the right.

North Ridge   300 feet   Difficult
The arête on the right-hand side of the crag, with a fine looking
pinnacle half-way up. Some loose rock. Start left of a black
hanging chimney.
1   150 feet. Gain the ridge by an open chimney and follow it
pleasantly to the pinnacle.
2   150 feet. Descend from the pinnacle to a gap and move easily
up to a steep nose which may be climbed slanting left (loose at
the top), or avoided by scrambling on the right. Pleasant slabs
lead to the top.

Twr Du

O.S. ref. SH 719135

Approach
From the North side of the mountain take the Fox's Path from
the Gwernan Lake Hotel, breaking off this at Llyn-y-Gafr and go
south-eastwards for just over half a mile to some huge boulders
which lie below the crag.

Character and Topography
The crag is north-west facing and about 400 feet high. There is
some good rock in places but the lower section is heavily
vegetated and it is a scrappy looking crag in its lower half. The
two lines of East and West Gullies are obvious. Between them
in the upper section is a compact-looking buttress. Right of this
across West Gully is the obvious arête of West Gully arête.

Descent
There is no easy descent except by going along the main Cader
Ridge and descending the Fox's Path. The quickest way but
tricky in its lower section, is to descend the first grassy-looking
gully to the right when facing the crag along the main ridge to
Cader Idris summit

East Gully   approx. 430 feet   Very Difficult
The obvious gully line to the left of the steep buttress. It is wet
and escapable in most places. Start below a leftward-slanting
groove.
1   120 feet. Follow the groove avoiding a steep section by
climbing the arête on the left to a grassy bay.
2   120 feet. The vegetated groove at the back of the bay is
followed to slabs; move right across these to reach the gully
line. Stance a few feet up the gully below a steep wet section.
3   130 feet. The wet steep section is avoided by going out left
onto the arête. Ascend leftwards to a corner and go up this then
move back right into a deep chimney.

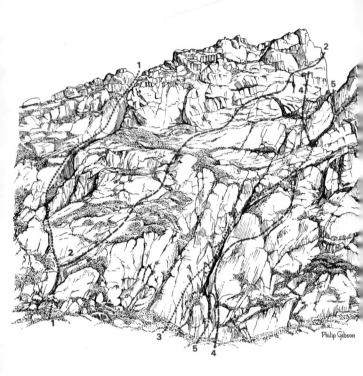

Philip Gibson

Twr Du

4 30 feet. Ascend the chimney, keeping to the left of a hanging rib.
5 30 feet. A chimney above is climbed passing a block at the top. Continue up the gully line for another 220 feet. No serious difficulties.

** **The Lamb** 500 feet   Very Severe   (1974)
Takes the easiest line up the central section of rock between East and West Gullies, finishing up the fine top pitches of Triad. Start 25 feet up East Gully where an easy traverse line right gains the cleaned area of slabs leading up to the steep central section.
1 140 feet. 4a. Traverse right and gain the slabs. Ascend these moving slightly left then go up to a short corner with a steeper smoother corner above.
2 90 feet. 4c. Ascend up to the base of the smooth corner, then go over a small overlap and traverse delicately right to a break. Take this then move right on good holds to a steep corner with a good ledge below it.
3 100 feet. 4c. Follow the steep corner moving out right onto the arête. Climb the wall above for 3 feet then go right to another arête. Ascend this on the right on good holds to a large ledge under an overhang.
4 100 feet. 4c. As for pitch 4 of Triad.
5 70 feet. 4a. Finish as for pitch 5 of Triad.

* **Western Gully Arête** 440 feet   Very Difficult   (1954)
The obvious striking arête 220 feet up the crag to the right of West Gully. Poor protection on pitch 3. Start below a rib 3 feet left of West Gully.
1 70 feet. Climb the rib then go up a grassy groove on the left to move back right into the gully. Stance as for West Gully and a jammed block belay.
2 70 feet. As for West Gully. The corner on the right leads to below some waterworn slabs, nut belays.
3 100 feet. As for pitch 3 West Gully. Crux. Follow the slabs first on the left then on the right to gain a vegetated ledge under a steep wall. Move up left into the gully, and ascend this for 20 feet to a stance on the arête on the right. Good spike belay.
4 40 feet. Go straight up the arête to a ledge below a steep wall, (chockstone pitch of West Gully on the left).
5 60 feet. Move right and ascend the right edge of the arête for 30 feet, go round onto the left side and climb a crack to a small stance with a large block belay.
6 100 feet. Continue just left of the arête, passing an overhang to ledges above. Ascend on easy ground above to a spike belay. Follow the arête for another 220 feet at Mod./Diff. standard to the summit plateau.

West Gully   440 feet   Severe
The gully/crack line with the big steep buttress on the left in the upper section and the striking arête on the right. The upper section is poorly protected with some doubtful rock. Start below the gully which is more of a crack to start with.
1   60 feet. Move in easily from the right then go up the crack with an awkward exit. Belay to some jammed blocks.
2   70 feet. The gully opens out. Climb a corner on the right and ascend to the base of some waterworn slabs; nut belay.
3   100 feet. Ascend the waterworn slabs moving up leftwards then go rightwards to gain a vegetated ledge below a steep wall. Move up left into the gully and go up this for 20 feet to a stance. Nut belay in the crack and a spike on the right arête.
4   40 feet. Go straight up the gully to a stance below a steep chockstone pitch; huge spike on the left.
5   100 feet. Climb the chockstone pitch above. Move out right for 3 feet across a little scoop, then climb straight up until a move left can be made to the bed of the gully at a vegetated ledge. Thread belay in the crack above.
6   70 feet. The gully now forks. Go up the right-hand branch moving left across into a crack; go straight up this, stepping out right to a big ledge. Scrambling leads to the summit.

** **Triad**   490 feet   Very Severe   (1957)
A line just to the right of West Gully, crossing this to finish up a clean section of rock on the right-hand side of the steep central buttress. Start as for West Gully.
1   130 feet. 4b. Follow the gully line for 20 feet then step out right to a small pedestal to go diagonally up right to gain a groove. Move up delicately right to a grassy ledge, then traverse back slanting up left to the arête. Climb this for 3 feet to a large ledge; then go up to the base of the waterworn slabs, nut belay.
2   50 feet. The waterworn slabs lead to a grassy ledge under a steep wall (part of pitch 3 West Gully). Peg belay removed.
3   140 feet. 4b. Step left easily into the gully bed. After 3 feet make a slightly descending traverse left on some sloping ledges to grass. Climb an easy broken rib to a weakness in the steep wall above; go up this to grass and after a few feet good holds on the left wall enable some blocks on a ledge to be gained. Climb directly above the blocks on excellent rock to a ledge under an overhang.
4   100 feet. 4c. A good pitch. Go up up right to another overhang. Traverse right under it to the base of a groove trending right; climb this to the top of a pinnacle. Move up from the pinnacle then go right to a small foothold on the arête. Climb up and traverse right to gain a scoop in a corner. Go up the corner to a ledge and belay.
5   70 feet. 4a. Step right and move up a slab into a corner. Ascend the crack above to the top.

Twr Groove 200 feet Severe   (1974)
Immediately right of Western Gully arête there is another gully
just right of an obvious groove. Start below the groove.
1 130 feet. Climb the groove by its slabby right wall to a good
stance and belay.
2 70 feet. Continue up the groove to where it steepens, then
gain another groove on the left using an obvious big hold on
the left wall. Ascend the left-hand groove to heather.

Escape is not easy and it is preferable to continue upwards on
steep heather and rock for about 220 feet to the summit plateau.

Cyfrwy   O.S. ref. SH 703135

Approach
For the section of crag between Cyfrwy arête and One Pitch
Gully, take the Fox's Path commencing from the Gwernan Lake
Hotel O.S. ref. SH 704159, up to Llyn-y-Cadair, then go of to the
right up the huge scree slope on the left under the Cyfrwy arête.

The Western wing of Cyfrwy is probably best gained by taking
the popular walkers' track up Cader from the National Trust car
park O.S. ref. SH 698152.

Character and Topography
Cyfrwy is a huge crag about 600 feet high at its highest and
about two-thirds of a mile in length. It faces north and its base
is over 2000 feet above sea-level. It has the reputation of being
loose and dangerous. When one looks at it from the Cyfrwy
arête this seems true, although the routes which are described,
with the exception of Lowrib and Squall, follow sound lines of
rock. The protection is adequate but not abundant due to the
compact nature of the rock.

The outstanding feature when walking up to this crag is the
left-hand bounding arête (Cyfrwy arête). Its jagged profile with
the flat-toped truncated pillar (The Table) at its foot stands out
clearly before any other feature is seen. Well below the table, at
the lowest section of the crag, is a fairly clean-looking buttress
(Table Buttress). A gully descends to the right of this buttress
from the gap behind the table. Right of the gully two huge ribs
run nearly the full height of the crag, the right-hand one being
the largest. Right again is an obvious diagonal gully. This is
Slanting Gully. A large fine-looking rib starts from the upper half
of the crag; Hyrib takes this.

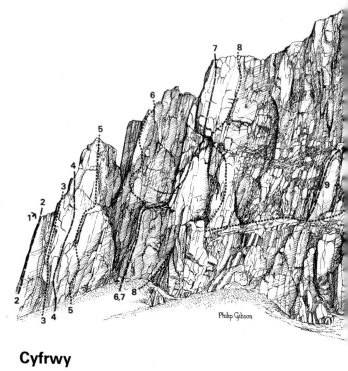

Philip Gibson

Cyfrwy

11	Hyrib	HS
12	Unity	S
13	Stross	HS
14	Obsession	VS
16	Gwydrin	E1
17	Dena	HS
18	Route 2	VS

Well over to the right is an area of fine-looking clean slabs, known as Slabby Buttress. The best routes on the crag make their way up these. The large obvious One Pitch Gully comes next, right of this the crag gradually tapers off, although about a ⅓ of a mile in length and is known as the Western Wing.

Descent
Descending from the main crag left of One Pitch Gully gain the main ridge at the top of the crag and traverse to the top of Cyfrwy Arête. Descend this down its easy top section for about 70 feet until a traverse can be made to enter the big scree gully on the right of the arête when looking down. Descend the gully to the crag base.

For the Western Wing gain a wide scree gully which is roughly half-way along this section of crag and descend this. The route Claw Mark is just to its right when looking down.

** **Cyfrwy Arête**   approx. 472 feet   Difficult   (1988)
Takes the left-hand bounding ridge of the buttress. The ridge has a very distinctive stepped outline; the largest step which is also the lowest is called The Table and has the form of a huge flat-topped pillar. A very good mountaineering route although the rock in places needs care. Start at a ledge 120 feet below The Table. This is gained by traversing in from the left above Table Buttress. This is a steeper section of rock at the lowest point of the crag.
1   60 feet. From the lowest rocks 20 feet left of the drop into the gully, climb an arête then a corner to the arête above.
2   60 feet. Continue along the arête to the top of The Table.
3   12 feet. Descend into the gap off the edge of The Table.
4   30 feet. Go left to a crack and ascend this to a small pinnacle on the left arête.
5   50 feet. Climb the arête above to a big ledge.
6   60 feet. Go up two walls with a ledge midway.
7   200 feet. Scrambling up short walls and spikes leads to the top.

TABLE BUTTRESS

A fairly clean steep buttress about 165 feet high, which forms the lowest section of rock below The Table on the Cyfrwy Arête. The gully descending from the gap behind The Table is immediately to its right.

* **Steric Slab**   130 feet   Hard Severe   (1942)
On the left-hand side of Table Buttress there is a noticeable clean edge of rock of which the right-hand side is formed by a smooth steep slab and the left by a chimney. The route takes the edge

and then the upper section of the chimney. Start with a scramble up to the base of the arête.

1   130 feet. 4b. Go up diagonally right on good holds to a large pointed flake on the right of the arête. A delicate rising traverse left leads to the edge of the arête. Climb up on good holds to a small ledge, step into a chimney and climb this to a ledge; then a short wall above leads to a wide terrace.

* **Nudging Groove**   170 feet   Hard Very Severe   (1974)

In the largest and most prominent arête of the buttress is an obvious groove-line. The route takes this groove. Rather poor protection on the first 40 feet which is also the crux. Start by a slab right of an overhang 30 feet to the left and below the insecure-looking pinnacle at the start of Table Direct.

1   100 feet. 5a. Climb the slab, going diagonally up left above the overhang to an arête then go up this to a peg in a little corner. Move left and traverse delicately across a groove to a rib then go straight up to a V-groove topped by an overhang. Ascend the groove, moving out right to the arête which is followed trending slightly right to a stance with good belays.

2   70 feet. 4c. Move up 3 feet then step left to an obvious groove and climb this direct to the top.

* **Pisa**   150 feet   Hard Severe   (1956)

A line of pillars up the wall to the right of Nudging Groove. Start up the gully to the right from the foot of the buttress at a leaning pinnacle (also the start of Table Direct).

1   50 feet. 4a. Go horizontally left across the wall for 12 feet to a vertical pillar. Ascend to the top of the pillar, then make a move left across a slab into the bottom of a broken groove (difficult). Go up the groove easily to a ledge on the right. Nut belays.

2   40 feet. 4a. On the left of the ledge rises another pillar. Climb to the right of this until the pillar top can be gained. Make an awkward move into a corner on the right and climb it to a ledge on the right. Stance.

3   60 feet. 4b. Ascend the steep slab above the ledge moving slightly left to a weakness. Belay on the big terrace beneath The Table.

Table Direct   170 feet   Very Difficult   (1951)

Below and to the right of Steric Slab is a short grassy gully slanting up rightwards between the buttress and some pinnacles. Start near the top of this gully where a pinnacle leans insecurely against the wall.

1   30 feet. Climb between the pinnacle and the wall then belay on a wedged stone at the top.

2   60 feet. A rising traverse leads easily up right for 35 feet, then go steeply leftwards on good holds to a large ledge.

3   50 feet. Ascend the crack in a corner on the right to a ledge.

4   30 feet. Go to the right end of the stance which overlooks the gully and ascend leftwards up the wall to the terrace under the Cyfrwy arête.

The following climbs take the big rib lines left of centre of the main crag between Table Buttress and Slabby Buttress, giving some of the longest routes on Cyfrwy.

Quartz Rib   290 feet   Very Severe   (1956)
The rib just right of the gully descending from behind The Table on the Cyfrwy arête. It has a noticeable white quartz line running down its edge. Vegetated in the lower part. Start as for Rib and Slab by an obvious narrow rib just right of the start of the gully.
1   140 feet. Ascend the narrowing rib which is in two sections. Then go up the vegetation above to a good spike belay, just right of a steep arête.
2   60 feet. Traverse left under the arête, then go diagonally left across slabs to an arête. Ascend this until an easy traverse back right can be made to a stance and thread belay.
3   90 feet. 4c. Go straight up from the belay for a short distance, step left and go up a crack to a scoop on the left under the bulging quartz arête. Pull over the arête, crux, (hold high on the left). Continue straight up the arête on good holds moving out right just below the top to a niche stance.

* Rib and Slab   460 feet   Mild Very Severe   (1960)
The big rib on the left of the crag with a noticeable butterfly overhang at 115 feet gives a good mountaineering route. Rather poor protection on the lower pitches. There is a bay at the entrance to the gully which descends from behind The Table on the Cyfrwy arête and a narrow rib runs up the right wall, finishing just to the left of the butterfly overhang. Start below the rib.
1   130 feet. Climb the narrowing rib, which is in two sections, to grass. Good nut belay on the right.
2   50 feet. 4b. Climb the steepening slab just left of the butterfly overhang for 35 feet slanting slightly right to the arête. Move round into a groove on the right. Follow this to a small ledge and good nut belays.
3   120 feet. Move right onto a slab and go up this to steep vegetation which is taken to the base of the upper slab. Large boulder belay.
4   140 feet. 4c. A good pitch. Ascend the slab by a crack (12 feet from the rib edge) over several small bulges, moving left near the top to the arête. Stance on the arête and a good spike belay 20 feet from the top.
5   20 feet. Doubtful rock leads to the top.

Squall 480 feet Hard Severe   (1974)

A similar route to Rib and Slab, but not as hard. Most of the climbing is Very Difficult with the big 4b pitch as the crux. Rock on the lower section is in a dangerous condition. Start by following a broken arête 35 feet to the right and below the noticeable rib of Rib and Slab. A shallow gully is on its right.

1 150 feet. Easily go up the arête to a groove just on the left of the arête then where it steepens go up the groove to grassy ledges on the arête. Spike belay up on the left.

2 50 feet. The arête continues; climb it at its weakest point on the left to grassy ledges. Good nut belay high above.

3 90 feet. Go up right to where the arête steepens; climb this on the right moving out left. Then go easily up the arête to vegetation with a large overlapping slab above. Large boulder belay on the left.

4 140 feet. 4b. A good pitch. Move 3 feet up and right on vegetation, then make a slightly rising traverse right for 20 feet above a small overhang until directly below a slot in a big overlap 50 feet above. Climb directly up to the overlap passing a flake. Move over the overhang with a good spike, and continue straight up a shallow groove to a small ledge with a large spike belay above.

5 50 feet. Climb the rock above moving to the left, finishing on the upper section of the Cyfrwy arête.

Lowrib 465 feet Hard Severe   (1974)

Takes the big rib just left of Slanting Gully, starting from the large terraces halfway up the gully. The climbing is about Very Difficult but due to some bad rock at the top of pitch 5 the route becomes rather serious hence the grade. From the terrace broken ribs and vegetation lead up to the main rib. Start under the most continuous and left-hand of the ribs at a cairn.

1 120 feet. Ascend the rib direct to its top; good spike belay.

2 40 feet. Traverse diagonally up right across vegetation to a huge spike. Move right off the top of this to ledges with spike and nut belays.

3 50 feet. Go up vegetation to a pinnacle. Climb this on the right, stepping off its top and moving left to a stance among large detached blocks.

4 60 feet. Go up the blocks, then move left to a groove forming the right-hand side of a huge spike. Ascend the groove to the top of the spike and continue up the short wall above to a small ledge with a good spike belay.

5 75 feet. Continue up the slab above taking the easiest line to a large ledge. The final section of this pitch has some distinctly worrying rock.

6 120 feet. Above is a smooth steep slab with a crack in it. Avoid this by moving down and traversing into the top section of Slanting Gully. Ascend this to the final section of the Cyfrwy arête.

Slanting Gully Grooves   300 feet   E1   (1970)
A line up the steep green slab on the left of Hyrib and above the
steep right wall of the upper section of Slanting Gully. Start
about 100 feet above the start of Hyrib in the upper section of
Slanting Gully. Gain a subsidiary groove left of the main slab.
1   70 feet. Ascend the groove, grassy at first, then a good crack
leads to an obvious move out right, to a stance and peg belay
below the slab.
2   110 feet. 5b. Move up and out onto the left edge to a cutaway,
using the slab and holds round the edge (old peg) then gain a
small ledge. Widely spaced holds on the inset slab above lead
to a move left into a grassy corner. Move up to an old peg belay
at a small pedestal.
3   120 feet. 4a. Ascend the groove above pleasantly to a steep
section, then climb up an awkward corner to a stance on the
ridge.

** **Hyrib**   380 feet   Hard Severe   (1960)
The line follows the rib on the right of Slanting Gully, starting
about half-way up the gully. Start by scrambling in from the left
across large terraces, to a water-worn groove just right of the rib.
1   90 feet. 4b. Ascend the groove, crux, then belay in the gully
bed above. Nut belays.
2   60 feet. 4a. Go diagonally left to the edge of the rib and climb
this to a stance and belay.
3   60 feet. 4a. Ascend the rib on large but doubtful holds to a
ledge.
4   70 feet 4a. Continue up the rib, taking a crack on the right to
a steeper section.
5   100 feet. 4a. Follow the slab on the left then move round to
the left along a grassy rake to a corner, spike runner. Ascend the
corner above, awkward move near the top, to the main ridge.

SLABBY BUTTRESS

The finest-looking section of the crag, taking the form of a huge
triangle. The base stretches from Slanting Gully to One Pitch
Gully. The left side is bounded by a shallow gully starting just
above the base of Slanting Gully, the right side by North arête.
Both gully and arête come together at the apex of the buttress.
The most outstanding features are two smooth clean-looking
slabs. The lower one, the finer, is situated just right of the upper.

Descent

There is no easy descent. For the climbs Stross, Obsession and
Route 2 go up the shallow vegetated gully slanting to the right
to the col behind the top of the buttress. Then follow the easiest
line trending right which is the top section of North arête. There
is some 300 feet of climbing at Moderate standard to the summit
ridge. Descend as for Cyfrwy arête.

* **Stross** 320 feet Hard Severe (1974)

Takes a line up the slabs to the left of Obsession, making for the chimney formed by a flake high up the buttress. Start 60 feet right of Slanting Gully and a few feet left of Obsession.

1 60 feet. A short cracked wall leads to a big ledge at 20 feet. From the left end of the ledge ascend a short groove to a stance on the right with a good thread belay.

2 70 feet. Climb trending left to an overhang and move into a groove on its right. Stance with nut and thread belay.

3 40 feet. Ascend the left-hand groove above to a ledge with loose blocks below a huge flake forming a chimney.

4 40 feet. 4a. Ascend between the flake and the wall until the flake looks very unstable. Move out right and climb a groove to a ledge with a leaning block in a corner. Good nut belay above.

5 110 feet. 4b. Go up the groove above the block to a large thread through its right edge. Climb the steep wall above the thread making a move right to a wedged flake. From the flake go up 3 feet and move right to ledges (then as for Obsession). Return left to a crack and go up this, stepping out right to another crack which is followed to the top.

** **Then There Were Five** 235 feet E1 (1983)

A good route. Start at the top of Obsession pitch 1 at a large spike belay.

1 80 feet. 5b. Step left from the spike belay and climb the steep clean blunt pillar to the ledge with a wedged block.

2 55 feet. 5b. Step off the top of the wedged block and climb up to good holds on the edge of the upper smooth slab. Move 3 feet left and climb the faint groove in the left edge of the slab to good ledges.

3 100 feet. 5b. Traverse right into the corner and climb this to the roof. Pull over this and continue up the corner above.

*** **Obsession** 370 feet Very Severe (1956)

A fine slab route taking an interesting line up the centre of the buttress, its upper section crosses the big upper slab from right to left. Start directly below overhangs some 22 feet left of the corner with the whitish water mark which lies directly under the lower slab.

1 120 feet. 4b. Go up the cracked slab below the overhangs for 40 feet and step left to gain the top of a large jammed block the underside of the block forms the lowest and most left-hand of the overhangs. Go straight up to a crack and climb this to a stance with perched blocks.

2 120 feet. 4c. Traverse right for 6 feet then climb straight up, moving out right to good holds. Ascend to a ledge with a good thread. From the groove, just right of the thread, traverse up diagonally left, making an awkward step above an overhang, then go straight up to a ledge with a jammed block. Step right

of the jammed block and climb a step-like groove until a good corner crack on the right can be gained. Stance with nut belays.
3   130 feet. 4c. Step back left into the groove at the extreme right of the big slab and ascend this to a crack (awkward move to reach a spike). Move left onto the slab then go up to a line of holds crossing the slab to ledges on the left. Go left again to a crack and ascend this, moving right to another crack which is taken to the top.

*** Gwydrin   190 feet   E1 (1982)

A brilliant second pitch which takes the centre of the smooth big lower slab. Start at a groove 6 feet left of a white water mark, directly under the lower slab, and about 15 feet right of Obsession.
1   90 feet. 4c. Climb the groove for 40 feet to a ledge (thread) below a steeper reddish groove trending slightly right. Climb this groove to the traverse line of Route 2. Traverse right to the stance on the right of the slab. Nut and thread belay.
2   100 feet. 5b. From the thread belay step back left onto the slab, move up and step left again, following a vague weakness in the slab some 6 feet left of the corner, until it ends. Make a delicate traverse left, peg, to a thin crack; climb this, moving right to a small ledge. Move up and go back left to follow thin cracks to the top of the slab, finishing close to the arête. Nut belay in a corner 23 feet above. Finish as for Route 2 or abseil down the route.

Dena   390 feet   Hard Severe (1959)

A line up the pillar to the right of Route 2. Some poor rock. Start below the lower big smooth slab at a vegetated groove.
1   70 feet. 4a. Ascend the groove with the white water mark on its left wall, to a stance below the big smooth slab. Thread and nut belay.
2   60 feet. Move round to the right to vegetation and climb this moving back left to a stance with perched blocks next to the smooth slab. Thread belay.
3   110 feet. 4b. Ascend the centre of the pillar above to a ledge with a shattered pinnacle. From the top of the pinnacle move straight up to an overhang, go over this (crux) and follow up the slab above to a large ledge, nut belays.
4   150 feet. Go up the shattered rib above to the top of the buttress.

* Route 2   325 feet   Very Severe (1959)

Another fine slab route, similar to Obsession, but crossing the lower big slab. The central section is unfortunately rather scrappy. Rather poor protection on pitch 5. Start under the lower big smooth slab in a corner with a long white streak running down its left wall. Start at the corner just right of this. Large block belay.

1 80 feet. 4b. Go up the groove or arête, grassy at the top, to a ramp under the big smooth slab. Thread and nut belays in a corner on the right.
2 40 feet. 4b. Traverse out horizontally left across the slab, following the obvious weakness. Go round the rib to a stance at the foot of a groove.
3 50 feet. 4a. Climb the groove to a ledge and thread belay (junction with Obsession).
4 70 feet. Climb up the left-hand groove to a stance with the upper big slab on the left. Large spike belay high above.
5 15 feet. Move right round the rib and climb this by a crack for 35 feet. Stance on a grassy ledge 10 feet to the right.
6 70 feet. 4c. Move back left to the edge of the slab, climb up delicately for 10 feet, crux, and go right to better holds in a small corner. From the top of the corner traverse back left to the edge, then go straight up to the top of the slab.

** **Pusher Man Variation**   100 feet   Hard Very Severe   (1974)
A very good pitch which is a hard variation of pitches 2 and 3 of Route 2. Start at the top of pitch 1 Route 2, below the big smooth slab.
1 100 feet. 5a. Take a slightly rising traverse across the smooth slab (starting 10 feet above the traverse line of pitch 2 Route 2), following a line of awkwardly spaced holds to the arête. Ascend the right edge of the arête with difficulty for about 25 feet to an overlap, go up left to a flake, then move left into a groove and climb easily up to the ledge at the top of pitch 3 Route 2.

North Arête   500 feet   Difficult   (1900)
Initially the left edge of One Pitch Gully, higher up becoming lost in mixed rock and vegetation. Start from the scree at the start of One Pitch Gully where a steepening rib goes up on the left forming the bounding arête of the gully.
1 100 feet. Go up the rib until it steepens then climb this on the right on big but doubtful holds to a terrace.
2 100 feet. Follow the arête keeping to its left to a ledge and good spike belay below a steep slab.
3 60 feet. Ascend rightwards to the arête overlooking the gully and climb two short walls above on the right to a large grassy bay.
4 120 feet. Easy climbing leads up the line of the arête.
5 120 feet. Ascend straight up to the top of a table-topped pinnacle.
About 300 feet of climbing at Moderate standard leads to the top.

One Pitch Gully
This obvious big wide gully, Very Difficult, is of little merit as a summer route, having only a single short chockstone pitch near the top.

WESTERN WING

The section of crag right of One Pitch Gully. The rock is probably more vegetated than the main crag although there are areas which are fairly clean. The crag tapers from being about 300 feet high near One Pitch Gully to 100 feet at the far right-hand end. The total base length is over a ⅓ of a mile. There is obviously scope for many more routes. The main features are deep wet cave-like gullies cutting into the crag at regular intervals. Some of these give excellent winter climbing.

CYFRWY PINNACLE

This is the pinnacle overlooking the entrance to One Pitch Gully and forming its right wall. It has faces to the east and north. The upper section of the east face gets the sun in the summer.

** **Red Crystals**   340 feet   Severe   (1982)
A pleasant line on the pinnacle east face. The first two pitches are as for Cyfrwy Pinnacle route. Start a short way up One Pitch Gully at a rib with a quartz streak, directly below the broken arête coming down from the Pinnacle.
1   120 feet. 4a. From the lowest point of the rib move first left then right to reach a ledge at 10 feet. Climb the crack above to the top of the rib (the rib can be avoided by scrambling to the right up vegetation). Continue up easier ground following the stepped arête coming down from the pinnacle. Flake and nut belays below a steeper section.
2   70 feet. 4a. Step right and climb a weakness in the wall to easier ground, still following the arête coming down from the pinnacle. Stance on a large horizontal ledge below the pinnacle proper.
3   70 feet. 4a. Move 20 feet left along the ledge to a vague crack with a thread 12 feet up. Climb up to the thread. Step left to a crack in a bulge and climb this. Move 3 feet left to a ledge and climb the knobbly wall on the left to a ledge below an overhang. Small spike and nut belays.
4   80 feet. 4a. Step left onto a spike. Move up the wall above until a step right can be made to a thin crack then make some difficult moves up this to good holds. Step right again, then traverse right for 10 feet to a ledge below a chimney/crack, and finish up this.

* **Cyfrwy Pinnacle**   330 feet   Very Severe   (1982)
The Pinnacle direct, following the arête throughout. An excellent top pitch. Start as for Red Crystals.
1   120 feet. 4a. As for pitch 1 of Red Crystals.
2   70 feet. 4a. As for pitch 2 of Red Crystals.

3 75 feet. Continue up the line of the arête, climbing a short chimney to a long narrow ledge below a headwall. Good nut slot round the edge to the right.
4 65 feet. 4c. Step round the edge to the right and climb up making an awkward move left to gain a groove in the arête. Take the groove to a roof, traverse delicately right under the roof to a crack, and finish up this.

** Mochyn 275 feet Very Severe (1983)
An enjoyable line up the clean face to the left of the deep chimney/gully to the left of Chinese Poppy. Start up the gully for 35 feet to an obvious ledge on the left below the intimidating overhangs.
1 100 feet. 4c. Move left to a recess, climb the rib on the left of this to steepening rock then make a rising traverse to the left to a shallow groove. Ascend this to gain a traverse line going back right to an exposed ledge above the overhangs. Nut and peg belays.
2 100 feet. 5a. Step back left and climb on good holds up to a small overhang. Make a short traverse right to a ledge below a corner, climb the corner to another overhang then make an awkward traverse right to a ledge on the edge of the gully.
3 40 feet. 4a. Climb the crack in the arête above to a good stance.
4 35 feet. 4a. Ascend the rib directly behind the belay block to the top.

Chinese Poppy 320 feet Severe (1974)
The buttress to the right of Cyfrwy Pinnacle has a distinctive vegetated ramp running diagonally from right to left. Mid-way up this ramp a deep gully cuts the buttress. The climb takes a line just to the right of this gully. Start from the ramp, below and to the left of an obvious pinnacle-like block.
1 60 feet. Traverse right to the base of the pinnacle then climb the arête on its left on good holds to a vegetated ledge, nut belays on the right.
2 60 feet. 4a. Ascend the leftward-slanting ramp above, keeping to its left edge which overlooks the gully. Ledge and belays at the top of the ramp.
3 70 feet. Move up and right to gain another ramp trending back left, climb this passing a large doubtful block then go out right to a good ledge with flake belays.
4 130 feet. Ascend easily up right to the top.

Trojan 300 feet Mild Very Severe (1974)
Well to the right of One Pitch Gully is an obvious big waterworn corner topped by a triangular overhang. Just left of it is a huge arched overhang. The waterworn corner and the overhang are set back and are approached by entering a small rocky amphitheatre. Start 12 feet left of the wet corner.

1 70 feet. 4a. Climb the left wall of the corner, trending slightly right up a weakness. Move left to some small ledges. Doubtful nut and peg belay (peg belay removed).
2 130 feet. 4b. Go back right and continue up the weakness until a move right can be made to a little ledge in the corner. Follow the corner until an obvious traverse line out left can be made across the slab; continue straight up to finish on a ledge just to the left of the triangular overhang. Nut belays.
3 70 feet. 4a. Take the chimney/crack above for about 65 feet then move out right to a ledge.
4 30 feet. Finish easily up broken rock above.

Claw Mark   430 feet   Hard Severe   (1974)
A line up the smooth clean slab well to the right of Trojan. A deep cave-like gully is just to its right. Pitch 1 gives the best climbing. Start 15 feet up to the right from the toe of the slab, at a weakness trending left.
1 130 feet. 4b. Ascend leftwards and follow a thin crack in the middle of the slab to a corner with a large block on the left. Go directly up the corner to vegetated ledges. Stance on a large ledge with a large flake belay.
2 140 feet. 4a. Ascend rock above the belay to vegetation. Climb the wall above keeping right of a large overhang, then go up a shallow groove, moving right to vegetation and a block belay.
3 100 feet. Scrambling leads to the top of a pinnacle.
4 60 feet. Descend into a gap and climb a smooth slab to vegetation.

Kurt Sumner on Sloose, Gist Ddu.   Photo: John Sumner

John Sumner and Bob Norris on Daisy Belle,
Bird Rock.

Photo: Coll. Sumner

RHINOG RANGE

Craig-y-Cae   O.S. ref. SH 708235

Approach
From Dolgellau take the A470 Trawsfynydd road for about 4 miles to the Tyn-y-Groes Hotel. On the left just past the hotel, a single-track gated road is followed to the edge of forest; discretionary parking for 2 or 3 cars on verges; National Trust land. The crag can be seen above the forest on the left. A short way into the forest a track rises south-west to emerge at the Nant Las watercourse. Keep right of this and go up rough-and-tumble ground to boulders under the crag.

Character and Topography
Craig-y-Cae faces east and is about 1300 feet above sea level. It is situated under the north-east side of Y Garn. The crag is only about 165 feet high but has many large roofs; there is also a lot of vegetation. The rock is less sound than it seems on first inspection.

The Central Buttress is obviously the main attraction. Immediately to its left is South Gully, steep, vegetated and having a tall narrow striking-looking roofed buttress set in it. Left of this is the vegetated South Buttress. Right of Central Buttress is the deep easy North Gully with again a vegetated buttress to its right – North Buttress.

Descent
Takes a wide terrace down over South Buttress.

* **Tririri** 200 feet Very Severe   (1966)
The left edge of Central Buttress. Start on the left-hand side of Central Buttress under South Gully.
1 50 feet. 4b. From the gully bed go over a small bulge and move right along a ledge for 3 feet then climb direct on sharp little holds to a large vegetated ledge below a wall (stance shared with Nichevo).
2 70 feet. 4c. Pitch 2 Nichevo. Move right and climb the wall above by a series of mantelshelves working up left, to land on a ledge at the edge of the gully. The vegetated gully is climbed moving back right to a tree on the arête.
3 80 feet. 4c. Pull over the bulge above the tree to reach a steep slab. Climb this direct in the line of a thin crack to a horizontal crack below a bulge. Go right and make an awkward move into the bottom of a crack. Ascend the crack to a big ledge. The vegetated wall above is followed easily on the left.

Craig-y-Cae

1 Tririri   VS
2 Nichevo   VS
3 The Hole   VS

* Nichevo   230 feet   Very Severe   (1958)
A climb of character, following the line of least resistance up the left-hand side of the buttress. Start a few feet right of South Gully below an obvious crack in a fairly clean wall.
1   50 feet. 4a. Ascend the crack to a large vegetated ledge on the left below a wall.
2   70 feet. 4c. Go right and climb the wall above by a series of mantelshelves trending left, to land on a ledge at the edge of the gully. The vegetated gully is followed moving back right to a tree on the arête.
3   40 feet. Traverse right from the tree on all fours along a slot through nests to a stance below a large chimney.
4   70 feet. 4a. Ascend the chimney. From its top go up a short vegetated wall on the left to the top.

The Hole   210 feet   Very Severe   (1974)
The climb gains the deep recess in the centre of the buttress then leaves it by an interesting traverse out left. Vegetated in its lower half. Start below the deep recess. A large holly tree is a few feet to the right.
1   60 feet. 4a. Ascend easily up the right wall of the recess and fight through a tree under the roof. Stance on the tree.
2   80 feet. 4c. Go delicately across the steep slab on the left to a holly tree, then take the obvious traversing line left on good holds to a crack. Go left again across a slab under a small overlap to the edge. Above the overlap is a crack in a steep slab slanting leftwards. Go up with difficulty to reach the crack and follow it for a few feet making a move right to good handholds and the large vegetated ledge under the chimney pitch of Nichevo.
3   70 feet. 4b. From the right-hand end of the ledge climb a groove up the right edge of a steep wall to the top.

Black Pillar   200 feet   Hard Very Severe   (1973)
A line up the wall directly above the large holly tree. Start in a little corner 3 feet left of the large holly tree.
1   100 feet. 5a. Go up the right edge of the corner to a ledge. Traverse right across the wall to its right edge; climb this for 3 feet then traverse back left to a ledge on the left edge. Take the steep groove directly above the ledge (crux) to a large grassy stance.
2   100 feet. 4b. Go right and ascend the slab to a groove (big pointed overhang on the right). Take the groove to the top.

* Fangorn   170 feet   Hard Severe   (1974)
Start below a narrowing slab in a corner, just above and a few feet right of the large holly tree. Flake belay.
1   70 feet. 4a. Climb the slab with widely spaced ledges to just below the top, then move right to vegetation. Pointed block belay on the left above the slab.

2 100 feet. 4b. From the top of the block step left and move delicately left across a slab to a ledge (big pointed roof 20 feet above). Move left again and ascend a steep groove in the wall above to the top.

Fangorn Right-Hand 90 feet Very Severe (1974)
A line following the break between two big roofs above the first pitch of Fangorn. Start by the pointed block at the top of pitch 1 of Fangorn.
1 90 feet. 4c. Go up easily into the corner above. Go over the initial overhang and climb a steep ramp above to ledges; ascend these to the corner with an overhang on the right. Ascend the right wall of the corner using a dubious flake to easier ground and the top.

NORTH BUTTRESS

* **Tribarfau** 210 feet Hard Very Difficult (1971)
Ascends the fairly clean arête just right of North Gully. Start on the right of the arête below a vegetated chimney.
1 30 feet. Climb a few feet by ledges to the right of the arête, then go up a little chimney. Move left onto a heathery ledge below a small overhang on the arête. Nut belay in a horizontal crack.
2 40 feet. Step right onto a steep little wall and with difficulty gain a hold above. Ascend the corner behind the tree on the right, then move left across a little wall to gain the arête. Block belay.
3 40 feet. Easy ground leads to the foot of the wall above. Large spike belay.
4 70 feet. Traverse horizontally right across a steepish wall to a large flake, then go round into a niche above an oak tree. Climb a chimney slanting up left to gain the arête again.
5 30 feet. Ascend slabs above to finish.

Craig Bodlyn
O.S. ref. SH 650237

Take the A496 coast road from Barmouth to Harlech to Llanddwywe. From there go inland up a long straight minor road to Cors-y-Gedol then a cart-track is followed for about 3 miles to Llyn Bodlyn and the crag.

The steep, tall crag of Craig Bodlyn is about 350 feet high, faces north and overlooks Llyn Bodlyn. The rock on the whole is sound with good friction. Unfortunately, due to the great deal of vegetation on the upper section, it takes a long time to dry out.

Craig Bodlyn

Philip Gibson

The most striking feature is the deep chimney-line of The Spade which goes the full height of the crag and cuts through some large overhangs. Left of this is the cleanish steep central section bounded on its left by the large corner-line of Inigo – also going the full height of the crag. Left of this is a big curving wall the left edge of which forms the edge of a deep wet gully.

Right of The Spade chimney-line is a steep though vegetated buttress with an obvious corner high up, taken by Strictus. Right again the crag loses itself in vegetation and short walls.

Descent
Gain the wide vegetated gully on the right of the crag (Strictus is the closest route to it) and descend this easily.

Porky 260 feet Hard Very Severe (1 pt. aid) † (1971)
A route up the left edge of the crag with a deep wet gully to its left. Start below an obvious corner at the top of pitch 1 of Mochan, where a large terrace comes in from the gully on the left.
1 60 feet. Ascend the easiest line up the corner to a large ledge below a chimney.
2 50 feet. The chimney leads to another big ledge.
3 80 feet. Traverse left from the ledge for a few feet then climb a shallow groove to blocks below an overhang; climb the overhang, peg for aid (in situ), and go up a groove above to a ledge under another overhang.
4 70 feet. Go right along the ledge for a few feet and climb a vague groove to gain a chimney on the right-hand side of a pinnacle. Follow this to the top.

* **Mochan** 360 feet Very Severe (1969)
The easiest line up this part of the crag. Start 12 feet right of a small tree at the lowest point of the cleaned slabs. The big obvious corner-line of Inigo is on the right.
1 100 feet. Go directly up the slabs to vegetated ledges. Block belay at the foot of the corner above.
2 60 feet. 4b. From the corner climb the arête on the right for a few feet then traverse right to a groove, and go up this to a vegetated ledge.
3 50 feet. 4a. Ascend the chimney cutting through the wall above to ledges, and ascend to the highest of these.
4 70 feet. 4c. Take the wall above to a horizontal crack, and move left to a vegetated ledge. Step up from the ledge and move right to the ledge above.
5 80 feet. 4b. Ascend the wall above, starting on the right, and slant left to finish to the left of a cutaway overhang. Belay above on the ledges on the right.

Mynydd Moel

1	The Sketch Man	HVS
2	Sundog	E2
3	The Bee	HVS
4	Twist Grip	HVS
5	Route Central	HVS
6	Rabble Rouser	E5
7	Ritander	VS

1 Upper Tier
2 Left-Hand Lower Tier
3 Right-Hand Lower Tier
4 First Crag

Craig Rhiwarth

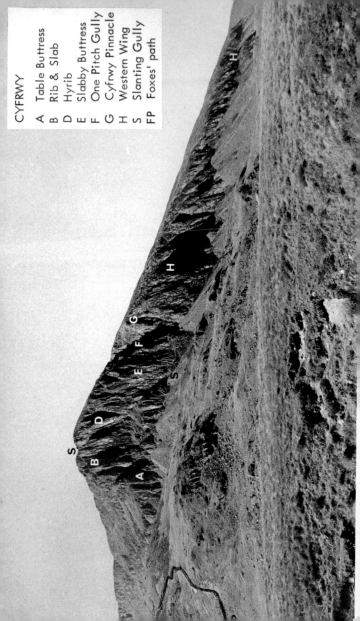

CYFRWY

A Table Buttress
B Rib & Slab
D Hyrib
E Slabby Buttress
F One Pitch Gully
G Cyfrwy Pinnacle
H Western Wing
S Slanting Gully
FP Foxes' path

Galium 330 feet   Hard Very Severe   (1969)
A line which makes for the big curved wall right of Mochan. Start from the top of a large embedded flake 10 feet left of the big corner of Inigo, below the cleaned slabs.
1   70 feet. 4a. Go up the steep slabs directly above the flake to vegetated ledges. Belay below an overhang.
2   60 feet. 5a. Gain the ledge above the overhang and take a fairly direct line to reach a groove above; go up this to a big ledge.
3   50 feet. 4c. Ascend the crack to the right of the chimney of Mochan, to another big ledge.
4   150 feet. 5a. Go up the wall to a horizontal crack; move right and gain the ledge above. Go right along the ledge to grass, then go up and back left. Traverse right and climb a groove above to the top.

Inigo 320 feet   Very Severe   (1967)
The obvious big corner-line going the full height of the crag. Vegetated in its lower section. Start directly beneath the big corner.
1   100 feet. 4b. Ascend the vegetated corner to a bulge, move right and continue in the corner to an overhang. Move right to a large vegetated ledge.
2   50 feet. 4b. Return left to below the overhang, climb this direct and take the steepening groove on the right to another large ledge.
3   120 feet. 4b. Ascend the corner above by its easiest line to a ledge below the last pitch.
4   50 feet. 4c. Go up the corner above to a bulge then go directly over this to the top.

* Nardus 330 feet   Very Severe   (1966)
Although it has a good central section, escape is possible at many points to Inigo. Start 12 feet left of the start of The Spade, at a cleaned groove.
1   120 feet. 4b. Ascend the groove to a ledge. Go up the wall above to a big ledge which goes left under an overhang and meets the corner-line of Inigo.
2   80 feet. 4c. Climb a shallow groove to the right of the overhang, moving left to a ledge on the arête. The easy arête is taken for a few feet then climb a groove on the right, capped by an overhang; step left at the overhang and ascend to some small ledges with nut belays.
3   40 feet. 4c. Ascend the arête direct via a little groove to good holds then move right to vegetated ledges.
4   90 feet. Take the easiest line above over vegetated ledges to finish just left of a large pointed spike.

Tenuous   275 feet   E3   (1 pt. aid)   †   (1969)
An intimidating line up the steep Central Buttress. Start from the big ledge above pitch 1 of Nardus.
1   85 feet. 5c. From the right-hand end of the ledge go up the steep wall until a traverse right can be made above the overhangs to reach a thin crack. Go up this using a peg for aid to reach a ledge.
2   100 feet. 5c. Move up then go back into the centre of the wall at the obvious horizontal break. Climb the wall above moving slightly right (difficult exit) to ledges.
3   90 feet. Vegetated ledges above lead to the top.

The Spade   340 feet   Very Severe   †   (1960)
The obvious deep chimney/gully line cutting through some large overhangs. Start below the chimney. Vegetated.
1   75 feet. Ascend vegetation to below the overhangs then move out right onto a ledge. A step up leads to a grassy ledge beneath a vertical V-corner.
2   20 feet. Climb the corner to another grassy ledge on the right.
3   50 feet. Go up delicately back left and move up to below the main overhang. Climb it direct to a small niche, then go up a small overhang above to a stance and belay in a cave.
4   30 feet. Exit leftwards, mantelshelf and return to the gully.
5   45 feet. The 40-foot chimney is strenuous.
6   60 feet. Move left again, mantelshelf, and go back into the gully. Go up into an overhanging cave making a step left to a large ledge and belay.
7   60 feet. Trend rightwards easily and follow the continuation line to the top.

Strictus   350 feet   E1   (1967)
Steep varied climbing making for the obvious corner high up the buttress. Start below a cleaned corner to the right of The Spade.
1   60 feet. Go up the corner to ledges.
2   60 feet. 4b. Ascend vegetation, trending left to a chimney cutting through a quartz band. Ascend the chimney to the top of a pinnacle.
3   100 feet. 5a. Move up and then go left across the wall to its left edge. Belay beneath a crack in the back of an obvious V-corner.
4   60 feet. 5b. Ascend the corner to a large ledge.
5   70 feet. Take the easiest line over vegetated walls above to the top.

Girdle Traverse   395 feet   E1
Start from the top of pitch 1 of Mochan.
1   60 feet. Pitch 2 of Mochan.
2   50 feet. Pitch 3 of Galium.

3   65 feet. 5a. From the big ledge beneath the horizontal crack, take an obvious line traversing right into the corner of Inigo. Belay on the right wall, stance as for Nardus pitch 2.
4   90 feet. 5a. Reverse a few feet of Nardus and move right to reach the obvious horizontal break crossing the steep central buttress. Go right along the break into The Spade; belay on the right beneath the V-corner of Strictus.
5   60 feet. 5b. Climb the corner as for pitch 4 of Strictus.
6   70 feet. 4c. Go right along ledges. Ascend a crack then follow vegetated walls to the top.

THE BERWYNS

Craig-y-Mwn

O.S. ref. SJ 074291

Situated in the southern part of the Berwyn close to Pistyll Rhaeadr, the largest waterfall in Wales. In summer this beautiful place attracts a lot of sightseers and walkers and it was a notable spot long before George Borrow went there, and it was singled out by Palmer as the finest falls in Britain. There is a good café beside the waterfall with car parking and toilets. Access to the waterfall valley is by narrow roads and lanes from Chirk (B450), Oswestry (B4580) and Shrewsbury (B4396), all converging on the village of Llanrhaedr-ym-Mochnant.

The crag faces north-east and is approached fairly easily by crossing the bridge beneath the waterfall, then by a rising traverse up left through woods and over scree to its base. The rock is of a volcanic type and is on the whole very sound. The crag has a distinctive undercut base and a height of about 140 feet.

* **Legionnaire's Disease**   140 feet   Hard Very Severe   (1985)
Follows cracks then a groove a few feet left of the obvious corner of Pardon Me for Breathing.
1   140 feet. 5a. Gain a ledge below a steep flaky crack, climb this (crux) and move left to a groove. Go up this to the top of the crag.

*** **Pardon Me for Breathing**   140 feet   E2   (1985)
The obvious corner gives excellent sustained climbing.
1   140 feet. 5c. Climb the corner (hard move at 15 feet), step right at the top and climb the steep continuation groove on big holds to a vegetated groove and the top.

** **Meisterspringer**   140 feet   E2   (1985)
The arête to the right of Pardon Me for Breathing. Start below the latter's groove.
1   140 feet. 5b. Gain a ledge on the right overhanging wall by a traverse from the left. Move up right to gain the arête at a ledge. Climb the right edge of the arête to reach a short overhung groove in the arête (peg); climb its right edge to easier ground and another ledge. Go up some detached blocks and finish out left.

* **Pale Rider**   140 feet   E4   (1985)
Start about 30 feet right of the Pardon Me for Breathing corner,
below the overhangs; overhung niche above.
1   140 feet. 6a. Gain the overhung niche (peg) and step left to
a flake (thread). Continue up the wall to the top.

* **Dovercourt Special**   140 feet   E2   (1985)
A weakness in the overhang with a groove above roughly in the
centre of the crag.
1   140 feet. 5c. Gain a large doubtful hold from the right (peg).
Move left and go up to the overhang (peg); pull over this
rightwards to reach the bottomless groove. Climb the groove
trending slightly left to the top.

Foundation and Empire   130 feet   E1   †   (1985)
The obvious overhanging chimney/crack in the centre of the
crag. Start at the same point as Dovercourt Special.
1   80 feet. 5b. A steep layaway leads to a ledge on the right
below the large overhangs (2 pegs). Swing out right boldly and
go up to gain a good ledge above.
2   50 feet. Continue up the crack to the top.

*** **Brothers In Arms**   140 feet   E3   (1985)
A superb route taking the overlapping wall just right of the large
overhangs. Start below a weakness in the lower band of
overhangs.
1   140 feet. 5c. Move up right to gain the wall below the
weakness in the first band of overhangs. Go through this
awkwardly to attain a large pocket in the wall below the second
band of overhangs. Avoid these by moving right then left to a
delicate slab (peg). Ascend this moving out left to finish up a
short juggy wall.

* **First Blood II**   120 feet   Hard Very Severe   (1985)
An obvious clean-cut groove at the extreme right-hand end of
the crag.
1   120 feet. 5b. Climb the groove with a difficult move low down
and a traverse to the arête just below a ledge. On the left of the
overhang above the ledge, climb the wall past a peg; steep
moves lead up and right to the prow and top.

Craig Rhiwarth   O.S. ref. SJ 055265

This crag and hill fort just above mark the most southerly point
of the Berwyn mountains, standing above the village of
Llangynog (535 feet) on the B4391 in the Tanat valley. Cars
should be parked in the village car park and not in the minor

road under the crag. The rocks belong to Miss Lloyd who lives in the village and she has been kind enough to allow climbing. Please respect this permit and obey the country code at all times.

Rhiwarth is composed of half-a-dozen small crags some 65 – 100 feet high, dotted low down on the hillside facing south. Four of the crags so far have been inspected; three of these are close together, forming a split lower and a continuous upper tier. They are also the lowest crags on the hillside with easy access from the minor road directly beneath them.

The granite-type rock is good on the lower tier but less so on the upper. The crags dry quickly, and having a sunny aspect make a visit worthwhile during the winter months.

FIRST CRAG

As its name implies the first crag to be seen when approaching from Llangynog along the minor road. The crag lies above and to the right of the last cottage along this road. Easy-angled scree with a slate ramp to its left.

A very steep squarish buttress, the routes start on the very steep wall just right of the trees.

Sledgehammer   80 feet   E2   †   (1986)
1   80 feet. 5c. Pockets to the left of Mismael (side runner placed from the ramp on the left). From the groove move right along a break, make a long reach to a good hold then follow the line of good holds trending right at the top to finish as for Mismael.

* **Mismael**   80 feet   E3   (1986)
The pocketed crack line just left of centre of the wall.
1   80 feet. 5c. From the block step left to the crack. Hard moves gain better holds which lead to a ledge and easier climbing to an oak tree.

** **Wingeing Pom**   110 feet   E1   (1987)
A rising traverse from right to left finishing up the obvious stepped crack at the top of the crag. A climb of increasing difficulty. Start at a groove on the right-hand side of the crag just left of a vegetated gully.
1   110 feet. 5b. Go easily up the groove to the overhang then traverse left below the overhang to a peg. Step left round an edge to the base of the stepped crack. Go up this strenuously then take a horizontal hand-traverse left. Finish up to a small tree.

Bionic Woman   80 feet   Very Severe   (1987)
Start as for Wingeing Pom.
1   80 feet. 4c. Go up the groove of Wingeing Pom to the
overhang. Make an awkward move up and right to easier ground
and the top.

The next three buttresses are grouped together about ¼ mile
right of the first crag. A small wood is directly below the
right-hand lower tier.

LEFT-HAND LOWER TIER

Phase Shift   60 feet   Hard Very Severe   (1987)
Start just left of the diagonal line of Silwood.
1   60 feet. 5b. Climb the short pillar with a difficult groove, peg.

Silwood   65 feet   Hard Severe   (1970)
1   80 feet. 4a. Ascend an obvious weakness slanting up right.

Ivy   80 feet   Very Severe   (1984)
The groove on the left of a smooth slab. Start below an oak tree.
1   80 feet. 4c. Climb through the oak tree to gain the groove and
climb this and a steeper continuation groove in the wall above.

Charisma   80 feet   E2   (1984)
1   80 feet. 6a. As for Ivy up through the oak tree, then traverse
the base of the smooth slab (peg) to a shallow groove; take this
and the steep continuation groove above.

* **Eden**   80 feet   E2   (1984)
1   80 feet. 5c. Ascend an obvious crack splitting the small
overhang at 20 feet and the continuation groove above.

Melangell   90 feet   Very Severe   (1970)
1   90 feet. 4b. Take the leftward ascending flake crack to a ledge
at half-height, then ascend a short wall up right to an arête. Gain
a corner on the right (Rose Corner) and finish up this.

The Slide   90 feet   Very Severe   4c   (1984)
The left arête of Rose Corner.
1   90 feet. 4c. Climb the steep leftward slanting ramp awkwardly
to gain a ledge on the left then finish as for Melangell.

* **Rose Corner**   85 feet   Hard Very Severe   (1962)
Easy for its grade.
1   85 feet. 5a. Climb the obvious corner, starting at a rose bush
on the right. Move right below an overhang at the top of the
corner and go up a short groove to finish.

* Ivory Tower   80 feet   Hard Severe   (1962)
The crack forming the left edge of a huge flake on the right edge
of the buttress.
1   80 feet. 4b. Take the crack to the top of the flake. Continue
up the broken groove above, moving left near the top.

RIGHT-HAND LOWER TIER

Bramble Pie   65 feet   Hard Very Severe   (1986)
To the left of the steep wall with The Cheshire Cat is an
easy-looking scoopy slab leading to an obvious leftward-
trending crack-line under a steep wall. Start below the scoopy
slab. Poor protection in the lower crux section.
1   65 feet. 5a. Gain the scoop from the right (crux). Pull over a
small overhang to gain the base of the leftward trending crack
line then go easily up this to a tree belay on the far left of the
crag.

** The Cheshire Cat   70 feet   E1   (1985)
The impelling thin crack line which starts half-way up the largest
unbroken wall; sustained.
1   70 feet. 5b. Go up steep rock directly below the crack-line,
moving slightly left to a resting place. Step back right to a hold
in the small overhang (peg) at the start of the crack proper. Pull
over the overhang and continue up the crack, keeping to its
left-hand side. Belay to the oak tree on the right. Abseil off.

The Gargoyle   65 feet   Hard Very Severe   (1985)
The obvious corner/chimney line direct to an oak tree.
1   65 feet. 5a. Climb the steep corner to gain a niche below the
huge chockstone. Pull over this and continue direct to the oak
tree. Abseil off from the tree or climb the continuation groove
at 4b; belay a long way back.

* Tanat   70 feet   Hard Very Severe   (1962)
Excellent rock, though protection is rather sparse. Start at the
lowest point of the crag.
1   70 feet. 5a. Step off a block and make a thin move left to gain
the arête; go up this moving slightly right to good holds below
a steep wall. Climb this direct to a ledge; move left to an oak
tree. Abseil off.

* The Hud   65 feet   E1   (1986)
Start right of Tanat below a short groove capped by a small
triangular roof, orange mark on rock at base of groove.
1   65 feet. 5b. Go easily up a chimney, then step right to gain
the groove. Pull over the roof on big jugs (peg) to the left. Gain
the traverse ledge of Quartizone Injection and move up to a peg
in the wall above. Finish up the little groove directly above.
Abseil from the tree on the left.

John Sumner on Vapour Phase,
Barmouth Quarry.

Photo: Coll. Sumner

Crack 2, Barmouth Slabs.   Photo: John Sumner

Quartizone Injection   100 feet   Very Severe   (1985)
Quite good climbing though meandering. Start at a detached slab leading up to a corner.
1   100 feet. 4c. Climb the slab and start up the corner, breaking out left. Reach a traverse line above the overhangs on the right and follow it to a tree; belay. Move back left cross a mossy slab and go up a vague crack leading to a ledge above; continue up the steep arête above first on its right then on the left. Finish up the arête direct on big holds.

* **Paper Lace**   100 feet   Hard Very Severe   (1984)
On the right-hand side of the crag is a gully separating a doubtful overhanging section of rock from the main buttress. This route lies just left of the gully and makes for a slab in a corner with a large pinnacle directly above.
1   100 feet. 5b. Go up to the slab and gain it moving up into the corner. Make an awkward move to the right edge of the corner and climb this to reach the right-hand side of the pinnacle; stance and belay. Step left from the pinnacle top to a ledge below an arête. Climb the right edge of this to the top.

UPPER TIER

At the right-hand end of the upper tier is a noticeable tower with a groove-line running up its centre; this is King of Maybe. Cavalier Attitude takes the right-hand edge of the arête right of King of Maybe.

Cavalier Attitude   80 feet   Hard Very Severe   (1985)
1   80 feet. Step onto the edge and climb slightly rightwards then go back left to gain the edge again. Climb directly up this to the top.

** **King of Maybe**   85 feet   Very Severe   (1962)
A sustained route.
1   85 feet. 4c. Gain a crack from the left (peg), go up into the groove to a bulge, then traverse left on big handholds. Go directly up to the summit block and take the short overhanging groove in this. Metal spike belay.

* **Thunder Road**   80 feet   Very Severe   (1962)
Well to the left of King of Maybe is a chimney/groove line going the full height of the crag.
1   80 feet. 4c. Climb this moving out left near the top, just below a small tree. Metal spike belay well back in a small outcrop.

Fifty and Rising   100 feet   E2   (1985)
A strenuous and technical route.
1   100 feet. 5c. Ascend the overhanging crack to an oak tree. Step right from the tree and climb up diagonally right to reach an easy slab above. Tree belay just below the top of the crag.

Stickle Back Man   90 feet   Very Severe   (1985)
Takes the undercut chimney/groove line starting half-way up the crag. Start by gaining an easy ramp below a large tree at the top of the crag.
1   90 feet. 4b. Follow the ramp rightwards then go up directly to the chimney line. Climb this to the top.

Chacmool   90 feet   Very Severe   (1985)
Start as for Stickle Back Man.
1   90 feet. 4b. Follow the ramp rightwards then go up to gain a leftward weakness crossing a slab and a groove to a ledge on the right of a groove. Climb the groove to a big tree at the top of the crag.

Luddites Demise   70 feet   Hard Very Severe   †   (1985)
A direct start to Chacmool.
1   70 feet. 5b. Start as for Chacmool then climb direct up steep rock to the groove.

* **Buzzard's Nest Crack**   80 feet   Hard Severe   (1970)
The big leftward-trending ramp line below a steep wall. A large tree at the top of the crag is just to its right.
1   80 feet. 4b. Climb a crack in a corner to gain the ramp and go up this to a steep little wall. Pull awkwardly over this and reach a ledge and tree belay. Climb a shallow groove on the right to the top.

On the continuation of the Rhiwarth escarpment on the hillside across a stream about ¾ of a mile to the east is a section of worthwhile rock. Two routes have so far been done.

Towards the right-hand end of this crag is a noticeable arête with a blank overhanging wall to its left. This forms the right wall of an obvious striking corner crack.

Class 87/2   80 feet   Hard Very Severe   †   (1987)
The obvious corner crack.
1   50 feet. 5b. Climb the corner crack with increasing difficulty to a large ledge.
2   30 feet. Follow the right edge then easy ground right to a tree.

Cloudwaltzer   80 feet   Hard Very Severe   †   (1987)
The groove immediately left of Class 87/2.
1   80 feet. 5b. Gain the base of the groove from the right. Climb this direct passing a peg at mid-height.

OUTLYING CRAGS

Barmouth Slabs   O.S. ref. 619165

These pleasant slabs are situated about one mile north of Barmouth Harbour, and can be approached via the public footpath starting from the harbour below Barmouth Quarry. They lie on the north-east slopes of Garn Gorllwyn (700 feet) close to the summit, and are some 70 feet high. The rock is good, giving mainly easy climbs often used by outdoor centres and outward bound schools in the district.

The crag looks smooth and rounded from a distance but on closer inspection it is found to be seamed with crack-lines. Starting on the left:

Crack 1   Severe. Crux near the top.

* **Xebec**   Hard Very Severe, 5a. Go up the middle of the slab between the two crack lines with a leftward slanting crack to finish.

Crack 2   Difficult

Zig Zag   Very Difficult. Only fair protection.

* **Main Slab**   Severe. Climb the middle of the slab into a scoop, then go directly to the top.

Crack 3   Very Difficult

Crack 4   Difficult. Not a definite crack line.

Crack 5   Difficult. Makes for the wide crack on the arête.

Stevie's Jamming Crack   Severe. This is the crack behind the large boulder over the back of the crag at the north end.

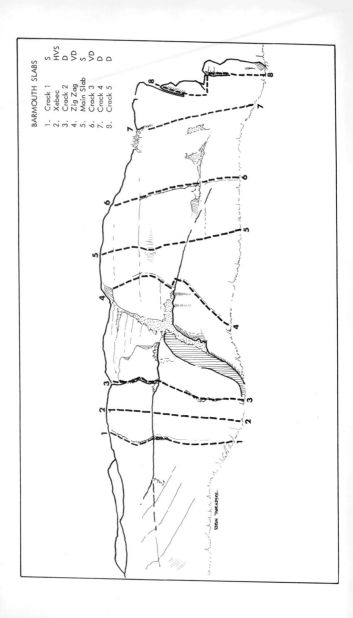

BARMOUTH SLABS

1. Crack 1   S
2. Xebec   HVS
3. Crack 2   D
4. Zig Zag   VD
5. Main Slab   S
6. Crack 3   VD
7. Crack 4   D
8. Crack 5   D

SIMON THURLIDWKE.

Barmouth Quarry

O.S. ref. 617157

This slate quarry facing south-east looks out over Barmouth Harbour, and has a public footpath leading up steps to it from the main road out of the town. The quarry is owned by the local council which STRICTLY FORBIDS CLIMBING. The following descriptions are for record purposes only.

*** Vapour Phase 170 feet E2 (1980)
A great line with good climbing which takes the big groove on the left-hand side of the crag. Start a little way down the scree slope. Good in situ peg protection, 2½ or 3 Friend nicely protects the crux.
1 120 feet 5c. Go up the groove to a steep section, pull over this passing an old spike (crux) then continue in the line of the groove moving over a nose and exiting left to the easier groove above. Large stance with huge spike belay under a wide crack in a corner.
2 50 feet. 4c. Ascend the wide crack above the stance.

* The Poisoned Dwarf 120 feet E2 (1980)
An obvious sharp arête right of Vapour Phase. Poor protection.
1 120 feet. 5c. Start just right of the arête and climb the wall easily to a peg. Move left to gain the arête and climb this making a very bold move to gain a large open niche. Move up and left out of the niche then go back right to finish up the right-hand side of the arête. Belay at the large spike as for Vapour Phase.

Southfork 110 feet E1 (1981)
To the right of The Poisoned Dwarf arête is a wall with an obvious crack in it (King of the Wild Frontier). Below the wall is a flat grassy area. This route takes a less obvious line 10 feet left of King of the Wild Frontier.
1 110 feet. 5b. Climb the wall easily to the base of a thin slanting crack. Make a difficult move left then go back right to the top of the crack. Follow a direct line up more broken rock to the large flake below the corner of Vapour Phase. Finish as for Vapour Phase or King of the Wild Frontier.

* King of the Wild Frontier 150 feet Hard Very Severe (1980)
The obvious crack in the wall with a grassy area below it. Good nut protection.
1 150 feet. 5a. Climb the crack to a slight ramp, move right and continue up the crack-line to the half-way terrace. Continue up easy-angled slabs to the top.

Barmouth Quarry

1 Vapour Phase   E2
2 The Poisoned Dwarf   E2
3 Southfork   E1
4 King of the Wild
   Frontier   HVS
5 Broken Arrow   HVS
6 Davy Crockett   VS
7 It's Looking Good
8 Houston   VS
9 Ethical Cruise   E2
9 Columbia   E1
10 The Floater   E3
11 Slipscream   E1
12 Total Perspective
   Vortex   E1

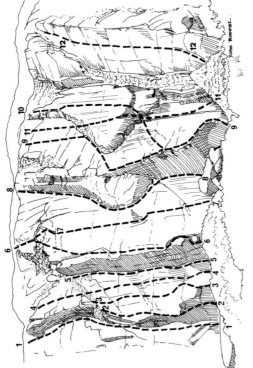

Broken Arrow   170 feet   Hard Very Severe   (1981)
The large corner right of King of the Wild Frontier.
1   110 feet. 5a. The corner crack is taken direct with the crux at fifty feet. Belay at the top of an earthy scoop.
2   60 feet. Wander up the slabs to the left.

Davy Crockett   150 feet   Very Severe   (1980)
The right-hand side of the arête forming the right edge of the large corner of Broken Arrow.
1   150 feet. 4b. Climb the slab on the right edge of the arête to an overhang, then step right to a crack. Gain the top of the crack and move back left to the right-hand side of the arête. Ascend this to the top. Vegetated ledges above lead to a good belay ledge on the right.

It's Looking Good Houston   140 feet   Very Severe   (1981)
An obvious crack-line in the wall mid-way between Davy Crockett and Ethical Cruise. Large nut protection.
1   140 feet. 4b. Climb the crack with a bulge at 20 feet, then continue up the crack until it peters out. Move left into a small bay and continue up another deeper crack-line to easy ledges. Good stance and belay just below the top.

* Ethical Cruise   175 feet   E2   (1981)
The groove capped with a large bulge.
1   120 feet. 5b. Go up the groove for 35 feet, then make some awkward moves up and left to some resting footholds. Continue leftwards with difficulty. An easy groove leads to an easy-angled area on the right and elusive belays.
2   55 feet. 4c. The groove on the left.

** Columbia   170 feet   E1   (1981)
The prominent arête between Ethical Cruise and The Floater.
1   130 feet. 5a. Move leftwards to the arête as for The Floater then climb up leftwards to a ledge on the arête. Continue up the edge passing a hidden peg in a small groove on the left up a broken section to an unusual bore hole. Move right to a spike belay on a large ledge.
2   40 feet. 4c. Finish up the pleasant wall above, moving left to a thin crack.

** The Floater   200 feet   E3   (1981)
Takes the big overlapped slab on the right-hand side of the crag. the first pitch follows a natural curving line into the weakness in the overlap, and the second takes the upper slab direct. Poor protection on pitch 1, no protection on pitch 2.
1   110 feet. 5a. Climb up moving right to a small ledge, then climb up leftwards to a ledge on the arête. Take the weakness diagonally right then a ramp leading right into the broken overhung corner. Good nut belay.

2 90 feet. 5b. Step out right into a shallow scoop in the steep slab above and climb the centre of the big slab to a horizontal fault at half-height. Climb up directly again for another 35 feet with an awkward move slightly right into a scoop. Traverse left to the arête and finish more easily up this.

Slipscream 170 feet E1 †   (1982)
A direct route up the Floater slabs.
1 130 feet. 5a. Climb up just left of a grassy corner at the right-hand end of the lower slab for 30 feet. Step left to clip a peg then go across to larger holds with difficulty. Continue up then right to the large recess. Ascend the right edge, hand-traverse the lip and go straight up the unprotectable slab above to a large grassy ramp.
2 40 feet. 4c. Climb the pleasant slab above, keeping just left of the corner.

* **Total Perspective Vortex** 150 feet E1   (1981)
Beyond The Floater slab is another big slab set at right-angles with three vague slanting groove-lines. This climb takes the central groove. At the base of the slab is a conspicuous white concrete-like mix. Three spikes in situ.
1 150 feet. 5b. Climb up the concrete mix to a little overhang. Climb the slanting groove above until it fades out at a niche. Step right and finish direct to the top.

Quarry Above Dinas Mawddwy   O.S. ref. SH
853139

The slate quarry facing north above the woods behind Minllyn hamlet.

Borderman 130 feet E3 †   (1986)
1 130 feet. 5c. Ascend the obvious corner groove with an overhang low down.

There are two short routes on a small slab on the front edge of the quarry.

Fringe Benefit 35 feet Hard Very Difficult   (1986)
1 35 feet. Take the obvious thin diagonal crack then go straight up to finish.

Ah-Ha 35 feet Very Difficult   (1986)
1 35 feet. Ascend the slab 15 feet left of Fringe Benefit Direct to the top.

Obi-Wan   150 feet   E4   †   (1986)
Takes the obvious curving groove in the wall round from
Borderman and then the slab just right of the arête.
1 150 feet. 5c. Climb the groove and then go right to the
obvious ledge near the arête. Move right round the arête to a
good foothold and two pegs. Technical climbing leads up to a
good foothold and another peg in a shot hole. Go up and right
to a good hold then back left to the tree. Ascend to the ledge
then traverse right past some dangerous rock to finish up
Borderman.

Winter Climbing

In Mid-Wales there are many snow and ice routes to be found during a hard winter. These are far too numerous to be given comprehensive treatment but the following are some of the better routes that have been identified in recent years.

ARAN AREA

CRAIG CYWARCH

Craig Maen Hir Ice Fall   IV
In Cwm Rhychain, the first obvious ice-fall right of Craig Maen Hir. There are two pitches, of 130 and 145 feet, which give steep ice.
First ascent: 2 March 1986, R Hastings, D Nicholl, P Burden

North Gully   IV
Needs hard frosts. The initial pitches are avoided. The Tombstone pitch is the crux, but with little snow then the pitch above is harder.
First ascent: 27 January 1979, J A Sumner, I R Tapley, A B Knox

Dinas Llywelyn Gully – Left Fork   II
A steepening ice pitch is found near the top.

Roddy   IV
The 80-degree ice pitch in the right-hand fork of Dinas Llywelyn Gully.
First ascent: 11 February 1979, P Douglas, J Codling

ARAN FAWDDY

Christmas Retreat Right-Hand Gully   III
The deepest of the three gullies to the right of Christmas Retreat above Craiglyn Dyfi and directly below Fawddwy summit. There is a cave pitch in the lower section and a steep exit.
First ascent: 1 February 1979, J A Sumner, R Thorndyke (AL)

Christmas Retreat Left-Hand Gully   II/III
Some good ice pitches.

* Aero Gully – Left-Hand Branch I
The wide gully above Craiglyn Dyfi, taking the left-hand branch in the upper reaches. It has easy-angled ice with a bulge near the top. This is the first gully to come into condition, and there is often a cornice.

Fawddwy Gullies 1 to 7 I/II
Mostly steep snow lying on the east face between the summit and Dyrysgol. Gully number 5 has a deep recess in the left-hand branch and it possibly has not yet been climbed.

ARAN BENLLYN

Tourist Gully III
At O.S. ref. 867233 is an obvious gully-line on the north side of the spur descending eastwards from the main Fawddy-Benllyn ridge. It has mostly steep snow with one ice pitch. Natural belays are scarce. There is often a dangerous cornice.
First ascent: 14 February 1970, J A Sumner, Miss J P Henrickson

* Winding Gully II
At O.S. ref. 866238, in the east face and well to the left of Benllyn's summit, is a shallow gully-line which makes for a 40-foot ice curtain. This is avoided on the right. Mainly easy-angled ice with occasional bulges. The ice curtain direct is grade IV.

** East Gully Direct IV
At O.S. ref. 868242. On looking at the east face of Benllyn an obvious feature is a great ramp which crosses the face from right to left starting under a steep and large section of rock roughly below the summit. From the ramp a big shallow gully ascends just left of the steep section. This is East Gully. Directly below and the ramp is a prominent ice wall. This gives a good 100-foot ice pitch which is 80-degrees for 50 feet.
First ascent: February 1970, J A Sumner, Miss J P Henrickson

* East Gully III
From the ramp ascend an ice pitch to an easy section then trend up right until a short ice-fall comes in from the left. Take this and its continuation to the top.

*** Sloose V
A magnificent outing which needs a hard frost. The first two pitches of Sloose lead to a huge jammed boulder then follow the steep wall between Sloose and Deadline.
First Ascent: 18 February 1979, J A Sumner, J Codling (AL), G Kirkham

ARAN PERIMETER

** **Craig-Wen Falls** III
At O.S. ref. 829174. Above Dinas Mawddwy on the left side of
Glasgwm at a height of about 1,706 feet. It takes a direct line on
the upper falls starting left of the pool at the base.
First Ascent: 20 December 1981, R W Symonds, C N Edwards

*** **Pistyll Gwyn** III
At O.S. ref. 885196 at the head of Afon Pumryd. 330 feet of
frozen waterfall with 50-60-degrees ice.
First ascent: 18 February 1979, C Powell, I Cowen, A B Knox
(shared leads)

* **Nant y Cafn Falls** IV
At O.S. ref. 895207. It is easily seen from the Pennant-Bwlch
Croes road. An ice slab with a vertical exit pitch leads onto easier
continuation ice.
First ascent: 1 March 1986, J A Sumner, C Nunn, S Coneys, M
Tolley

** **Nant Efail-fach Falls** III
At O.S. ref. 899162 below the west side of hillock Y Foel at 1,560
feet. There is an 85-foot tapering ice pitch. Abseil from the tree
at the top.
First ascent: 2 March 1986, J A Sumner, J Roe, J Mountain

* **Little Eiger** III
Immediately right of Nant Efail-fach Falls is a long ice runnel.
Climb this for 150 feet then traverse left to continuation ice with
a steepening at the top.
First ascent: 2 March 1986, J A Sumner, J Roe, J Mountain

DOVEY FOREST

QUARRY ABOVE DINAS MAWDDWY

** **Central Ice Flow** V
At O.S. ref. 852139 above the woods behind Minllyn hamlet.
Pitch 1 is a big vertical ice curtain leading to a large ledge. Pitch
2 is taken on the left up a steep corner, traversing out right under
ice mushrooms.
First ascent: Pitch 1, 2 March 1986, A Grondowski, C W Little
Pitch 2, 1 March 1986, J A Sumner, C Nunn, S
Coneys

** The Ice Pillar IV
Lower down and left of Central Ice Flow is a superb 26-foot ice pillar. Climb the free-standing pillar and a groove above to a tree. Abseil from the tree.
First ascent: 2 March 1986, A Grondowski, C W Little

CRAIG MAESGLASAU

*** Maesglasau Falls IV
At O.S. ref. 826141. In the centre-head of the cwm is this 660-foot frozen waterfall. Ice peg belays. The line is taken right of the water gutter and the central 230-foot section is very steep ice.
First ascent: 17 February 1979, J A Sumner, G Kirkham

CADER IDRIS GROUP

CRAIG CAU

Little Gully II
There is an awkward cave pitch near the top.

** East Gully III
The crux is a 100-foot ice groove near the top.

*** Great Gully III
Harder if all the pitches are taken direct.

The Baron V

MYNYDD MOEL (SOUTH FACE)

Bifrost IV
An obvious watercourse flowing down a slabby area on the south face. Approach by track to Llyn Cau. All pitches are taken direct with the crux, a 25-foot ice curtain, near the top.
First ascent: February 1977, M Fenton, A Jones (AL)

PEN-Y-GADAIR CRAG

* Central Gully III
At O.S. ref. 710132 where the summit cliff overlooks the llyn of the same name. The crux is in the upper section of the central gash at an ice chimney with a capstone.

** **Gwth**   IV
At the extreme right-hand end of the buttress with Central Gully note an obvious ice ramp about 65 feet high at an angle of 60-degrees. Climb this and two rope-lengths above follow an ice runnel. The ice wall of Gwth will be seen on the left side of a narrow, steep-walled gully. Take steep ice for 130 feet to easier icy ground and a finish on the summit plateau of the mountain.
First ascent: 12 January 1985, J A Sumner, I Warner

* **Rattler**   III
A vague gully system midway between Gwth and Central Gully but good ice normally shows in the upper section.
First ascent: 19 January 1985, J A Sumner, C W Little

TWR DU

** **West Gully**   III/IV
The 100-foot ice smear on the second pitch varies from verglas to thick green ice.

White Adder   III/IV
A distinctive set of ice grooves 230 feet right of West Gully. Five pitches of good ice/snow lead to the ridge.
First ascent: 1 March 1986, C Dawson, D Kilborn

CYFRWY

* **One Pitch Gully**   I/II
One short awkward chimney pitch with good protection.

Slanting Gully   III
There is an ice pitch in the lower section and an awkward cave pitch in the upper part.

*** **Colonial Virgin**   V/VI
Immediately left of Trojan. The route takes a line under the huge curved roof, exiting via an icicle. Go up steep ice under the roof to a chockstone belay. Traverse out right and go up to the icicle. Climb this and a steep slab to a second icicle.
First ascent: 12 January 1985, M Fowler and party

*** **Trojan**   V
As for the summer route except on the first section where an obvious groove in the corner is climbed. Sustained ice climbing at 70-degrees lasts for 350 feet. Poor stances.
First ascent: January 1979, J Codling, J A Sumner (AL), G Kirtham

** **The Shining**   IV
The deep narrow gully immediately right of Trojan. Climb the gully to a cave under the ice curtain. The curtain and ice bulges above lead to another cave. Take an ice chimney/groove to snow, then a short ice pitch to the final capstone and finally move out right.
First ascent: 16 February 1986, J A Sumner, S Coneys

** **Barn Door**   III
Start at a wide gully 500 feet right of Trojan. This grade I gully leads to an ice-fall on the left, giving the main 130-foot pitch. Avoid the steep lower part by a rising traverse left to blocks. Traverse back right to the centre of the ice wall and climb this slightly right. If the initial steep lower part is climbed direct, the grade would be IV.
First ascent: 23 December 1981, S Howe, A Meadows

Graded List of Climbs

The following is a list of climbs of Very Severe and above in increasing order of Difficulty. Routes with the † have been left out. Aid points are in brackets.

VS
Derwent
The Steeple
Jungle
Click
The Dome
Melangell
Rib and Slab
China Shop
Trojan
Bundu
The Slide
The Scythe
Grimbarian
Bluebell Babylon
Box Trick
Styx
The Beak
Chamool
Lanchester
Stickle Back Man
Short Circuit
White Rock
Curly Fringe Frown
Apollo
Bionic Woman
Mud Slide Slim
Girdle, Rhygan Ddu
Oread
Tri-Grainian
It's Looking Good Houston
Tappers arête
Pear Tree Blues
Davey Crocket
Thunder Road
Trick In The Tail
Quartizone Injection
Mochan
Snodgrass D.C. Direct
Cyfrwy Pinnacle
Doom

Man of Kent
Ritander
Raindrop
Ivy
Triad
Brick-a-Brac
The Fortyfier
The Yellow Policeman
Obsession
Piledriver
The Lamb
Di Fledermaus
Nichevo
Dinner and the Duo
Inigo
Touchstone
Lincoln Green
Black Wall
Great Spotted Booby
The Hole
Midlander
Tririri
Lectern Direct
Nardus
Battered Caravanserai
Stygian Wall
Georg Machine
King of Maybe
Central Rib
Spike Wall
Route 2
Mochyn

HVS
Alicia
Acheron
Rose Corner
Sweet Baby James
Cavalier Attitude
Delft
Tanat
Kathmandu
King Of The Wild Frontier
First Visit

Legionnaire's Disease
Where Eagles Dare
Wedgewood
Blatch's Folly
Giotto
Sloose
First Blood II
The Big Cleft
Lone Ranger
Baskerville
The Gargoyle
Quartzberg
The Sting (1 point)
The Sketch Man
Gate Of The Winds
Gwith o' Wynt
Xebec
December Grooves
Taranu Crack
The Crab
Migraine
The Comedians
Bramble Pie
Morning Crescent
Paper Lace
Twist Grip
Scimitar
Moai Man
The Grey Citadel
Aardvark
Broken Arrow
Iceman
The Scarecrow
Dawns Left-Hand
Quartz Buttress
Lucy In The Sky
Bird In Flight
Thyme
Lost Man
Gorilla's Armpit
The Graveyard
Paperback
The Magic Dragon
Pamplemousse
Ringwraith
Dancing Man
Sveinstock
Girdle, North Buttress
Crack of Cau

The Bolero
Beggars Banquet
Girdle, Diamond Wall
Nudging Groove
Plankwalk
Pusherman Variation
The Worm
Route Central
Black Pillar
Electric Rail
The Whisper

E1
Brick Wall
Shade of Pale
Judge and Two Convicts
Wingeing Pom
Carrion
The Hud
Southfork
Adrenalin Trip
Hades
The Mule
Kathmandu Direct
The Bee
Bird of Time
Deadline
Columbia
Charon
Girdle N.E. Buttress
Total Perspective Vortex
Girdle Craig Rhwyddfor
Loki
Scourge
Daisybell
Jugs Groove
Soldier
The Cheshire Cat
Quartz Wall
Then There Were Five
Slanting Gully Grooves
Keel Haul
Gwydrin
Frigid Pink
Voie Suisse

E2
Dream Racer
Ethical Cruise

Heist
Little Red Rooster
The Overlap
Ice Man Direct
Vapour Phase
Tumblin' Dice
Chariots Of Fire
Sundog
Meisterspringer
Roumagaou
Leander
Idris Corner
Pardon Me For Breathing
The Technician
Powder Monkey
Dovercourt Special
Hard Rain
Fifty And Rising
The Poisoned Dwarf
Spartan
The Gods Themselves (1 point)
The Great Mogul
Cat o' Nine Tales
Trouble Maker
Eden
Black Shiver
Second Foundation
Tyburn Gate
Heretic
Charisma
Green Wall

E3

Purge
Darker Angel
Brother In Arms
The Grafter
Mismael
The Diamond
Diamond Eliminate
Bomber
Pluto
Darkness On The Edge Of Town
Strobe
Rolair
Bear Cage
The Floater
Pink Panther
Alecto (1 point)

E4

The Mind's Eye (1 point)
Crozzley Wall
Old Glory (1 point)
Systems Of Romance

E5

Messiah
Rabble Rouser
Hungry Hearts

First Ascents

pre-1880	**Central Gully** (Pen-y-Gadair)	Possibly F H Bowring
1888 May 18	**Cyfrwy (The Eastern) Arête**	O G Jones (solo)
1895 May	**Great Gully**	W P Haskett Smith, O G Jones, E L W Haskett Smith,

A section of this climb fell away shortly after the first ascent.

1895 May 19	**East Gully** (Craig y Cae)	W P Haskett Smith, Dr. W E Sumpner, O G Jones,
1900 Sept. 3	**North Arête** (Cyfrwy)	T K Rose, F W Rose
1902 Aug. 28	**East Gully** (Twr Du)	S Ridsdale, H L Jupp, Mrs J Phillips
1902 Aug. 29	**West Gully** (Twr Du)	S Ridsdale, H L Jupp, Mrs J Phillips
1903 June	**Pencoed Pillar**	M Dalton, H G Dalton
1907 Easter	**Little Gully** (Cywarch)	A E Bramley, P S Minor, C H Pickstone
1907 Easter	**Great Gully** (Cywarch)	No party named
1907 Easter	**North Gully**	S Houghton, G T Ewen and others
1941	**Souwester Gully** (Gist Ddu)	R C Evans
1941	**Slab and Arête** (Gist Ddu)	R C Evans
1941	**Devious** (Gist Ddu)	R C Evans, E Ker
1942 June 30	**Steric Slab**	E L Furness, J H S Gilham
1950	**Kurzweg**	P R J Harding, N L Horsfield
1951	**Langweg**	D Kay

Direct up the pinnacle of Maen Hier. Route not in text.

1951 June 19	**Table Direct**	R E Davies, H E Chatburn
1952 Aug. 30	**Central Route**	R E Lambe, Miss M A Dunn
1953 May 17	**Diagonal Arête**	R E Lambe, S H G Taylor (AL)

*The route was originally done by climbing the first three pitches of
Central Route. G Jarvis, R Thorndyke, B Knox added pitches 1 and
2, 24 August, 1970.*

1953 June 3	**The Nose of Old Man of Cywarch**	R E Lambe

Route not in text.

1953 June 13	**Steilweg**	R E Lambe, R O L Clarke
1953 June 14	**Incapability**	E Byne, C W Ashbury
1953 Sept. 26	**Oread**	E Marshall, K A Wright, R Simpson

*Pitch 3 added by A J J Moulam, R E Lambe 1 April, 1956, which is
more in keeping with the rest. The original way took the line
Will-o-the-Wisp..*

1954 Oct.	**Western Gully Arête**	R Handley, B Cook
1955 June	**Light and Shade**	D M Adcock
1955 June 4	**Buzzard's Balcony**	J A Sumner, G F Williams (AL)
1955 July 9	**Stygian Wall** (1 pt. aid)	J A Sumner, D M Adcock (AL)
1955 July 10	**The Wall**	J A Sumner

*On Craig Maen Hier. A top-rope was used for the last few feet.
Climbed free in 1970 by J Sumner, J P Henrickson.*

1955 Oct. 22	**First Visit**	H Smith, C T Jones, K J Clarke
1955 Oct. 22	**Hope Street**	A B Afford, E Griffin
1955 Nov. 27	**Clubs**	R J R Vereker, J D Nicholson
1955 Dec. 4	**Cerebos**	J A Sumner, A Mills
1955 Dec. 4	**Garden Path**	R E Lambe, V Leese

Left of Square Gully, Tap-y-Gigfran. Route not in text.

1956 March 4	**Pigsty** J P Downes, A B Knox, R E Lambe	

On the crag at the top of Hiden Cwm taking a line left of knife-edged rib.

1956 March 31 **Black Wall** W J Finlay, A B Knox

Pitches 3 and 4 were added at a later date by W J Finlay and R E Lambe, 3 April, 1956.

1956 March 31 **Hopsit** (some aid) A J J Moulam, R E Lambe

Aid was used to gain the tree on pitch 3.

1956 April 2 **First Anniversary** R E Lambe, Mrs. R E Lambe

1956 April 3 **Sifta** J A Sumner, D G Chisholm, W J K Finlay, R E Lambe

1956 May 26 **Acheron** A J J Moulam, R E Lambe

A fine piece of route finding. Pitch 1 added 30 May, 1970 by A J Swindale, A B Knox. The original way took the wet start of Vulcan.

1956 May 26 **Relaxation** A J J Moulam, R E Lambe

1956 May 26 **Jungle** D T Roscoe, Miss A W Newton

1956 May 27 **Bluebell Babylon** A J J Moulam, R E Lambe

1956 May 27 **Bubble Wall** J A Sumner, D M Adcock

1956 June 17 **Midlander** P M Biven, H T H Peck

1956 June 24 **Obsession** A B Black, H Gartside, Miss S Grantham, G Payne

A climb called Route 1 done in 1959 followed approximately the same line by R Handley and W Richardson.

1956 June **Pisa** A B Black, E Swann, J Alexander

1956 June **Quartz Rib** A B Black, E Swann, J Alexander

1956 July 8 **South Face Crack** B C Roach, W Drew

1956 **Purge** (A2) J A Sumner, D M Adcock

Pitch 1 by D G Chisholm, A B Knox, on 10 June 1956.

Pitch 2 by J A Sumner, D G Chisholm on 1 April, 1956.

'About a dozen pegs required for each pitch. Some are in place. Some wedges will also be found useful.' Mainly on etriers.

1956 July 10 **Square Chimney** A Mills, T Wheeler, R Hancock

1956 Aug. 5 **Thung** G F Williams, D M Gilbert, A Mills

Pitch 1 was added by A Ward and A J Swindale 5 July, 1969. The original way took to the trees and vegetation on the right.

1956 Sept. 22 **Capability** M H Jahn, R E Kendal (AL)

Start to Jack o' Diamonds right of Incapability. Route not in text.

1956 Sept. 22 **Jack o' Diamonds** M H Jahn, R E Kendal (AL)

1956 Sept. 23 **Styx** D M Adcock, G F Williams

1956 Nov. 4 **Portcullis** A B Knox, R E Lambe, K H Higgens

1956 Nov. 18 **Dirty Knave** P Burden, J A Sennett (AL)

Took a line right of Hot Pants. Route not in text.

1957 May 5 **Triad** R Handley, F Allen, J N Millward

1957 May 26 **Knockdown** A B Knox, J P Downes (AL)

Muir Goch. In Hidden Cwm where the gully forks.

1957 June 23 **Shady Saunter** A B Knox, J P Downes, L S Galpin

1957 Sept 1 **Van Wall** J P Downes, A B Knox

Arête right of Pigsty in Hidden Cwm. Route not in text.

1957 Nov. 10 **Ceramic Chimney** T W Goodwin, G A Martin

1958 March 1	**Ronkleboot Chimney** G Martin, T Goodwin, J Downes, N Smyth, A B Knox	

1958 March 1   **Ronkleboot Chimney**   G Martin, T Goodwin, J Downes, N Smyth, A B Knox
On Far North Buttress, Cywarch above right-hand end of the ledge. 'This poor inoffensive route was beaten into submission very promptly by a very strong party who gave it no quarter, after being repulsed by a couple of other lines on the same crag, which were found too steep (i.e. overhanging).'

1958 March 2   **Solo Crack**   A B Knox
Left of S & D. Route not in text.

1958 March 23   **Nichevo**   M J Harris, R J Jones

1958 May 31   **S & D**   G A Martin, T W Goodwin, A B Knox, Miss M Andrews

1958 June 1   **Barbican**   A B Knox
On the entrance side wall of Hidden Cwm. Route not in text.

1958 Aug.   **Bundu**   G A Martin, J G Wilding

1985 Aug.   **Wig Walk**   J G Wilding, G A Martin

1958 Sept. 14   **The Hoe**   A B Knox
On the entrance side wall of Hidden Cwm. Route not in text.

1959 May   **Guano Pinnacle** (Bird Rock)   C J S Bonington, M White
Bonington also just failed on The Bastion which was not climbed until 1975.

1959 May 17   **Dena**   K A Podmore, G Bailey, R Jones

1959 June 8   **Route 2**   D Burgess, J R (Nat) Allen

1959 June 8   **Route Central** (1 pt. aid)   J Brown, H Smith
Climbed free by J A Sumner and N Cauldwell June, 1981.

1959 Summer   **Hades**   C J S Bonington, I Douglas
A line which had been atempted many times without success by different parties. Pitch 1 previously climbed by D Adcock and A B Knox 1958.

1960 Whitsun   **Hyrib**   J R (Nat) Allen, W Hayden, F Allen

1960 July 2   **Rib and Slab**   D Burgess, J R (Nat) Allen

1960 July 2   **Ritander**   D Burgess, J R (Nat) Allen

1960 Aug. 27   **The Spade**   J R Lees, I F Cartledge

1962 July 8   **Flake Wall**   S J Salt
On the small buttress in the gully between Tap Rhygan Ddu and Tap-y-Gigfran. Route not in text.

1962 Summer   **Siesta**   F Williams, A N Other
The start of real activity at Bird Rock.

1962 Summer   **Pedestal Route**   R Owen, D Rudder (AL)

1962 Summer   **Ivory Tower, Rose Corner, Tanat, King of Maybe, Thunder Road**   B Phillips, P Hill, J Jenks

1963 April 3   **Sloose**   J Brown, G D Verity

1963 May 1   **The Trench**   J Brown, G D Verity, G Mansell

1963 May 2   **The Wing**   J Brown, G Mansell

1963 May 2   **Pile Driver**   J Brown, G Mansell

1963 June 8   **Grass**   J Brown, J Smith, C E Davies, D Alcock
Thought not worthwhile.

1963 June 8   **Abdication**   G Mansell, G D Roberts, M E McMorland

1963 Aug. 5   **White Ribbon**   B Wright, Mrs D Wright, Miss M Perrin
Pitch 2 was climbed previously by B Wright and J Hunt via the grass terrace June, 1961.

1964 May	**Daisy Bell** L K Forsey, D Davies (AL)
	Originally climbed with a lot of aid.
	Done free probably by J Codling and party 1978.
1964 June	**Mother's Pride** Mrs J Wilding, C U Cockshott (AL) Miss C U Cockshott
1964 June 10	**The Beak** A Howard, A Green
1964 June 14	**The Gizzard** A Howard, A Waterhouse
1964 June 14	**The Talon** A Howard, A Waterhouse (AL)
1964 June 21	**Postscript** A B Knox
	A few feet left of First Anniversary. Route not in text.
1964 Aug. 30	**Trend** D W Matthews, E J Perrin
1964 Aug. 30	**Grad** D J Steele, A B Knox (AL)
1964 Nov. 22	**The Diagonal** A Howard, D Davies (AL)
1965 May 16	**Curl** D J Steele, A B Knox
1965 July 3	**Wright's Route** B Wright, J Hunt
1965 Dec. 26	**Christmas Retreat** J G Wilding, R Thorndyke
1966 March 19	**Northerner** (2 pts. aid) D K Scott, R Gillies
	On the second ascent a block came off with the second below the aid peg. The block was used as one of the main holds for the leader. The route has not yet had a third ascent.
1966 May	**Nardus** M Anthoine, I F Campbell (AL)
1966 May 28	**Tririri** J F Murray, C J James
1966 May 29	**Gardener's Rib** A B Knox, F R Edgar, Mrs P M Edgar
	A vegetated line right of Flanker. Route not in text.
1966 June 4	**Spartan** D Cuthbertson, G Caine (AL)
	A fierce lead. A peg was placed for protection above the overhang.
1966 June 4	**Sheep's Climb** A B Knox, J Wiltshire, S Bingham, J Lockett, Miss J Shaw
1966 June 5	**Flanker** A B Knox, S Bingham
1966 July 2	**Mint Cake** A J J Moulam, G J Lambe, R E Lambe
	A line on Craig Llam in Cwm Bydyre. Route not in text.
1966 Summer	**The Rockery** W Baker with two O.B.S.S. pupils
1966 Sept. 3	**Peal** Mrs R Fairbrother, E R Fairbrother
1966 Sept. 3	**Recuperation** J A Sumner, Mrs S A Sumner
1966 Sept 24	**The Arch** J A Sumner, J C I Saxton
1966 Sept. 24	**Plankwalk** M Boysen, J Jordan
1966 Sept. 24	**Quartz Buttress** A Nicholls, A Rhodes, D Little (AL)
1966 Sept. 25	**Aardvark** M Boysen, A Williams, D Little
1967 April	**Strictus** M Anthoine, I F Campbell (AL)
1967 April	**The Jug** R A Wilson, P Surfleet
1967 April	**Birdcage** R A Wilson, P Surfleet
1967 April	**Rockerfeller** R A Wilson, P Surfleet
1967 April	**Girdle Traverse** (2 pts. aid) R A Wilson, P Surfleet, P Doncaster
	Climbed free by K Bentham, D W Shaw 16 May, 1976.
1967 June 10	**Charon** J A Sumner, Mrs R Fairbrother
	Originally climbed with 3 points of aid.
	Climbed free by J Codling, G Davies 1 September, 1979.
1967 July 2	**Compensation** R E Lambe, G J Lambe
	The best line on Creigiau Camddwr. Route not in text.
1967 July 9	**Rolling Stone** P Treble, D Bone, J Kelley

1967 July 15	**The Green Sweater** A B Knox, R E Lambe (AL) G J Lambe
	A vegetated line on the right-hand side of Tap Dwyren. Route not in text.
1967 July 23	**China Shop** D Thornley, B Benson
1967 Aug.	**Inigo** M Anthoine, I F Campbell (AL)
1967 Sept. 24	**Lectern Direct** D Thornley, J A Sumner
	The oak tree was also used for aid. On Lectern Direct the arête to the right was climbed..
	Originally done taking the veg. start of the arch and then known as Lectern, J A Sumner, Mrs R Fairbrother, E R Fairbrother (AL) 14 January, 1967.
1968 May 11	**Christening** J A Lockett, A Bland (AL)
	The rib on the left edge of Tap Mawr Pella. Route not in text.
1968 May 11	**Girdle Tap Rhygan Ddu** D Thornley, J A Sumner (AL)
1968 May 19	**Odin** A C Scott, J G Wilding, P Chalmers
	A vegetated line on the left-hand side of Tap Mawr. Routes not in text.
1968 May 21	**Unity** P Sidoli, R Berry
	A vegetated line on the left edge of Slabby Buttress, Cyfrwy – Route not in text.
1968 May 25	**Restoration** J G Wilding, P J George
1968 May 28	**Encore** A C Scott, J P Downes
	A vegetated line left of Peal. Route not in text.
1968 July 7	**Dunsinane** A B Knox, P Cockshott
1968 July 27	**The Technician** (3 pts aid) D Thornley, J A Sumner (AL)
	Previously called Crucifix.
	The crux section of the groove was whittled down from 3 pegs for aid to one with shared efforts.
	Climbed free by J Codling.
1968 Aug. 4	**Yggdrasil** R E Lambe, Miss F M Lambe, J C Coppard
1968 Aug. 4	**Ring Wraith** R Thorndyke, J P Downes
1968 Aug. 27	**The Gem** J A Sumner, J P Downes
1968 Aug. 29	**The Grafter** (5 pts aid) J A Sumner, G Kirkham (AL)
	Originally climbed with 3 points of aid on the first pitch and two on the second.
	Climbed free by M Elwell and A Grondowski 12 April, 1980.
1968 Aug. 30	**The Comedians** J A Webster, R Thorndyke
1968 Aug. 31	**The Wizard** A B Knox, H Lawton
1968 Sept. 13	**Sveinstock** (1 pt. aid) D Thornley, D L Walker
1968 Sept. 14	**Sickle Wall** R Thorndyke, H Lawton
1968 Sept. 17	**Half-Moon Crack** H Lawton, A B Knox
1968 Nov. 3	**Doom** (aid) J A Sumner, A Gillis (AL)
	Several pegs were used on the first ascent.
1969 April 6	**Surrealistic** A J Swindale, G R Herus (AL)
1969 May	**Mochan** M Anthoine, A S Hunt (AL)
1969 May 3	**Ace of Spades** D Mason, P Dawson (AL) P Chalmers
	A line up the left edge (overlooking gully) of North Wing Upper Buttress, Tap-y-Gigfran. Route not in text.
1969 May 24	**Room at the Top** J A Webster, R Thorndyke (AL)
1969 May 24	**Paper Back** (3 pts aid) R Thorndyke, J A Lockett
	The aid was nuts.

1969 May 24	**Girdle North East Buttress** J A Sumner, J Entwistle (AL)	
1969 May 24	**Gornik** J A Sumner, J Entwistle (AL)	
1969 May 24	**Scourge** (3 pts aid) G Kirkham, T Thorndyke	

Originally climbed with 2 pegs and a nut for aid.
Climbed free by D Beetlestone, P Gibson, G Gibson 17 May, 1980.

1969 May 25	**Apollo** G Kirkham, A B Knox

Pitch 1 was led the previous day, 24 May, 1969 by A B Knox, H Lawton.

1969 June	**Purge** (3 pts aid) N Robertson, D McGonigal

Climbed with 2 points of aid on the first pitch and 1 point on the second.
Climbed free by J A Sumner, R Whitehouse 29 August, 1979.
Originally climbed as an artificial route by J A Sumner and party in 1956.

1969 June	**Tenuous** M Boysen, M Anthoine
1969 June 4	**Taranu Crack** R Thorndyke, L Foden, R D Cryer
1969 June 13	**The Big Cleft** D Thornley, J A Sumner

Pitches 1 and 2 climbed previously by G Jarvis and J Tooke Easter, 1969.

1969 July 12	**Phoebus** A B Knox, R E Lambe (AL)
1969 July 19	**Click** J A Sumner, Miss J P Henrickson
1969 Aug. 5	**Barad D'ur** R Thorndyke, J A Webster
1969 Aug. 9	**Man of Kent** (2 pts. aid) R Thorndyke, J A Webster, T Thorndyke

A peg and nut were initially used to climb the steep wall direct on pitch 3.

1969 Aug. 9	**Girdle North Buttress** J A Sumner, D Thornley, (AL)

Pitch 7 added by F Van Den Broeche, J A Webster August, 1975.

1969 Sept.	**Galium** M Anthoine, D Alcock (AL)
1969 Sept. 20	**Whirligig** R Thurman, J G Wilding
1969 Sept. 27	**Keel Haul** J A Sumner, Miss J P Henrickson

Led after protection peg on pitch 2 had been placed by abseil.

1969 Sept. 31	**The Whisper** J A Sumner, Miss J P Henrickson
1969 Oct. 5	**Quartz Vein** G Jarvis, A B Knox
1969 Oct. 5	**Troom** D Walker, A Ward
1969 Oct. 11	**Hell's Gate** G Jarvis, L Nuttall

Second could not follow pitch 2.

1969 Dec. 6	**Dungeon Flea** J A Sumner, Miss J P Henrickson

A line up the rock and heather buttress between Phoebus and Lethe. Route not in text.

1969 Dec. 7	**Lethe** J A Sumner, Miss J P Henrickson
1969 Dec. 26	**Flu '69** I R Tapley, A Ward
1969 Dec. 27	**The Grey Citadel** G Jarvis, A B Knox

Second could not follow pitch 5.

1970 Feb. 14	**Tourist Gully** J A Sumner, Miss J P Henrickson

Most prominent of the gully lines on the north flank of the spur which descends eastwards mid-way between Aran Fawddwy and Aran Benllyn. This route which is better in winter is not in the text.

1970 April 11	**Stronghold** J A Sumner, Miss J P Henrickson, I R Tapley
1970 April 18	**Portcullis Arête** A J Swindale, L Pedrisa

Arête above Portcullis. Route not in text.

1970 April 19	**Battlements** J A Sumner, I R Tapley (AL) Miss J P Henrickson
1970 May 2	**Concorde** R Thorndyke, Mlle M Laforest

1970 May 10	**The Magic Dragon** R Thorndyke, I R Tapley (AL)
	Pitch 5 added by R T Thorndyke, P Blatch 26 May, 1973.
1970 May 17	**Where Eagles Dare** I R Tapley, R Thorndyke (AL)
1970 May 17	**Scimitar** J A Sumner, A J Swindale
	Pitch 3 originally took the arête.
191970 May 25	**The Scythe** A B Knox, I R Tapley (AL)
1970 May 30	**Box Trick** J A Sumner, Miss J P Henrickson
1970 June 6	**Vulcan** G Kirkham, J A Sumner (ALt)
	Pitches 1 to 4 previously climbed by G Kirkham, A Storey 3 August, 1969.
1970 June 14	**Delli** A B Knox, R Chapman
1970 July 18	**The Little Red Helmet** R Thorndyke, T Thorndyke
1970 Aug. 8	**The Archer** A J Swindale, A B Knox
1970 Aug. 8	**Inclination** A B Knox, A J Swindale
1970 Aug. 23	**South West Arête** R Thorndyke, G Jarvis (AL)
1970 Aug. 24	**Oh Calcutta** G Jarvis, R Thorndyke, A B Knox (AL)
1970 Aug.	**Silwood, Melanger** D Bishop, D Thomas (AL)
	Probably climbed before.
1970 Aug.	**Buzzards Nest Crack** D Shone, D Bishop
1970 Aug. 25	**Porcupine** G Jarvis, R Thorndyke (AL)
1970 Aug. 29	**Obvious** R Thorndyke, T Thorndyke
1970 Aug. 29	**Schnellweg** J A Sumner, Miss J P Henrickson
1970 Aug. 30	**Slanting Gully Grooves** D Burgess, J R (Nat) Allen
1970 Aug. 30	**Tambourlaine** R Thorndyke, T Thorndyke (AL)
1970 Sept.	**The Perishers** R Thorndyke, T Thorndyke
1970 Sept. 6	**Monolith** R Thorndyke, G Kirkham (AL)
1970 Oct.	**Sundowner** P Dawson, D Mason
	Between Phoebus and Dungeon Flea. Route not in text.
1970 Oct. 18	**Tombstone Blues** G R Herus, R Thorndyke (AL)
1970 Dec. 20	**The Dome** J A Sumner, R Cully (AL)
1971 Feb. 28	**Thin Man** J A Sumner, Miss J P Henrickson
1971 March 27	**The Yellow Policeman** R Cully, J A Sumner (AL)
1971 April 11	**Left-Hand Break** J A Sumner, Miss J P Henrickson
1971 April	**Porky** M Anthoine, N A Phillippe (AL)
1971 April 11	**Tilt** J A Sumner, Miss J P Henrickson
1971 April 11	**The Nest** J A Sumner, Miss J P Henrickson
1971 April 11	**Grit** J A Sumner
	Miss J P Henrickson held rope.
1971 April 13	**Elephant Walk** A B Knox, I R Tapley (AL)
1971 May 1	**The Overlap** J A Sumner, R Thorndyke, R Cully
	After inspection on a rope.
1971 May 2	**Hot Pants** D Mason, P Dawson
1971 May 31	**Jugs Groove** (4 pts. aid) J A Sumner, G R Herus
	Originally climbed with 2 points of aid on the first pitch and 2 points on the second.
	Climbed free by J Codling, D Jones 5 August, 1979.
1971 Sept. 19	**Tribarfau** A B Knox, C G Powell, R E Lambe (AL)
1972 Jan. 2	**Mud Slide Slim** G R Herus, R Cully (AL) D Brown
	All three pitches were thought to be the same standard.

1972 April 4	**Will-o-the-Wisp** J A Sumner, Miss J P Henrickson

D Brown, J Bromwich, P Dawson helped on the initial cleaning of this route.

1972 May 7	**The Mekon** A J Swindale, J Bromwich
1972 Summer	**High Girdle** M Anthoine, D Alcock (AL)
1972 July 17	**Hotspur** A B Knox, T Bland
1972 Aug. 26	**Moai Man** J A Sumner, Miss J P Henrickson, D Brown

Pitch 3 added at a later date by J A Sumner, Miss J P Henrickson, A B Knox 2 September, 1972.

The peg on pitch 2 was placed from an abseil.

| 1972 Sept. 24 | **High and Dry, Jambiri** C G Powell, J Powell |
| 1972 Sept. 30 | **Deadline** J A Sumner, D Shepherd, A Ward |

Top-roped first.

| 1973 March 9 | **Black Eyes** J A Sumner, I R Tapley |

Assistance with cleaning the route was given by Jill Sumner and Alison James.

1973 May 19	**Girdle** D Shepard, J A Sumner (AL)
1973 May 27	**Gryptych** A B Knox, P Miles, J Bromwich
1973 May 29	**Echo Wall** J A Sumner, Jill Sumner

On Clogwyn yr Ogof. A zig-zag line up the wall finishing up the left arête. Route not in text.

| 1973 June 10 | **Guillotine** R Thorndyke, J A Webster (AL) |
| 1973 June 24 | **Oak Arête** J A Sumner, Jill Sumner |

The long arête on the left of Craig-y-Gornel, starting from the toe of the buttress. Route not in text.

| 1973 July | **Black Pillar** M Boysen, D Little |
| 1973 Aug. | **Strobe** (1 pt. aid) G R Herus, J A Sumner (AL) |

Climbed free by A Grondowski, C Little 10 June, 1979.

1973 Aug.	**Delft** F Van Den Broeche, J A Webster
1973 Aug. 27	**Pamplemousse** K Bentham, J A Sumner (AL)
1973 Oct. 21	**Touchstone** J A Sumner, R Thorndyke
1973 Oct. 27	**Crack of Cau** J A Sumner, K Bentham

A nut and sling was found beneath the major difficulties, left by A B Black and party on an earlier attempt.

| 1973 Oct. 27 | **Marsum** B J Marsden, G Summers (AL) |

There were signs that it had been climbed before.

1974 Jan. 21	**Chouca Rib** J A Sumner, R Thorndyke (AL)
1974 Feb. 3	**Great Spotted Booby** R Thorndyke, J A Sumner (AL) R F Short
1974 Feb. 17	**Picket Line** P Blatch and others
1974 Feb. 17	**Plume** J A Sumner, A B Knox, G Summers
1974 March 17	**Curly Fringe Frown** J A Sumner, Jill Sumner
1974 April 7	**White Lady** K Bentham, D W Shaw
1974 April 7	**Dawn's Left-Hand** K Bentham, D W Shaw
1974 April 10	**Black Shiver** (5 pts. aid) K Bentham, D W Shaw (AL)

Sling used for aid while cleaning pitch 1.

Four points of aid originally used on the crux.

| 1974 Easter | **Twr Groove** J A Sumner, I R Tapley |

There were signs that pitch 1 had been climbed before.

| 1974 April 14 | **The Baron** K Bentham, R Thorndyke |

1974 April 16	**The Sting** P Blatch, A B Knox (AL)
	Two points of aid were originally used on the first pitch.
1974 April 16	**Central Rib** D W Shaw, K Bentham (AL)
1974 April 18	**Sybarite** (5 pts. aid) D W Shaw, K Bentham
1974 April 19	**Battered Caravanserai** K Bentham, D W Shaw (AL)
1974 May 8	**Tremor** K Bentham, D W Shaw (AL)
1974 May 15	**Terraneai Rib** K Bentham
1974 May 19	**Trojan** J A Sumner, R F Short, A Jones, G P Cockshott
1974 May 25	**Moving Finger** K Bentham, D W Shaw (AL)
1974 May 26	**Bird of Time** K Bentham, D W Shaw (AL)
1974 May 26	**The Sufri** K Bentham, D W Shaw
1974 May 27	**Nudging Groove** J A Sumner, M J Cameron (AL)
1974 May 30	**Darker Angel** D W Shaw, K Bentham (AL)
	The aid points were originally used on pitch 4.
1974 June 15	**North Ridge** C P Cockshott, Gill Thorndyke, T Thorndyke
	Probably climbed before.
1974 June 15	**The Bee** (1 pt. aid) J A Sumner, G Summers
	Climbed free by J A Sumner, D Lee June 1981.
1974 June 23	**Morning Crescent** J A Sumner, A Jones (AL)
1974 June 23	**The Lamb** J A Sumner, A Jones (AL)
	First section of the route had obviously been climbed before.
1974 Aug. 4	**Claw Mark** J A Sumner, R F Short
	An old peg was found at the top of pitch 1.
1974 Aug 4	**The Gods Themselves** D W Shaw, K Bentham
1974 Aug. 11	**Chinese Poppy** J A Sumner, G F Jarvis
1974 Aug. 18	**Stross** J A Sumner, D Power (AL)
1974 Aug. 27	**Squall** J A Sumner, D G Chisholm
	First section had obviously been climbed before.
1974 Aug. 29	**His Satanic Majesty** D W Shaw, K Bentham (AL)
	(The Revelation 13: 5-8! Ed.).
1974 Aug. 30	**Low rib** J A Sumner, J P Downes, I Cowan
	Probably climbed before.
1974 Sept. 14	**Pusher Man Variation** G R Herus, J A Sumner
1974 Nov. 10	**The Bolero** J A Sumner, R F Short
	Top pitch extended. J A Sumner, R F Short 24 August, 1975.
1974 Nov. 17	**The Hole** R F Short, J A Sumner (AL)
1974 Nov. 24	**Fangorn** J A Sumner, I Cowan
1974 Dec. 1	**Fangorn Right-Hand** J A Sumner, R F Short
1975 April 25	**King Edward's Army** D W Shaw, K Bentham
1974 April 27	**Deadpan** D W Shaw, K Bentham (AL)
1975 April 27	**The Graveyard** J A Sumner, R F Short
1975 May 9	**Abraxus** K Bentham, D W Shaw (AL)
1975 May 17	**Bassillades** D W Shaw, K Bentham (AL)
1975 May 17	**Twist grip** J A Sumner, I Warner
1975 May 18	**Mere Gill** K Bentham, D W Shaw (AL)
1975 May 18	**The Steeple** J A Sumner, A B Knox, I Warner
1975 May 24	**Tatham Wife** K Bentham, D W Shaw (AL)
1975 May 25	**Snodgrass Diversification Company** K Bentham, D W Shaw (AL)
1975 May 30	**The Gulch** D W Shaw, K Bentham (AL)

1975 June 7	**Gotterdamerung** (1 pt. aid) K Bentham, D W Shaw (AL)
	Climbed free by L McKinley, D W Shaw May, 1976.
1975 June 22	**Gorilla's Armpit** J A Sumner, M J Cameron
	Direct finish added 4 November, 1969 by J A Sumner, I R Tapley.
1975 June 28	**Lucy in the Sky** J A Sumner, R Thorndyke (AL)
1975 Aug. 6	**The Mule** J A Webster, F Van Den Broecke
1975 Aug. 10	**Alecto** (6 pts. aid) J A Sumner, R F Short
	The aid was used on pitch 2.
	Whittled down to 1 point of aid by A Grondowski and M Elwell April, 1980.
1975 Nov. 22	**Dinner and the Duo** J A Sumner, I Warner
1975 Dec. 5	**December Grooves** J A Sumner, D Thornley
1976 Feb. 21	**A.G.M.** J A Sumner, I R Tapley (AL) D G Armstrong
	First pitch cleaned by D G Chisholm, D G Armstrong.
1976 May 8	**The Diamond** (2 pts. aid) K Bentham, D W Shaw
	Originally climbed with 1 pitch of aid on each pitch.
	Climbed free by D Wiggin, J Codling (AL) M Elwell, March, 1978.
1976 May 8	**Derwent** G Jarvis, T Lugg
1976 May 9	**Sweet Baby James** J A Sumner, D G Armstrong
1976 May 9	**Tappers Arête** J A Sumner, D G Armstron
1976 June 6	**Migraine** I R Tapley, J A Sumner (AL)
1976 July 28	**Fritz the Cat** I R Tapley, Miss A H James
1976 July 31	**Flashback** J A Sumner, E R Fairbrother
1976 Aug. 14	**Carrion** A Simpson, J A Sumner (AL)
	Pitch 1 climbed previously by G Herus, J A Sumner, August, 1973.
1976 Aug. 29	**Stiff Lower Lip** C Powell, D Kent
1976 Aug. 29	**Stiff Upper Lip** C Powell, D Kent
1976 Aug. 29	**Lifeline** D Walker
1976 Aug. 30	**Trouble Maker** (2 pts aid) J A Sumner, D L Walker
	Previously called Nigger in the Woodpile.
	Climbed free by J A Sumner 15 September, 1979.
1977 May	**Here Comes the Sun** L McKinley, D W Shaw
1978 Feb. 4	**A Touch of Class** J A Sumner, I R Tapley (AL) G Sumner
1978 March	**Diamond Eliminate** D Wiggin, J Codling (AL) M Elwell
1978 April 23	**Pear Tree Blues** J A Sumner, I R Tapley
1978 June	**Ethical Voyage** D L Walker, J Roberts
1978 June 24	**Koh-I-Noor** J Codling, M Elwell
1978 July 12	**Hard Rain** (1 pt. aid) G Herus, J A Sumner
	Climbed free by T Bristlin, J Codling.
1978 Aug. 29	**Powder Monkey** J A Sumner, C G Powell, M S Harris
1978 Aug.	**Tumblin Dice** G Herus, R Bradley (AL)
	Pitch 1 climbed previously by G Herus and G Caine.
1978 Aug. 21	**Pink Panther** J Codling, M Elwell
	Originally climbed with 1 point of aid.
	Climbed free by D Wiggin, A Grondowski (AL), C Little, 5 May, 1979.
1978 Sept. 3	**Kathmandu** J A Sumner, R T Thorndyke
1978 Sept. 20	**Heretic** J Codling, Jerry Codling
1978 Sept. 21	**Quartz Wall** J A Sumner, G Kirkham
1979 April 14	**Blatch's Folly** J A Sumner, I R Tapley
1979 April 14	**Ice Man** J A Sumner, I R Tapley

1979 April 15	**Ice Man Direct** J A Sumner, I R Tapley
	Originally climbed with 1 point of aid.
	Climbed free by N Longland, E Murray 4 July, 1980.
1979 April 16	**Raindrop** G Jarvis, G Armstrong, C P Cockshott
1979 May 19	**Baskerville** J A Sumner, I Warner
1979 May 26	**Systems of Romance** D Wiggin, A Grondowski
1979 June 10	**Cat o' Nine Tails** J Codling, R Cope, J A Sumner
1979 July 6	**Dancing Man** J A Sumner
	A B Knox held rope.
1979 Aug.	**Purge**
	Free.
1979 Sept. 1	**Kathmandu Direct** J Codling, G Davis
1979 Sept. 8	**The Great Mogul** J Codling, P Gibson
1979 Sept. 8	**Old Glory** J Codling, P Gibson
1979 Sept. 16	**The Fortifier** J A Sumner, Ruth Fairbrother
1980 Feb. 24	**Bird in Flight** J A Sumner, M Tolley
1980 April 20	**Girdle Traverse** J A Sumner, D L Walker, M Tolley
1980 May 4	**Gate of the Winds** J A Sumner, D L Walker
1980 May 10	**Loki** J A Sumner, D L Walker
1980 May 11	**Lost Man** J A Sumner, D L Walker
1980 May 17	**Bear Cage** G Gibson, D Beetlestone, P Gibson
1980 May 17	**Messiah** J Codling, D Jones, T Bristlin
1980 May 18	**Pluto** J A Sumner, M Tolley
1980 June 12	**Buzzards Groove** D L Walker, D W Walsh
1980 June 26	**Tyburn Gate** J A Sumner, D L Walker
1980 July 3	**Right Little Lady** D L Walker
1980 July 5	**White Rock** D L Walker, J A Sumner (AL)
1980 July 5	**Quartzberg** G Gibson
1980 July 5	**Bomber** J Codling, J A Sumner, D L Walker
1980 July	**Electric Rail** J Codling, P E Douglas (AL)
1980 Aug. 9	**Roumagaou** P Gibson, J A Sumner (AL)
	Pitch 2 climbed previously by D L Walker, July, 1980.
1980 Aug. 10	**The Crab** J A Sumner, P Gibson (AL) R F Short
1980 Aug. 23	**The Minds Eye** G Gibson, P Gibson, J A Sumner
1980 Aug. 24	**Soldier** G Gibson
	Second could not follow.
1980 Aug. 30	**Crozzley Wall** (pitch 2) J A Sumner, P Gibson
	First pitch added later by M Elwell, J A Sumner, 24 April, 1982.
1980 Sept. 6	**Steel Breeze** G Gibson, P Gibson
1980 Sept. 6	**Adrenalin Trip** D L Walker, J A Sumner, P Gibson
1980 Sept. 27	**Judge and Two Convicts** J A Sumner, G Summers, J Phillips
1980 Nov.	**Frigid Pink** J A Sumner
	Second could not follow.
1980 Dec. 20	**King of the Wild Frontier** D Wiggin, J A Sumner, S Darlington
	This line had probably been climbed before by A Hughes, H Boswell,
	October, 1971.
1980 Dec. 27	**Vapour Phase** J A Sumner, M Tolley (AL)
1980 Dec. 27	**Davy Crockett** J A Sumner, M Tolley
1980 Dec. 27	**The Poisoned Dwarf** A Grondowski, M Elwell
1981 Jan. 1	**Xebec** J A Sumner, A Grondowski

1981 Jan. 1	**Southfork** A Grondowski, J A Sumner
1981 Jan. 31	**Georg Machine** J A Sumner, M Ridgway
1981 Feb. 14	**The Floater** A Grondowski, J A Sumner (AL)
1981 March 28	**Ethical Cruise** J Codling, T Bristlin
1981 March 28	**Broken Arrow** J Codling, T Bristlin
1981 April 4	**Shade of Pale Right-Hand** J A Sumner, I R Tapley
1981 April 18	**Green Wall** J A Sumner, I R Tapley
1981 April 20	**It's Looking Good Houston** J A Sumner, M Cameron, Jill Sumner
1981 May 9	**Heist** J A Sumner, C Seymour
1981 May 10	**Columbia** J Codling, D Astbury
1981 june 7	**Total Perspective Vortex** J A Sumner
	Jill Sumner held rope.
1981 June 21	**Dream Racer** J A Sumner, R Thorndyke, N Caldwell
1981 July 4	**Beggars Banquet** J A Sumner, A B Knox
1981 Aug. 16	**Sundog** J A Sumner, D Lee (AL)
1981 Sept. 5	**Rabble Rouser** J Codling, J A Sumner
1981 Sept 5	**The Sketch Man** J A Sumner, R T Thorndyke
1981 Sept. 13	**Lone Ranger** J A Sumner, N Caldwell
1981 Oct. 4	**Little Red Rooster** J A Sumner, S Lewis
1982 Feb. 13	**Tower of Babel** J A Sumner, K D Sumner, G Lambe
	Pitch 3 climbed previously by A B Knox, P Williams, P Cockshott, I R Tapley 3 April, 1972.
1982 March 7	**Lanchester** J A Sumner, N Caldwell
1982 April 4	**Lincoln Green** J A Sumner
	A Green held rope.
1982 April 24	**Rolair** J A Sumner, D Clilvered
1982 May 16	**Idris Corner** J A Sumner, I Warner
1982 May 17	**Short Circuit** J A Sumner, R F Short
1982 May 30	**Darkness on the Edge of Town** M Elwell, T Bristlin
1982 June 13	**General Galtieri** J A Sumner, A Green
1982 Aug. 14	**Gwydrin** J A Sumner, I Warner
1982 Aug. 28	**Red Crystals** J A Sumner, I Warner
1982 Sept. 3	**Cyfrwy Pinnacle** J A Sumner, A Green
1982 Sept. 18	**Trick in the Tail** J A Sumner, G Lambe
1982 Sept. 18	**Gwith o' Wynt** J A Sumner, G Lambe
1982 Sept.	**Slipscream** J Codling, S Allen
1982 Oct. 30	**Crozzley Right-Hand Finish** J Codling, C Seymour
1983 May 5	**Shade of Pale** J A Sumner, I Warner
1983 June 25	**Alicia** J A Sumner, A Clements
1983 July 9	**Leander** J A Sumner, R Cottell
1983 July 17	**Then There Were Five** I R Tapley, J A Sumner (AL)
1983 July 31	**Mochyn** C Nunn, J A Sumner (AL) I Warner
1983 Aug.	**Safe as Sausages** J A Sumner, I Warner
1983 Nov.	**The Worm** J A Sumner, I Warner
1984 May 13	**Thyme** J A Sumner, C Nunn
1984 June 10	**Chariots of Fire** J A Sumner, P Harding
1984 June 16	**Baptême de L'air** J A Sumner, P Harding
1984 July 21	**Voie Swisse** J A Sumner, P Harding
1984 Aug 12	**Grimbarian** J A Sumner, D Gale, Jill Sumner
1984 Aug. 18	**Hungry Hearts** A Grondowski, J A Sumner

1984 Sept. 3	**The Scarecrow**	J A Sumner, S Smith
1984 Sept. 15	**Paper Lace**	J A Sumner, Jill Sumner
1984 Autumn	**Eden**	C Nunn
1984 Autumn	**Ivy, Charisma, The Slide**	J A Sumner
	With various partners.	
1985 March 9	**Pardon Me For Breathing**	J A Sumner, C W Little, A Grondowski
1985 March 9	**Brothers in Arms**	A Grondowski, C W Little, J A Sumner
1985 March	**Fifty and Rising**	A Grondowski, C W Little, J A Sumner
	D Bishop and D Thomas did first section up to the tree, 1970.	
1985 March 31	**Legionnaire's Disease**	J A Sumner, C Nunn
1985 June 2	**Meisterspringer**	J A Sumner, Jill Sumner
1985 June	**Luddites Demise**	C Nunn, S Coneys
1985 Oct. 26	**Pale Rider**	M Elwell, A Grondowski
1985 Oct.	**Chacmool, Stickle Back Man, Cavalier Attitude**	J A Sumner with various partners
1985 Sept. 14	**First Blood II**	C W Little, C R Little
1985 Sept. 28	**Live is Life**	J A Sumner, C W Little
1985 Sept. 29	**Dover Court Special**	J A Sumner, C W Little
1985 Oct. 19	**The Cheshire Cat**	J A Sumner, Jill Sumner
1985 Oct. 19	**The Gargoyle**	J A Sumner, Jill Sumner
1985 Oct. 19	**Foundation, Empire**	C W Little, I Cowan
1985 Oct. 26	**Die Fledermaus**	J A Sumner, K D Sumner
1985 Oct. 26	**Second Foundation**	C W Little, I Cowan
1985 Oct. 26	**Auto Man**	C W Little, I Cowan, C R Little
1985 Dec.	**Quartizone Injection**	J A Sumner, R Norris
1986 May 26	**Fringe Benefit**	M Little, C R Little, E Little
1986 May 26	**Ah-Ha**	C R Little
1986 May 27	**Borderman**	C W Little, A Grondowski
1986 June 8	**Mismael**	C Nunn, S Coneys
1986 June 12	**Sledgehammer**	C Nunn, D Gale
1986 July	**Tri-Grainian**	J A Sumner, Jill Sumner
1986 Aug. 23	**Giotto**	J A Sumner, Jill Sumner
1986 Sept. 7	**Bric-a-Brac**	J A Sumner, Jill Sumner
1986 Sept. 14	**Brick Wall**	J A Sumner, R Norris
1986 Sept. 20	**Obi-Wan**	C W Little, C R Little
1986 Oct. 12	**Bramble Pie**	J A Sumner, Jill Sumner
1986 Nov. 29	**The Hud**	J A Sumner, R Norris
1987 May 26	**Wingeing Pom**	J A Sumner, I R Tapley
1987 May 26	**Bionic Woman**	J A Sumner, I R Tapley, Jill Sumner
1987 Aug.	**Phase Shift**	J A Sumner, Jill Sumner
1987 Aug. 29	**Cloudwaltzer**	J A Sumner, Jill Sumner
1987 Oct. 17	**Class 87/2**	J A Sumner, R Norris

Index

Rescue

In the event of a serious accident where assistance is required, a message giving all the factual information about the person(s), location (crag, climb, pitch etc.) should be passed on to the Police by dialling 999.

The Police will contact the respective Rescue Team/Post, and as co-ordinators will obtain further assistance (e.g. helicopter) as directed by those effecting the rescue. The nearest Mountain rescue Centre is at the Aberdovey Sea School.

There is now a rescue post in Cwm Cywarch situated in part of the generator building, just behind Bryn Hafod, O.S. ref. SH 854195. The post contains a stretcher plus all lowering gear (ropes, etc.). The key is kept on the notice-board on Bryn Hafod.

There is a hospital Dolgellau equipped to deal with minor injuries. Tel: Dolgellau 422479. The nearest hospital with an X-ray Unit it at Aberystwyth. There is also a doctor in Dolgellau. Tel: Dolgellau 422431.

When climbing in this isolated area it is important to remember just how isolated it is, compare to Snowdonia for example. The best advice to climbers is to **TAKE GREAT CARE** at all times and try to avoid accidents at all costs. Don't forget that in the event of an accident it may be a considerable time before a rescue operation can be set in motion.

After an accident, please report in writing directly to the Hon. Secretary, Mountain Rescue Committee, 9 Milldale Avenue, Temple Meads, Buxton, Derbyshire, giving particulars of: date of accident, extent of injuries, name, age and address of the casualty, details of the MRC equipment used and the amount of morphia used (so that it can be replaced).

Normally this will be done by the local Police and/or the Rescue Post/Team involved, who will also require the names and addresses of the person(s) climbing with the injured party.

Avoid making rash, or unconsidered statements, to the Press; refer any journalists to the mountaineer who has overall charge of the rescue.

HELICOPTER NOTES

In the event of a Helicopter evacuation **ALL** climbers **ON** or **OFF** the cliff should take heed. A helicopter flying close to the cliff will make verbal communications very difficult, and small stones etc. will be dislodged by the rotor downdraught. All loose equipment must be secured and climbers in precarious positions should try to make themselves safe. A smoke grenade may be dropped from the helicopter to give wind direction.

The person with the injured party should try to identify their location. **NO** attempt should be made to throw a rope at the helicopter, but assistance should be given to the helicopter crew/personnel if requested.

A helicopter will always be flown into the wind to effect a rescue and on landing there are three danger points: the main rotor, the tail rotor, and the engine exhaust. The Helicopter should not be approached until directed to do so by the air crew.

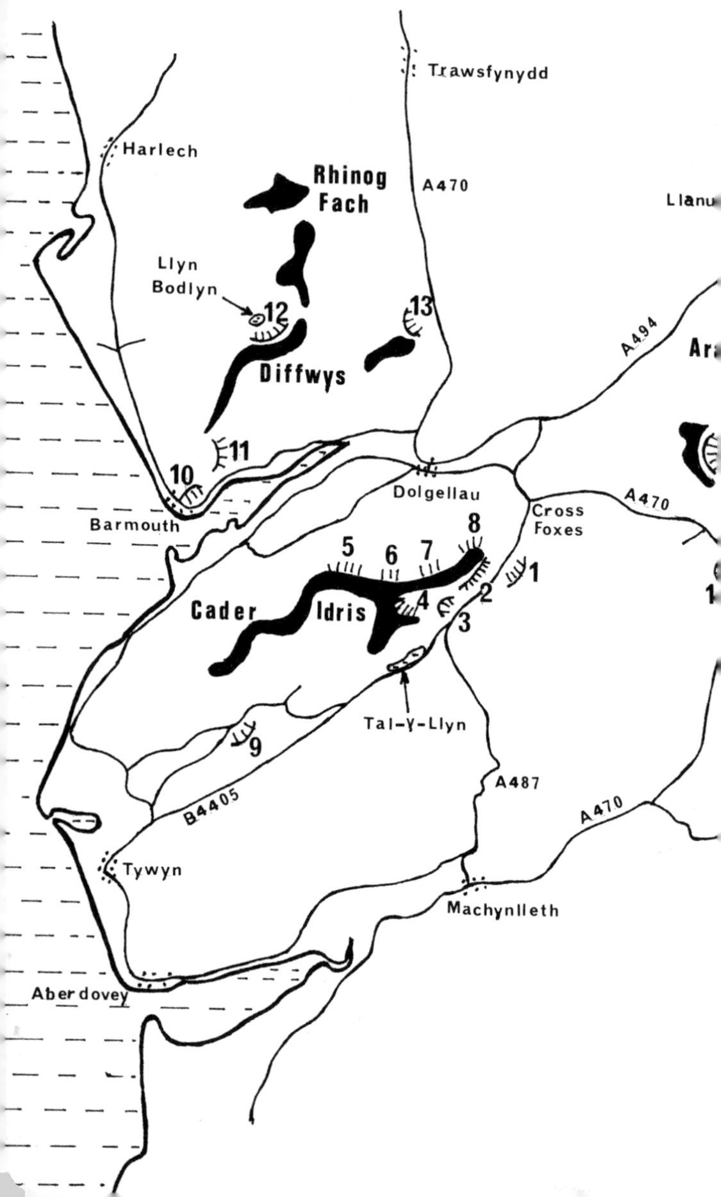

Trawsfynydd

Harlech

Rhinog Fach

A470

Llanu

Llyn Bodlyn

12

13

A494

Ara

Diffwys

11

10

A470

Barmouth

Dolgellau

Cross Foxes

A470

8

5   6   7

1

Cader   Idris

4   2

3

9

Tal-y-Llyn

A487

A470

B4405

Tywyn

Machynlleth

Aberdovey